GOD
J̶SATAN
JOB
& FRIENDS

A TRIBUTE TO AND IN MEMORY OF
JOHN W. SANDERSON, JR.

Books Brothers Press
15 Westchester Drive
Asheville, NC 28803

Editor: Nat Belz
Cover illustration: Natalie Belz
Design and production: Nat Belz
Printed in the United States of America
V6.0

TABLE OF CONTENTS

MARK BELZ

PREFACE

WHILE THE AUTHOR takes responsibility for the content of this writing, it is by no means a product of his study and thinking alone. Principal credit must be given to his friend and teacher, the late John W. Sanderson.

Rob Sanderson, John and his wife Pearl's youngest, graciously consented to write a piece for this book (p. 311), a tribute to his father. It is wonderfully helpful in providing a portrait of John Sanderson the man, one who shunned a worldly career in favor of a humbler life as a servant of God. John Sanderson's students and colleagues all recognized that having him around was something very special, because all knew that he could have achieved a mark in the world that, as Rob says, would have placed him in the encyclopedia. But to our great benefit, he chose to exercise his gifts in a much smaller world.

John Sanderson loved the Wisdom Literature in Scripture, and particularly the Book of Job. I was privileged to hear him expound the book three times: once in January, 1962, when he spoke for two weeks in daily chapel at Covenant College, once in 1975 when he delivered his most detailed exegesis of the book in a series of lectures at Covenant Theological Seminary, and once in 1981 when he taught an evening class at Covenant Seminary. Each time was a bit different, but his major thesis remained the same: that the theme of Job is not "why do the righteous suffer," but rather, "How does the revelation of God's glory reflect on man's response to that glory, that faith which binds man back to God?"

I take responsibility for the content of this book, in part because I cannot saddle Sanderson with what I say. If he were still with us, he surely would disagree with some of it. On the other hand, I found his lectures convincing, and thus I have adhered pretty closely to his thinking, and have attempted to identify those thoughts that came directly from him by footnote, direct quote, or otherwise. The reader is authorized to blame the author for the balance of the writing.

The three series of lectures mentioned were the only available sources of Sanderson's work on Job. He never wrote on the book. I did have my notes, or some of them, from the 1961 lectures, but was just 18 years of age when I attended, so such was of little value. As a result, no reference is made to the 1961 lectures.

I also had a set of notes for the 1975 lectures, but found it unnecessary to reference them, because those lectures were captured on audiotape, and are available for listening at the Presbyterian Church in America Historical Center in St. Louis, Missouri. These lectures are cited extensively in this writing, footnoted by tape number such as "7 JWS 75-120D-A" (the "7" identifying the tape number; the "75-120D" referencing the historical center's library number; the "A" indicating the side of the tape). Unfortunately, Sanderson's last lecture in the 1975 series, covering the last two chapters of Job, is lost. The only source available for this material is that contained in his 1981 lecture series.

While no tapes are available for 1981, Sanderson sent me his original lecture notes for that series a few years before he died. They proved helpful, but Sanderson, in marked contrast to the author, was a scholar. Some of these notes fall well outside my expertise. But some, rather than being in Hebrew or Greek, were, thankfully, in English!—and therefore of great help. These notes are cited simply as "John W. Sanderson, Lectures (1981)." At this writing, they are not publicly available.

In addition to the substance of the exegesis of Job obtained from these sources, Sanderson's methodology and style influenced me greatly. In his preaching and teaching he was strictly exegetical. In 1981 I asked him how he prepared sermons. He told me that he'd typically begin eight days before he was scheduled to preach. He'd read the text—whether one verse or several chapters—at least once on that day, as well as on the next two. He disciplined himself not to make notes during these three days. On the fourth day he'd take a blank sheet of paper to remind himself that he wasn't yet ready to come to any conclusions (Sanderson liked to use the Latin term *tabula rasa*, meaning "blank tablet," or "an absence of preconceived ideas or predetermined goals"). On the paper he'd list all of the thoughts generated in his brain during the previous three days, when he studied the text. There was to be no order imposed on these thoughts. On the fifth day he'd review what he had jotted down, organize the thoughts, outline them, and compare his outline to the text. Then he would just wait for the appointed day, letting the text and his outline percolate. He was then ready to preach.

I have recounted this in some detail, because I believe his methodology was a product of his theology. Sanderson had enormous reverence for Scripture, and for the work of the Holy Spirit in the heart of the reader and preacher. Parishioners and students who sat under Sanderson will testify universally that every sermon or lecture he delivered evidenced Sanderson's confidence in the Word of God—the confidence being, that if a person just meditated on a passage, something amazing would eventually appear, a truth there all along, but perhaps not recognized. He disciplined himself to let Scripture work on him, rather than the reverse. He never embellished the Word, nor felt it particularly necessary to make it interesting to the hearer. He believed that Scripture, aided and enlightened by the work of the Holy Spirit, made itself more interesting than he could. All of these factors evidenced a rare humility in a man so gifted.

To say that Sanderson refused to impose his ideas on Scripture, or to embellish the text, is not to say that he didn't illustrate. He was the master of illustration. I was taking notes during a lecture when he gave this one:

> On a sunny Saturday afternoon, I decided to wash the car. I poured a little liquid detergent into an empty bucket, half filled it with warm water in the house, swished the soapy water around, and went outside to fill the rest of the bucket with cold water from the tap on the side of the house. When the water reached almost the top of the bucket, I turned the spigot off.
>
> It was a sleepy summer day, and I was in no rush. I stood there philosophizing for a few seconds, looking at the spigot. A small drop of water was beginning to form on it, sparkling in the sunlight, looking like it might fall into the bucket, but wasn't yet quite big enough. I asked myself, "Should I wait for that drop to fall, or should I just take the bucket now and get to work? Will that drop of water really make any difference in the overall project I have in mind, that is, washing the car?"

Sanderson was illustrating Isaiah 40:15: "Surely the nations are like a drop in a bucket; they are regarded as dust on the scales," and told us that that little drop of water, in the Lord's view, is the United States of America, the Soviet Union. In the Lord's "overall project," he said, mighty nations don't make that much difference.

SANDERSON INSISTED THAT his students read the Book of Job as a whole, "in one sitting," before attempting exegesis. In his opening lecture in the 1975 series, he told the class: "What I would like each of you to do, some time this week, is to schedule a period when you can read the whole book of Job in one sitting. Try to do that, so that you can sit down and read it without any interruption. In this way the unity of the book will come across to you, and I think it was a book that was meant to be considered in one piece." So Sanderson would urge the readers of this book to do the same. And the author has found, when he has had the opportunity to teach the book, that it is essential that the members of the class possess some understanding of what happened, for example, at the end of the book, in order to fruitfully evaluate and interpret what comes before. The end of the book proves to be a lens through which the rest of the book can be interpreted.

If this book accomplishes nothing else, I hope, and I trust, that it will prove to be a tribute to John Sanderson's love for the Word of God, and that it will stand as one student's long overdue expression of gratitude to him, now with Jesus, for sharing that love with all the rest of us.

JOHN SANDERSON thus was and is the author's primary guide and motivator. Others encouraged me to write on Job, but I believe everyone who explicitly did so also sat under Sanderson. He moved them and they moved me. My sister Sara Drexler was the first to do so, I think because both of us have taught Job in the adult education setting; we are soul-mates as far as Sanderson and Job are concerned. Without Sara's initial encouragement about twenty years ago, I doubt that I would have undertaken the task. Rob, John Sanderson's son and my lifelong friend, when he became aware of my effort, pushed me to keep at it. Will Barker, professor to me both at Covenant College and Covenant Theological Seminary, has encouraged me too, and has the stature as a scholar to make me feel it is maybe important. Of course my wife

Linda, a writer far superior to me, has been of support all along the way, pointing out my errors (not limiting them to those in the manuscript), and helping me with diction and literary style. Mary Beth McGreevy has edited the manuscript, lending both her theological and editorial skills to the project.

To each of these dear brothers and sisters, I express my thanks.

I.

JOB THE MAN

CHAPTER 1:1-5

WE WOULD ALL like to be like Brother Job, but only on his good days. We'd like to be able to select certain parts of his life and discard the rest.

In the beginning of his life, Job had everything that most men and women strive for, and apparently had achieved it with integrity. In worldly terms, Job could sleep well at night. And once he got to the top, he managed his status and possessions without abusing either power or wealth. He was gracious, humble and godly. He had a stellar reputation well beyond his own community.

GOD'S APPROVAL OF JOB

His earthly success, though, would have meant nothing if he had not had God's approval. But God did approve of Job, in the strongest terms. The Lord described him as a "blameless and upright" man who "feared God and shunned evil" (1:1). God's blessing was on Job in every aspect of his life.

In fact, God bragged on his servant: "there is no one on earth like him" (1:8; 2:3). Along with Noah and Daniel, Job is held out as the righteous man *par excellence*.[1] The Apostle James also cites

---

1   Eze. 14:14, 19.

Job as a man of perseverance and patience.[2] It's quite an honor for God to certify you in Scripture as a "righteous man," "blameless and upright," and then have the prophets and apostles chime in.

JOB'S WEALTH

Job was also affluent. The author of the book meticulously lists Job's portfolio. In addition to his seven sons and three daughters, "[h]e possessed 7,000 sheep, 3,000 camels, 500 yoke of oxen, 500 female donkeys, and very many servants." He was the "the greatest of all the people of the east[3]" (1:2-3). Job was not left to wonder where his next meal was coming from.

A man's wealth in Job's world, where agriculture was king, was measured not so much in silver and gold, but in sheep, camels, teams of oxen, donkeys and servants. Fields, grain and other livestock were surely indicia of wealth as well. Probably the greatest sign of wealth in that day was children.

Job's contemporaries, like ours, held those who have great wealth in high esteem.[4] But when the material possessions disappear, or when the rich man or woman dies, the high esteem disappears too, just because it was the riches that gave the person that high esteem. Later in the book the author makes it clear that Job knew this. And King David said:

> For he sees that even the wise die;
> the fool and the stupid alike must perish
> and leave their wealth to others.
> Their graves are their homes forever,

---

2   James 5:11.

3   Literally, "sons of the East."

4   Jesus' disciples displayed the same. When the rich young ruler turned away from Jesus because of his wealth, Jesus told them that "[i]t is easier for a camel to go through the eye of a needle than for a rich person to enter the kingdom of God." The disciples had thought the opposite, and asked, "Who then can be saved?", showing their assumption that material wealth was evidence of righteousness, bringing a person closer to entering the Kingdom of God than those with less. (Mk. 10:23-31).

their dwelling places to all generations,
though they called lands by their own names.
(Psa. 49:10-11)

In the Lord's eyes, it is not wealth that makes a man great, and though Job's possessions had nothing to do with his greatness in God's eyes, the Lord is the one who blessed him with them, and used them as he worked in Job's life. Job's possessions are tied to what happened to him in Chapters 1 and 2, where all he had was taken away. They are also relevant to the last chapter of the book, where they were restored times two. His possessions are among the first and last things mentioned. They serve as bookends for the writing.

JOB'S PERSPECTIVE ON WEALTH

We can put one concern to rest. Job was not in love with his possessions. The Lord certified Job as "my servant" (1:8; 2:3). A servant of the Most High God cannot serve both God and his possessions. Jesus said:

> No one can serve two masters. Either you will hate the one and love the other, or you will be devoted to the one and despise the other. You cannot serve both God and money. (Mt. 6:24)

There is a proscriptive element in what Jesus said, because he clearly means that we *ought not* to serve money. But the substance of this verse is not really a command. Rather, the Lord is stating a fact of life: it is *impossible* to do both. It doesn't work. Trying to serve both is like jumping off the garage roof in an attempt to defy the law of gravity.

The Lord could not have claimed him as his "servant" if Job had been in love with, if he depended upon, if he served, his money. Indeed, the rich young man had to turn away from Jesus because he was in love with his wealth.[5] Even he, an unbeliever,

---

5   Mk. 10:17-31.

realized that he couldn't love both. Those two worlds are mutually exclusive. A man may try to do both at the same time, but it's not just an uphill battle—it's hopeless and undoable. More than that, if one loves God, he will (like the Lord) despise money where it otherwise would have dominion over him. But if he loves his money, he will despise the Lord. This is a radical truth, and Christians as well as non-believers constantly attempt to straddle the fence. But you can't straddle the fence. Jesus' statement makes that clear, and our experience bears it out.

Job's example demonstrates another truth too: a person may be blessed with great wealth and still be God's servant. Jesus said that you cannot *love* both; he did not say that you cannot *have* both, and this isn't just semantics. It may be difficult to have both, but the Lord has blessed some with that ability. From common observation, their number is few, but they are there. Long ago I heard a preacher say that God does two great miracles in a rich man's life: he liberally saves him, and then makes *him* liberal with what he has, using it for the Kingdom of God.

Job also understood where his wealth came from. Jesus talked about someone who didn't understand this in Luke 12:

> The land of a rich man produced plentifully, and he thought to himself, "What shall I do, for I have nowhere to store my crops?" And he said, "I will do this: I will tear down my barns and build larger ones, and there I will store all my grain and my goods. And I will say to my soul, 'Soul, you have ample goods laid up for many years; relax, eat, drink, be merry' " (Lk. 12:16-19).

It's significant that every personal pronoun in this passage refers to the rich man. This self-consumed fellow thought in terms of himself and nothing else. It was in fact God's good earth that yielded an abundant harvest, but his response was not to be thankful for what he had received from God, but to worry about self-preservation, wondering what in the world he was going to do since he didn't have enough room to store his crops. Though it had been given to him, he selfishly considered it his because he was the one who stored it up. The Lord was not on his radar, and that made him act the fool. He was even a bigger fool in this regard than the devil, because Satan knew where Job got his wealth. The devil had reported to the Lord that that "[y]ou have blessed the work of his hands, and his possessions have increased in the land" (1:10).

But Job understood who it was that gave him his wealth. After everything had been taken from him, Job said "The LORD gave, and the LORD has taken away; blessed be the name of the LORD." (1:21). It was only because Job understood that everything he had was a gift from God that he could remain standing after losing it all.

JOB'S REPUTATION

Not only did he have great wealth, but Job had the respect of others, and status. He was the greatest man among all the people of the East (1:3). Though we do not know the exact location of the land of Uz,[6] it was in what was considered "the East" in Job's day. His reputation apparently had spread well beyond the land of Uz. He was highly esteemed by others. He was a righteous man, a fair man. He had a good reputation because he "feared God and turned away from evil" (1:1). People see that, and Scripture tells us that a good reputation is important—not just among friends and fellow believers, but with the outside world.[7] Clearly Job had this attribute.

---

6 Uz is mentioned twice in Scripture in addition to Job 1:1. It appears in Jer. 25:20, and in Lamentations 4:21. The Lamentations text says: "Rejoice and be glad, Daughter Edom, you who live in the land of Uz," leading some scholars to conclude that Uz is identified geographically with the land of Edom, south and a little east of Judah.

7 1 Tim. 3:7.

JOB'S FAMILY

There is more to say about this remarkable man. Many years ago I was a member of a law firm specializing in trial work. Trial law is difficult, and takes an enormous amount of time and energy. Preparation, research, interviewing witnesses, taking, defending and reviewing depositions, working on opening and closing statements, preparing exhibits—these tasks are all-consuming, especially as the trial date approaches. It is often said that to be a good trial lawyer, you can't be a good family man or woman, and as I have observed the lives of many successful trial lawyers, I think there is more than a kernel of truth in that assessment. It isn't unique to a law career, either. In every vocation, if you want to excel you are going to have to concentrate on your career to the exclusion of some other things in your life. Sadly, family life is one of the first things that suffers. It just doesn't seem possible to cover all the bases.

Job, however, had a successful career *and* a good family, as evidenced by the fact that his adult children got along well. He had seven sons, who "used to go and hold a feast in the house of each one on his day, and they would send and invite their three sisters to eat and drink with them" (1:4).

Is anything more fulfilling in this life than for parents to know that their children are living in harmony with each other? Job experienced that great blessing. But he did not take it for granted.

JOB PRAYED FOR HIS CHILDREN

Job knew his family was a gift from the Lord, and regularly interceded for them. Whenever his sons and daughters got together and would "eat and drink," Job surely was concerned that the celebration, involving alcoholic beverages,[8] could open the door to misbehavior. He knew about such dangers. Most parents

---

8   See 1:13, where the "sons and daughters were eating and drinking wine in their oldest brother's house."

do. When your teenage daughter is out late at a party, you worry about her: she might have a car accident, or worse. As the hour grows later and later, a parent's concern rises, and the prayers grow more and more fervent. Surely Job had these concerns. Neither he nor his children had Chevrolets, but maybe there were camel accidents, and Job had 3,000 camels for the kids to ride.

Job's ultimate concern for his children, however, had to do with their relationship to the Lord. Too often, even as believing parents, we do not have our priorities in order with regard to our children. We typically pray for their physical wellbeing, their relationships with others, their grades, and so forth. We are relieved when we see those prayers answered, and God does answer such prayers. But believing parents who are truly concerned for their children will pray beyond those things, as Job did. The ultimate concern of his prayers was for their spiritual wellbeing.

It doesn't take much reflection to recognize that these ultimate matters are what truly concern us too. We want those things most of all for our children, and, given the choice, we would forfeit earthly wellbeing in exchange for eternal wellbeing. But we too easily put such considerations aside for the moment, focusing on safe passage through the events of this twenty-four hour day rather than eternity. We just want our son or daughter to get home tonight in one piece.

Job worried that it was possible that his children, during such family reunions, had "cursed God in their hearts" (1:5). The phrase "curse God" appears here and in three other places in the book. Satan twice assured the Lord that Job would "curse God" if God brought trouble on him (1:11, 2:5). After the trouble came, Job's condition could not have been more painful, nor his outlook more bleak. After Job's second devastation, his wife also advised Job to "curse God" (2:9).

CURSING GOD

It would be profitable to exegete the Book of Job by focusing on those two words, "curse God," because one of the fundamental questions raised is "is God just?" Of course man is in no position to make such an assessment, but if the answer to that question were to be "no," then cursing God would in fact be justifiable.

Job allowed for the possibility that his children were capable of, and perhaps had committed, that great sin. It's impossible to imagine a more blasphemous, self-damning act than to curse God. It sounds like the unforgivable sin. But here we learn something about the man Job, and his theology.

First, Job understood that the very nature of sin is to "curse God." Every sin is subsumed under that phrase, because to intentionally disobey God is to cast him away, to deny his divine authority, and to defy his very being. It is equivalent to telling the Creator God to "get lost," or "go straight to hell." It's that bad; such is the essence of a curse. And though we would never speak those words, we may think the equivalent in our hearts. Job knew his children were susceptible.

But second, Job believed that such a heinous thought or statement was not beyond the pale of God's mercy. If he had believed otherwise, he would not have interceded with God, by way of continual sacrifice and prayer, for his children. Job had confidence that God would forgive even what may seem like the ultimate, unforgivable sin. Job believed that God's mercy had no limit.

Third, Job (like Abel) understood that God required a sacrifice of blood. We do not know exactly when Job lived, but it was after Abel, and almost certainly was in the age of the patriarchs. God had revealed to Cain and Abel that blood sacrifice was required—not just God's preference, but his command. This was looking forward to the blood sacrifice of God's own son, and Job surely did not have that precise knowledge. But Job did know that God himself orders the manner in which man is to approach and worship him. Men and women do not call the shots. Job was obedient to the Lord in worship.

JOB THE ELDER

From this scriptural description of Job, it's clear that he would have been highly qualified for the office of elder in the New Testament church. The Apostle Paul, in his letter to Titus, says that "an overseer, as God's steward, must be above reproach" and can qualify for the office if "his children are believers and not open to the charge of debauchery or insubordination."[9] Among other things, "[h]e must manage his own household well, with all dignity keeping his children submissive, for if someone does not know how to manage his own household, how will he care for God's church?"[10] Job also appears to qualify as "the husband of one wife,"[11] even though his wife fell down on the job pretty badly, as recorded in Chapter 2.

JOB ON THE BOARD OF DIRECTORS

Job also would have been an outstanding pick for a corporate or institutional board of directors. Many years ago, some folks lacking good judgment chose me to serve on the board of trustees of a college. During my stint, we were lectured by some experts the college had employed in the area of development. These out-of-towners (all experts are) were educating us as to what a good board member looks like. I well remember shriveling down in my chair as they put those qualifications on the overhead, summarized by three words beginning with the same letter, "W." They were Wealth, Work and Wisdom. They put Wealth first, because, after all, they were development people, and that W was first in their book.

---

9   Tit. 1:6-7.
10   1 Tim. 3:4-5.
11   1 Tim 3:2.

I began to feel like a fish out of water. We were told, in so many words, that we might be barely suited for the board if we possessed just one of the W's, much better if we had two, and off the charts if we had all three. All I took home from that lecture was that I was a man without "W's." I really should have resigned my position right then and there.

But Job had them all. We already know that he was industrious, because he started small (8:7), and built a substantial estate, earning two quick W's. As we progress through this study, we will see that he was a man of wisdom as well. He was a Three W Man. Any corporate or institutional board would absolutely die to have Job on "board."

JOB, GOD'S SERVANT

However, the most significant aspect of this great man was that he was a servant of the Most High. God himself calls Job his servant (1:8; 2:3). Job offered sacrifices for his children; he was on his knees before the Lord; he worshiped Jehovah God. This is how the story begins, and it is how it ends 42 chapters later: Job on his knees, in prayer. In between, Job suffered loss in every sense of the word. There were all kinds of questions. Job became bewildered, angry and doubtful. But these things turned out to be part of his journey—an excruciating one—and from beginning to end, Job remained a servant of the Most High God.

God's righteous servant was about to undergo trials, loss, pain and hardship that would exceed that imposed on any other human being mentioned in the Bible, apart from Christ himself. We are never told specifically why. But his story gives us insight into more important matters, both in this life and that which is to come. The Lord is not going to squander Job's great suffering. He is going to bring something wonderful from all that Job experienced, not only for Job's benefit, but also for the good of all believers who "follow in his train." Job is one of those great Old Testament witnesses, meant to strengthen and encourage us, so that we can "run with endurance the race that is set before us."[12]

---

12   Heb. 12:1.

FOR REFLECTION

I.

Considering Job before he was struck with disaster, in what ways are you like him? In what ways different? Do you identify with him, or do you feel like he's someone so different from you that you can't?

2.

Do you see any problems, or dangers, in Job's life—things that might be warning signs to him, or concerns that he should have, given his wealth, family and station in life?

3.

If you are a parent, do you pray for your children as Job did? What can parents learn from Job in his relationship with his children, and how he prayed for them?

2.

A STRANGE MEETING

CHAPTER 1:6-8

THIS WAS NOT a little get-together over coffee. It was an epic confrontation between God and Satan. The participants were all heavenly beings; no mortal took part or was present. It was mysterious, other-worldly, and though revealed to us, impossible to fully comprehend. There is nothing like it in Scripture, and certainly not in human history apart from Scripture.

JOB NOT INVITED

Although Job was the primary topic of discussion in this meeting, he was not there, and didn't even know that it had been scheduled. In fact, there is nothing in the entire forty-two chapters of the book indicating that he ever learned about what happened between God and Satan in this exchange. It is likely that we are informed of something here that Job didn't learn until he went to heaven. We thus have a distinct advantage, and must keep that in mind as we evaluate and judge Job throughout this study.

GOD HOSTED THE MEETING

The author begins the description of this event almost casually, with the words "One day..."—not unlike the manner in which an author would begin a novel. But this is not a novel. It occurred. It is part of God's special revelation to us. And on this particular day "the sons of God[13] came to present themselves before the Lord, and Satan also came among them" (1:6). This makes it sound like it was a regular occurrence, and maybe so. But it happened in a world normally hidden from human view and beyond human understanding.

This amazing event, and how it was arranged, is obscured from our limited vision. But we can find solace from the manner in which this meeting was called to order. We are given some information on that point. The angels "came to present themselves" before the Lord. He did not "come to present himself" to them. It was his convocation, not theirs. No one can call him to a meeting, and no one can attend a meeting he arranges, apart from his invitation.

The devil is wrong as night about almost everything, but this is one thing he realizes. He hates to admit it, but understands clearly that God is in charge. He has a good memory, though in most areas of his thinking he scuttles what he should have learned in the past so that he can go his own way. He is unteachable, but he does know that he has to yield to the sovereign Creator. For the devil, it is not a 'lesson learned' but a perennial necessity.

GOD IN CONTROL

We find comfort in this. Particularly when we consider the Lord's relationship with Satan, it is crucial for us to know that God is sovereign, not only in the ultimate but the immediate; not only in the past but in the present and future. He controls every atom of the universe—he always has, and always will. The solace

---

13   Or, "angels" (NIV).

we derive from this pervades all the events of our lives. As we think about the past, for example, every one of us has memories of things we did, or had done to us, that make us cringe. Like close calls.

When courting my future bride in the fall of 1964, we were traveling in a green Volkswagen bug to a jewelry store in North Carolina where I hoped to get a good deal on an engagement ring. There were hardly any of Eisenhower's new interstates at that time, and we were following the signs for state highways, often confusing. We approached what turned out to be an unmarked railroad crossing. There was a red pickup truck right in front of us and I don't *think* I was tailgating.

All of a sudden the pickup truck disappeared. I slammed on the brakes. All we could see was a grayish-black blur about 10 feet in front of us. It was boxcars, indicating a train! They were come and gone in a flash. We never saw a locomotive. It was then that we once again saw the truck, neatly sliced in two, both pieces on the other side of the track. Thankfully, its driver was opening the door of the remaining front half of his vehicle, unharmed.

We had been able to stop just in time, although my pulse rate had gone from about 70 well into the thousands.

SETTLED LONG AGO

Maybe what happened there, now fifty years ago, seems to be just an amusing anecdote to others. But it has never been so to us. Recalling the event has caused me to wince, even shudder.

In the last few years, though, I have been more at rest regarding the 'near miss' as I have begun to think more about God's sovereignty in the *past*. What occurred was under God's absolute control. It was indeed a close call, but there was actually no chance that the train would hit and kill us, or the driver of the pickup ahead of us. Nor must we be forever burdened with that memory.

We can find enormous relief in contemplation of God's past sovereignty.

The same assurance is there for the Christian in the big events of life, even when the result is the opposite. Tragedies such as fatal accidents, or the death of a loved one, are nightmares. Couldn't it have been prevented? This question can haunt the person who has suffered the loss for the rest of his or her life. Of course greater care on the part of one of the drivers in a car accident might have prevented it. We should be careful, and due care can make all the difference. Preventive actions that we take, like almost all other actions, are known as "second causes," or "contingencies."

But the end result is altogether in God's hands. We can take inestimable comfort from that fact. We can cease the nightmare of worrying about what might have been, because though it was a tragedy, and though someone might have been to blame, God was in complete control of those contingencies.[14] There was not one atom spinning out of his sovereign, eternal, beneficent design.

Job was going to need this kind of assurance, not only as his story unfolds here, but for the rest of his earthly life. His sufferings were to come to an end. But he lived for 140 years[15] after the trial was over, and he surely asked himself at times if things might not have been different. We can't blame him if he did. But Job never relinquished his faith in his God, and thus could rest in the goodness and magnificence of what the Lord was doing in every event of his life—even these unparalleled tragedies.

---

14 To say that an event occurs because of second causes is not at loggerheads with the doctrine of the sovereignty of God. The Westminster Divines wrote that "God from all eternity did by the most wise and holy counsel of his own will, freely and unchangeably ordain whatsoever comes to pass; yet so as thereby neither is God the author of sin; nor *is violence offered to the will of the creatures, nor is the liberty or contingency of second causes taken away, but rather established." Westminster Confession of Faith*, Chapter III, Section 1 (emphasis added).

15 42:16.

God was in control of this meeting, and all resulting events in Job's life. Questions are asked, mystery pervades, but nothing is, or ever really was, up in the air. It could not have gone one way or the other. Job could later rest in that sublime and unshakable truth.

ATTENDEES AND LOCATION

Those present were the Lord and the "sons of God," likely meaning his angels. The only angel identified by name is the fallen one, Satan, "the Prince of Darkness grim."[16] It's safe to say that Satan was attempting to hide his dark and grim self here, masquerading as "an angel of light."[17] Of course, such an attempt was ridiculous since he was presenting himself before the One who created him. Satan is a spectacular being—clever, brilliant,[18] and inestimably mightier than we are[19]—but he also has a certifiable history of insanity. He's captain of that band of beings who claim to be wise, but are really fools.[20] That becomes evident in this passage, as well as just about every other time Satan is mentioned in Scripture.

We may picture this meeting as being in heaven, God's abode. But if, when Jesus testified that he "saw Satan fall like lightning from heaven"[21] he was referring to an event that took place at or near creation, I think it is doubtful that this occurred in heaven, because it would seem inconceivable that Satan has ever been allowed to return. There is a good deal of debate on when he was thrown out. But of course the Lord can meet anywhere he wants.

---

16 "A Mighty Fortress Is Our God," Martin Luther (1483-1546), stanza 3.

17 2 Cor. 11:14.

18 Isa. 14:12-14; Eze. 28:2-7.

19 "On earth is not his equal./Did we in our own strength confide/Our striving would be losing." "A Mighty Fortress Is Our God," stanzas 2 and 3.

20 Rom. 1:22.

21 Luke 10:18.

A ROARING LION

The Lord addressed Satan with a question: "Where have you come from?" It may be that the Lord was singling him out as an imposter. We might say something like "how did you get in here?"

It wasn't as though the Lord didn't know where Satan had been, or how he had gotten in. God knew his every move, where he had been, and what he was up to. And the devil knew that the Lord knew, but his insane insolence interfered with the facts.

In any event, the Lord asked the question, and demanded a response. Satan gave an offhanded, flip answer: "From roaming through the earth and going back and forth in it" (1:7). You know, just touring, bopping around, sightseeing, vacationing.

There was some truth in Satan's answer. But it was not "the truth, the whole truth and nothing but the truth." He meant it to give the impression that his gallivanting about was innocent and harmless. Did he really think he could slip that one past the Lord? It was a lie. He wasn't on vacation. Satan, the Prince of the Power of the Air,[22] had, in fact, been roaming throughout the earth, but he was on the prowl:

> Be sober-minded; be watchful. Your adversary the
> devil prowls around like a roaring lion, seeking
> someone to devour (1 Pet. 5:8).

Though Satan claimed to be out there just "roaming," God knew what his true intentions were, and who he was after. The Lord was going to ferret the truth out of him, like an adult confronting a disobedient child trying to avoid punishment by lying. An adult presses the dishonest child for details.

MY SERVANT JOB

The Lord did so here by asking Satan another question: "Have you considered my servant Job?" (1:8). God brings the

---

22   Eph. 2:2.

subject up, identifying Job, but it wasn't as though Satan hadn't thought about God's servant. Satan already had his sights set on Job in particular, as indicated in his prepared response that followed. The Lord wasn't going to delay the issue; he was getting right to the point. I know you are on the prowl, and Job is your quarry. He is the one you have your eyes on.

GOD'S SOVEREIGN PURPOSES

Then God does something that may be hard for us to understand. He tells Satan: "there is none like him on the earth, a blameless and upright man, who fears God and turns away from evil" (1:8). It's as though the Lord was goading the devil to take action against Job! And Satan didn't need much goading, because if there's any mortal that he wants to destroy, it is a saint who is blameless, upright, who fears God and turns away from evil.

So why emphasize that, Lord? If you love Job, if you are his shield and protector, and if "the LORD will keep you from all harm—he will keep your life,"[23] then why push this door open, purposefully identifying poor Job, Satan's obvious prey? Sanderson says the answer is found in the sovereignty of God:

> First of all, we see God's sovereignty. In theological circles today, the word "sovereignty" has a much narrower meaning than it does when you read about it in the Bible. And this is unfortunate. We talk about the sovereignty of God, and we talk about the five points of Calvinism, and things of that sort, which is all very good and all very true, but the sovereignty of God is a much broader term than that. For example, in the discussion between God and Satan, Satan comes in and presents himself before the Lord, and the Lord says, "What have you been doing?" And Satan says, "Well, I've

---

23   Psa. 121:7.

been sort of roaming around in the earth, looking for some trouble." And the Lord says, "Have you considered my servant Job? There's nobody like him in all the world."

Who started all Job's trouble? God did it! God did it! Well, what right does God have to do that? I mean here's a man who is just leaning over backwards to be holy and righteous and sanctified and all the rest of it. I mean, what in the world?

Okay, let's come face-to-face with the sovereignty of God. God has the right, no question.

Have you considered my servant Job? [24]

Yet the Lord has guaranteed us that he will keep his promises, and his great, immutable assurance to his children is that we will prosper, that we have a hope and a future.[25] That's his sovereignty too. He will get the job done, and do so perfectly. Every detail will be accomplished, and prove to be in our interest and favor. Furthermore, the Lord will do it in a timely way—his schedule, not ours—and what seems like delay is no delay, for "[t]he Lord is not slow to fulfill his promise."[26]

Much of the Book of Job revolves around the Lord's opening question and statement to the devil. Job will constantly wonder why God seems to be after him. It would be easy to explain, perhaps, if we were simply to respond that God really wasn't after Job; that Job's calamities were due to the powers of evil alone, or to a devil out of God's control for a time. In that case, Job and the Lord would have spent the rest of the book fending him off, hopefully finally defeating him, as a *Star Wars* kind of epic battle. The problem with that explanation is that it is false, because God

---

24   2 JWS 75-120A-B.

25   Jer. 29:11.

26   2 Pet. 3:9.

is sovereign, and because the battle has already been won, forensically, in Christ.

SUFFERING FOR THE SAKE OF THE NAME

Part of the explanation, as already mentioned, is that God knew exactly what Satan was thinking. He knew not only that Satan had set his sights on Job, but also the reason. It was precisely because Job was a righteous man, and as God says to Satan, "my servant." Throughout the whole of Scripture, "from the blood of righteous Abel to the blood of Zechariah the son of Barachiah, whom you murdered between the sanctuary and the altar,"[27] God has placed his servants in harm's way. So any mystery here is a mystery surrounding every man or woman of God.[28] Perhaps the difference here is that God's determination to put Job at risk is set forth so starkly.

The Lord did the same with the Apostle Paul, and his intentions to do so were revealed almost immediately after Paul was converted. Paul was trying to peel the scales off his eyes, just blinded by his vision of Jesus on the road to Damascus, when the Lord told Ananias, who feared Paul because of his murderous rampages against Christians, to meet with and befriend Paul. Ananias was understandably queasy about this assignment, and resisted, but the Lord told him to

> Go, for he is a chosen instrument of mine to carry my name before the Gentiles and kings and the children of Israel. For *I will show him how much he must suffer for the sake of my name.* (Acts 9:15-16).

---

27 Mt. 23:35.

28 All of God's people can expect this: "Indeed, all who desire to live a godly life in Christ Jesus will be persecuted" (2 Tim. 3:12); "When [Paul and Barnabas] had preached the gospel to [the people of Derbe] and had made many disciples, they returned to Lystra and to Iconium and to Antioch, strengthening the souls of the disciples, encouraging them to continue in the faith, and saying that through many tribulations we must enter the kingdom of God." (Acts 14:21-22).

In the events of Paul's life following his encounter with Ananias many specific reasons for God's placing him in harm's way are revealed. Paul even explains many of them as he goes along.[29]

ANSWERS KNOWN ONLY TO GOD

We will find in studying the life of our brother Job that specific reasons for his suffering are more difficult to find. Some are there, and when discovered they bring awe and wonder. Job, though, couldn't see those things yet. In the end, God's overarching purpose was made clear to Job, but still, very few of God's specific purposes are revealed in the text.

We may take consolation here, as always, in the infinite wisdom of God. Of course there is nothing contingent or 'preliminary' about God's sovereign wisdom. But Job's life, like ours, was an ongoing process. If we are honest, and not pacified with pat answers, we have to admit that in the process of our lives (especially the Monday through Saturday part) we often question both the wisdom and the sovereignty of God.

Hard times—particularly those that seem interminable—raise such questions *especially* because we already have a conceptual understanding that God is all-wise and sovereign over every atom in the universe. It is just because of this that when trouble arrives, we raise the same questions Job raised. If God were not sovereign about every sparrow that fell to the ground, answers might seem easier. But he is sovereign over all. And that is why the Book of Job is at once so difficult and relevant for us.

---

29   For example, Paul told the church at Corinth that "we do not want you to be unaware, brothers, of the affliction we experienced in Asia. For we were so utterly burdened beyond our strength that we despaired of life itself. Indeed, we felt that we had received the sentence of death. But that was to make us rely not on ourselves but on God who raises the dead." (2 Cor. 2:8-9).

SATAN'S RESPONSE

Then Satan responded to the Lord. He didn't directly answer God's question "Have you considered my servant Job?" but his response belies the fact that he had been giving Job a whole lot of consideration. He had thought not only about the fact that Job had a good relationship with the Lord, but why. Satan believed he had figured out why God loved Job and Job feared God.

Satan thinks he is an expert at what makes the 'world go 'round.' And in truth, it is his domain. He is the Prince of the Power of the Air.[30] He knows that whatever control he may have been given in this world is subject to the Lord's ultimate authority, but he tries, unsuccessfully, to ignore that fact. It seems that he perpetually thinks somehow he can do an end run on God.

So Satan now takes upon himself the task of explaining the workings of the universe to the Lord of Glory, his Creator, the Maker of the universe, and the one who literally makes the world go around. The devil is an angel for sure, but he is also a fool, not embarrassed or cautious about rushing in where other angels fear to tread.

---

30   The Apostle Paul tells us that Satan is "the ruler of the kingdom of the air, the spirit who is now at work in those who are disobedient." (Eph. 2:2).

FOR REFLECTION

1.

From the text, is there any evidence as to why God called this meeting of angels, and if so, what reasons, if any, might he have had? Then, apart from the text, can you speculate as to why?

2.

What has been the most traumatic event in your life? As you look back on it, do you find yourself at peace about it, or not? How would you say God's sovereignty relates to it?

3.

Does it make you nervous, or concerned, to think that God might have conversations with Satan about you, similar to the one he had with Satan about Job?

3.

WHAT MAKES JOB TICK?

CHAPTER 1:9-11

SAINT LOUIS, like most river and coastal cities in the United States, has its waterfronts filled with all the gambling casinos the city fathers and mothers can cram into the limited space available. Though I've not yet had either inclination or enough spare cash to patronize them, I've seen the ads. The commercials don't exactly have what one might call a "heavenly" perspective, unless you think heaven is filled with slot machines and endless piles of poker chips. (Some people do think that.)

One of these ads featured a man and woman, average in appearance, poking quarter after quarter into the one-eyed bandit standing before them. Nothing. Another quarter or two. The machine is silent, and the tension rises. Then all of a sudden the machine in front of them explodes. Nickels, dimes and quarters come gushing out on the floor in front of them. Paper currency swirls around their heads. Soon the money is up to their ankles, then knees, waists and necks. They are drowning in money, all the while giddily pumping their fists in the air. A man's sinister "voice-over" then speaks to us, the hypnotized viewers, as the picture fades: "WE know what floats your boat!" A wink, a nudge, and a subliminal "C'mon, folks. We *all* know."

SATAN THOUGHT HE HAD JOB ALL FIGURED OUT

That's what Satan claimed to know, too, as he responded to the Lord's affirmation that "there is none like him on the earth, a blameless and upright man, who fears God and turns away from evil" (1:8). Satan had already considered that fact—note that he didn't deny that Job was all that God said he was—and had settled on the reason:

> Then Satan answered the LORD and said, "Does Job fear God for no reason? Have you not put a hedge around him and his house and all that he has, on every side? You have blessed the work of his hands, and his possessions have increased in the land. But stretch out your hand and touch all that he has, and he will curse you to your face." (1:9-11)

Satan had Job 'taped,' all figured out. He knew why Job appeared righteous before the Lord. It was because Job knew which side his bread was buttered on. For Job, Satan was saying, it's a good deal. Job wasn't the "genuine article." He wasn't in true fear of the Lord at all. Job was faking it, putting up a front that would become evident to everyone—including God—if his material wealth were to be taken away from him. Job was a sham. Satan knows what floats Job's boat; he knows what makes Job tick. It isn't the Lord, or Job's faith. It is his flocks and herds, his money, his reputation, his fields, his servants, and his children. Take those things away and just see how blameless and upright your so-called servant is. He'll curse you to your face. You'll see, God.

Maybe the devil had convinced himself of this because it's all that he understands. He's deluded. He believes a lie, "is a liar, and the father of lies."[31] He preaches lies. And just as the casino ad proclaims, Satan thinks he knows what 'floats your boat.' It's money and all that it can buy. The devil cannot see anything different,

---

31   Jn. 8:44.

and gives it no count. This is so because it's his nature, and why he was thrown out of heaven. He is willfully blind to and ignorant of what binds a believer to the Lord. He once knew better, but rejected the truth long ago.

SATAN INSULTS JOB

In his explanation of Job's righteous behavior, Satan insults Job. His theory is that Job is shallow, as he is, interested only in what worldly goods he has, earthly comfort, physical wellbeing, utterly materialistic, like the couple in the casino ad. Job, Satan says, found out that God was a good source of material things and was interested in God, pretending to be a good man, so the stream of income would continue. *God was a good deal.* But none of it was genuine. God was merely a means to an end. That's all that Job cared about. Job was a fraud.

SATAN DEFAMES JOB

Satan not only insults Job, but defames him. The law defines defamation, libel or slander, as making a statement (in any form, oral or written) injurious to another's reputation, when the speaker knew or should have known the statement to be false. The statement must be made, or "published," to one or more person, someone other than the individual who is being defamed. Here, all these requirements are met, and the 'third person' is God. The devil's intent was to defame Job in God's eyes.

That Satan libeled Job should come as no surprise, because most of the devil's time and effort is spent manufacturing false accusations against God's children.[32] Any one of us who knows that his sin is atoned for by the blood of Christ, and that he is thus delivered eternally from God's wrath and curse—that he is

---

32   "And I heard a loud voice in heaven, saying, 'Now the salvation and the power and the kingdom of our God and the authority of his Christ have come, for the accuser of our brothers has been thrown down, who accuses them day and night before our God.' " (Rev. 12:10).

no longer under law, but under grace—will find himself on the receiving end of Satan's incessant defamation before the Lord.

SATAN ACCUSES JOB

I wonder if we fully appreciate the fact that someone is constantly accusing us—specifically and by name, as the Great Accuser did here. Satan is determined to write every person alive out of the Lamb's Book of Life. Satan accused Job and he accuses us. Hard, direct evidence was more difficult to collect in Job's case than in mine.[33] But Job was a sinner, too:

> As it is written: "None is righteous, no, not one;
> no one understands; no one seeks for God.
> All have turned aside; together they have become
> worthless; no one does good, not even one."
> (Rom. 3:10-12)

Satan's prosecutorial attempts are doomed to fail, but not for lack of evidence. He has to go no further than this passage in Romans to make his case. But he cannot grasp, nor does he wish to understand, our invincible defense. That is why he misread Job's relationship to God. He has no appreciation for the basis of Job's standing with the Judge of all the earth. He holds no regard for the fact that we are already justified in the sight of God.[34] He does not understand, nor does he have any desire to understand, that we have already become the righteousness of God in Christ.[35]

This truth, of course, applies to all believers, to all those chosen by God's grace. When the devil was attacking Joshua the high priest, Zechariah the prophet said:

---

33 This surely must be the reason Satan singled out Job as a target. If he could successfully convict a man whom God holds out to be "blameless and upright" (1:8; 2:3), convicting the rest of us would seem to be an easy task.

34 Justification is defined as "an act of God's free grace, wherein he pardons all our sins, and *accepts us as righteous in his sight*, only for the righteousness of Christ imputed to us, and received by faith alone" *Westminster Shorter Catechism*, Q. 33. (emphasis added)

35 2 Cor. 5:21.

Then he showed me Joshua the high priest standing before the angel of the LORD, and Satan
standing at his right hand to accuse him. And the
Lord said to Satan, "The LORD rebuke you, O Satan! The LORD who has chosen Jerusalem rebuke
you! Is not this a brand plucked from the fire?"
(Zech. 3:1-2)

And in a summation, the Lord, through the Apostle John, tells
us what the end of this self-appointed prosecutor will be: "the
accuser of our brothers has been thrown down."[36]

The Great Accuser, not God's children, will be the one behind bars. And he's not going to get another go-round. God's
judgment will be final and eternal.

This characterization of Satan as the "accuser" is front and
center as the Book of Job unfolds. He is standing to one side, hidden from Job's view and hearing, shouting accusations at God's
servant through others. He sets the stage here at the beginning,
and though he isn't mentioned again until the end of Chapter 41,
his work, his words, and his accusations pervade.

SATAN INSULTS GOD

Most egregiously, Satan was insulting, or blaspheming, the
Lord himself. He was claiming that Job was not only a fraud, but
getting away with it. He was saying that God was capable of being
hoodwinked. He was insulting the Lord of Glory, intimating that
a mortal man is able to 'put one over' on his Creator.

Satan was alleging that God and Job were in a symbiotic relationship. The dictionary defines this as "the relationship between
two different kinds of living things that live together and depend
on each other." Satan was telling the Lord, to his face, that he, the
Lord of Glory, depended on Job. Why had God "built a hedge"
around Job? Satan implied that God favored Job because Job

---

36   Rev. 12:10.

praised and blessed the Lord. You do a favor for me, and I'll do one for you. You scratch my back, I'll scratch yours. To say such is a horrible insult even to one person in relationship to another—but to impugn the Lord of Glory? Saying that he conducts his relationship with us based on such vanity? That's incomprehensibly blasphemous. In short, Satan was saying that God himself was subject to Satan's stated principle of 'what makes the world go 'round.' Satan was telling God what made God tick, too.

THE THEODICY PROBLEM

Satan was confident of his own worldview, and sure of his reasoning as to why Job and the Lord were on good terms. So confident, in fact, that he challenged God to "touch all that [Job] has, and he will curse you to your face." If the Lord would give him permission, Satan would prove what made Job tick.

Of course, the Lord could have turned Satan aside at any point, but chose not to. Instead, God granted him the very permission he sought. The Lord answered: "Very well, then, everything he has is in your hands, but on the man himself do not lay a finger" (1:12). Why did God let Satan get his way, when he could have stopped him dead in his tracks? Sanderson wonders about that too, and comments:

> We need to notice that the Lord here is allowing
> Satan a great deal of freedom. This is one of the
> great mysteries that we find in the Scriptures, and
> in all of Christian thinking: the relation of God
> to evil. St. Augustine was quite concerned about
> this whole problem. He called it "theodicy," and
> he wrote a great deal about theodicy. What is the
> relationship of God with evil? Well, here we see
> one of the elements in the doctrine, and that is
> that in many instances God gives evil a free reign.

Do you want to do some harm, Satan? Here's Job,
go ahead.[37]

But though God's giving Satan permission to attack Job has
a dimension of mystery beyond our comprehension, we can be
assured of this crucial fact: God was in control. Even Satan knew
this, because he didn't say "if *I* touch everything he has," but "if
you touch everything he has." Satan knew that if the Lord didn't
do it, or allow it, it wasn't going to happen. Additionally, when
the Lord gave Satan permission, he drew a line that Satan could
not cross: "Only against him do not stretch out your hand." The
Lord was boss, and would remain so throughout. It's utterly insane that the devil would embark upon this project knowing that
God was setting the boundaries. But that's the nature of the beast.

UNDER COVER OF DARKNESS

It's also the nature of the beast, as he pursues an evil, destruc-
tive scheme, to do so outside the presence of the Lord. After he
got permission from the Lord, the author says simply: "So Satan
went out from the presence of the LORD" (1:12). Judas did the
same when Satan entered him at the Last Supper, immediately
before he betrayed Jesus:

> So, after receiving the morsel of bread, he imme-
> diately went out. And it was night. (Jn. 13:30)

What Satan was about to do would not bear the light of day
either.

FOR REFLECTION

I.

Do you think there was any truth in what Satan said about Job, and implied about all believers, that their love for God is motivated by what blessings he gives them?

2.

Why do you believe God gave Satan permission to attack Job?

3.

Limiting your response to what you see in Job 1:9-11, is there any comfort that you could have given Job, if both of you had known about this conversation and what was coming? Are you comforted by anything you see in these three verses?

4.

JOB'S PREPARATION

BEFORE RECOUNTING the devastation Satan brought
upon Job, it is crucial to see how Job had prepared for, or
how the Lord had prepared him for, what was about to
hit him. He had no idea what was coming, but he was ready.

READY OR NOT

None of us know what tomorrow will bring. We may take
protective measures, and hope that no ill will come. But of course
we don't know. All we know is that tomorrow is coming, and no
one can stop it.

The citizens of Joplin, Missouri had no idea what was about
to hit them on Sunday, May 22, 2011. On that day, just after 5:30 in
the afternoon an EF5 tornado, tracking from west to east, touched
down a little southwest of the unsuspecting city. There was virtually no warning of its approach. As it tracked over residential
neighborhoods, the tornado intensified exponentially. Photo-
graphs taken afterward showed entire subdivisions leveled by the
twister. Three-hundred pound parking stops, anchored with steel
rebar, were torn up and thrown 50 yards away. St. John's Regional
Hospital was destroyed. The resultant damage was in the billions
of dollars. One hundred fifty-eight people were killed.

How can you prepare for this kind of catastrophe? You can't. We have done all we can think of, including the installation of sophisticated alarm systems, tested at 11 sharp on the first Monday morning of every month, triggered by trustworthy meteorological reports. We know we're supposed to head for the basement. We've built storm-safe buildings and bunkers. We take many precautions, but still, Missouri lost 158 people within a few seconds, and there was nothing any of us could do about it but clean up the mess.

Job was about to lose everything he had, and it would be in an instant too. He could be no more prepared for the physical ruin and the loss of precious lives than the residents of Joplin on that Sunday afternoon.

But in the ways that really mattered, he was prepared.

JOB'S ESTATE PLAN

We hear advertisements on the radio and television urging us to plan our estates. We are invited to financial planning seminars; the seating is always claimed to be limited and we need to sign up immediately if we want to get in. We are told that an expert estate planning advisor will be the presenter. He or she will assure that no matter how small or large our portfolio may be, if we plan (and, by the way, put the money in their hands) we can have a bright future, financially speaking. And those of us who haven't put together a good plan (or maybe any plan at all) are made to feel that we have neglected the most important thing in life.

The most qualified presenter is one who has already done it. Job would have been right up there with the best. For one, I would be interested to hear how he did it, and I'd sign over my portfolio to him and pay a fee for his services (it would be a challenge for Job because my portfolio consists of a maxed-out credit card, but I bet he could do it).

Job would have been a good candidate to lead such a seminar right up through the end of Chapter 1, verse 12. As mentioned, he had everything the world could offer, and his successes garnered great respect from his peers.

So what was the shape of Job's own estate at this point, just before calamity struck? According to American standards, it was perfect. It was even diversified, with several kinds of livestock, so that if a camel disease wiped out the camels, he'd still have his oxen. In current terms, he had achieved the great American dream.

The great financial institutions of the country tell us about it all the time, because they know that's where our interests lie. Plan, plan, plan—and then stick to your plan. If you just follow our arrows on the floor while you're in your productive years, if you come to us for guidance, we'll see to it that you can live comfortably now, put your kids through college (Job had ten of them), and relax about your retirement. We'll see to it that you have enough money to maintain your standard of living all the way along, and go to the grave a comfortable, joyful, happy, and fulfilled man or woman. If, of course, such things are all that fulfilling.

Job could have even looked forward to a second career in his retirement, occasionally giving financial seminars on the subject of how to obtain that universally desired result. He wouldn't have to of course; he had enough salted away so it could be done at his discretion. But he could if he wanted.

ETERNAL ESTATES

Christians, in particular, need to pause at the end of verse 12 and ask themselves a question: is what Job had, in these terms, enough? Is it what we look forward to, and presently labor for? If it is basically what we worry about—and the ads are aimed at dealing with our worry—then the answer is mostly "yes," because it has begun to consume us. We have bought into the American dream wholesale.

It is good to plan,[38] save, and support our families,[39] but these things in and of themselves have no ultimate value. None. If we settle for such, we have not only been disobedient to the Lord, but have seriously shortchanged ourselves because the estate plan God offers is infinitely better—it is eternally fulfilling; it is the ultimate.

It isn't that money and property aren't good, because they serve an important purpose in our lives. God means for us to use what he has given us. But when it becomes too loved, too important, too exalted, it becomes an abomination to the Lord. And if you were to stand up at a financial planning seminar and say that the subject at hand wasn't really all that important to you, you'd be ridiculed, just as Jesus was.[40]

Job demonstrated how he viewed his estate through his prayer. His hopes and dreams were not temporal, but eternal. When he prayed for his children, he probably did pray for their safety and physical wellbeing, although it's not recorded. What is recorded is that he prayed that they would not curse God in their hearts. That was his interest. He focused on their *eternal* wellbeing. He obviously was not all that concerned about providing a large inheritance for them. His interest, his investment, was in eternity. Jesus said:

> Do not lay up for yourselves treasures on earth,
>   where moth and rust destroy and where thieves

---

38 Jesus said: "For which of you, desiring to build a tower, does not first sit down and count the cost, whether he has enough to complete it? Otherwise, when he has laid a foundation and is not able to finish, all who see it begin to mock him, saying, 'This man began to build and was not able to finish.' " (Lk. 14:28-30).

39 "But if anyone does not provide for his relatives, and especially for members of his household, he has denied the faith and is worse than an unbeliever." (1 Tim. 5:8).

40 "The Pharisees, who were lovers of money, heard all these things, and they ridiculed him. And [Jesus] said to them, 'You are those who justify yourselves before men, but God knows your hearts. For what is exalted among men is an abomination in the sight of God.' " (Lk. 16:14-15).

break in and steal, but lay up for yourselves treasures in heaven, where neither moth nor rust de-
stroys and where thieves do not break in and steal.
For where your treasure is, there your heart will
be also. (Mt. 6:19-21)

As we'll see throughout the rest of the Book of Job, Job had
obtained this kind of estate plan. Live or die, his plan was perfect
because it was anchored in the promises of God, not the counsel
of men. Whatever earthly treasures he had put away for the future
were about to evaporate, and he was prepared for that contingency, because he was depending entirely on something inestimably
better, something eternal.

But he was going to be put to the test.

FOR REFLECTION

1.

When you hear the term "estate plan," what comes to mind? In your mind, might there be a suitable biblical definition of this term, and if so, what might it be?

2.

In light of what Jesus said in the Sermon on the Mount (Mt. 6:19-21), do you believe that it's possible to save money, and accumulate an estate for your family, and still be obedient to his command not to "lay up for yourselves treasures on earth"?

3.

If your entire material estate were to be suddenly wiped out, would you still have an estate? What would it consist of?

5.

SATAN'S FIRST ASSAULT

CHAPTER 1:13-22

VERSE 13 of Chapter 1 is one of the great turning points in the Book of Job. Every bit of the American dream is going to go up in smoke in the space of about fifteen minutes. And it's going to happen because of a great battle that had been waging ever since Eve ate the fruit of the Tree of the Knowledge of Good and Evil.

SATAN VS. EVE'S GRANDSON

After Eve sinned, and Adam followed, the Lord spoke to Satan, who had lured Eve into sin:

> I will put enmity between thee and the woman,
> and between thy seed and her seed;
> it shall bruise thy head,
> and thou shalt bruise his heel. (Gen. 3:15, KJV)

Man has been in cosmic conflict with the devil from Genesis 3:15 on. The disaster that awaited Job was fallout. Sanderson says:

> The conflict now starts between Satan and the seed. This is one of the examples of the enmity that starts way back in the third chapter of Genesis, where Satan and the seed are going to battle it

out. This is a battle that comes to its climax only
at the cross, because only Jesus Christ is able, ultimately and finally, to deal with Satan.[41]

Job may not have known that his calamities were Satan's
work, but he did learn, as his world collapsed around him, that
someone more powerful than he was going to have to deal with it.
And as time goes on, he's going to start wondering if anyone more
powerful than he was actually going to deal with it at all.

SATAN'S POWER ON EARTH

Before looking at the specifics of the calamities Satan wreaked
on Job, we must take notice of his power. God has given him this
power, and he exercises it regularly in the world.

This power is far beyond human power, and really beyond
our understanding. Satan is going to take everything Job has, and
is going to afflict him with life-threatening disease. He will use the
natural elements, bands of Sabean terrorists, and other means to
accomplish his purposes.

Let's say that I wanted to get rid of you, or maybe just hurt
you in every way possible. Let's also say that the Lord gave me
permission to do so. How would I go about it? Send a storm to
knock down the house your children were in? Send fire from
heaven? Cause a band of Sabean terrorists to kill your employees?
Afflict you with boils from head to foot? I'd need a lot more than
permission.

But Satan has those powers, and he uses them to the full extent (though always within the limits the Lord has prescribed).
We make a great mistake if we think we can handle this evil being
on our own. We are no match, and we had best realize this at the
outset, because "[i]f we in our own strength confide, our striving
would be losing."[42] And though Job didn't know that Satan was

---

41 3 JWS 75-120B-B.
42 "A Mighty Fortress Is Our God," Martin Luther (1483-1546), stanza 2a.

back of what happened to him, he certainly understood that he was no match for whoever was at work.

JOB'S FIRST DEVASTATION

Job's first calamity happened on a day when he was preparing sacrifices and would be praying for his sons and daughters,[43] who were "eating and drinking wine" at the oldest brother's house. This, as we have seen, was Job's regular custom.

A messenger came running, and told Job: "The oxen were plowing and the donkeys feeding beside them, and the Sabeans fell upon them and took them and struck down the servants with the edge of the sword, and I alone have escaped to tell you!" (1:14-15). Oxen, donkeys, and servants—gone.

News sometimes comes trickling in, but in this case a tsunami of bad news had begun—a tsunami because it was going to come at Job wave upon powerful wave, leaving no time between for him to recover. While the first messenger was still speaking, another messenger came and said, "The fire of God fell from heaven and burned up the sheep and the servants and consumed them, and I alone have escaped to tell you!" (1:16). All Job's flocks of sheep and another crew of his servants—gone.

While this second bearer of bad news was still speaking, a third came: "The Chaldeans formed three groups and made a raid on the camels and took them and struck down the servants with the edge of the sword, and I alone have escaped to tell you!" (1:17). Now even more of Job's servants, and all his valuable dromedaries—gone.

Then a fourth and final messenger came while the third was still speaking, and told Job something that made the first three volleys of news seem like good news. "Your sons and daughters were eating and drinking wine in their oldest brother's house, and behold, a great wind came across the wilderness and struck the

---

43   See 1:4-5.

four corners of the house, and it fell upon the young people, and they are dead, and I alone have escaped to tell you!" (1:18-19).

SHOWDOWN

Satan's first round was complete. He had utterly devastated Job. He had taken away everything Job possessed, even his children, and now was Satan's set time for Job to curse God to his face.[44] Satan had claimed that God had "put a hedge" around Job[45] and now that hedge was gone. It was the showdown Satan wanted, and he was about to prove to God what it was that made Job tick.

JOB'S REACTION

No man or woman, including Job, could receive this news stoically, not unless they had become so numb to life that they were like a dead stump. Job was no stoic, evidenced by his life described in the first part of Chapter 1, and particularly at this very moment, when he was about to offer sacrifices and pray for his children. No matter what philosophy, worldview, or theology one had adopted, a person would be emotionally devastated. Job had this kind of expected reaction, because he got up from his prayers for his children, tore his robe and shaved his head[46] (1:20).

And like a man shot with a rifle, Job fell to the ground.

Here Job was, having hit the dirt with a thud, face down. He was ravaged, shocked and overwhelmed at the unbelievable blitz of horrible news he had just heard. He would later testify that "What I feared has come upon me; what I dreaded has happened

---

44   1:11.

45   1:9.

46   In the Old Testament, shaving the head was a sign of mourning. The prophet Micah told the Israelites to "[m]ake yourselves bald and cut off your hair, for the children of your delight; make yourselves as bald as the eagle, for they shall go from you into exile." (Mic. 1:16).

to me" (3:25, NIV). In a blink, a wonderful life had turned into the nightmare of nightmares.

IF ONLY IT WERE A NIGHTMARE!

If Job was like those of us who remember September 11, 2001, he was wishing it was just a nightmare. On that terrifying day, I was on the road in northern Missouri, and my wife called me on my cell to say that there had been a terrible accident in New York City; an airplane had crashed into the north World Trade Center tower. Then, a few minutes later, she called again to say that a second plane had hit the south tower. We knew then that this was no accident—we were under attack.

As the news continued to develop during the afternoon hours, with news of a hit at the Pentagon and a fourth plane crashing in Pennsylvania, the whole day became surreal. When we finally went to bed in the wee hours of the next morning, I truly wondered if this had been just a bad dream. We all hoped that it was, but of course it wasn't. It was real, terrifying, and impossible to process. Job surely went through something like this, and like us on 9/11, realized, sooner or later, that the terrible news was true. It's just there, and you have to deal with it. You have no choice.

JOB WORSHIPS

But there are two more words—momentous ones—appearing at the end of verse 20. They tell us everything we need to know about Job. He fell to the ground, "*and worshiped.*"

This is something that the world cannot fathom. Neither can believers, apart from the work of the Holy Spirit in their minds and hearts. Job himself likely didn't fully appreciate this fact about himself; believers just can't until the moment comes upon them. But he was *prepared* for this moment, prepared in ways that he probably didn't even realize. It may well have been a surprise to him that when he fell down, he discovered that he was instantly moved to worship his God and Creator.

Have you experienced this? Many believers have. It may not be that you have been through the kind of disasters that Job went through, but it is the same experience, because when you are devastated you are brought to your knees, or even further down—flat on your face in the dust. I've been there more than once, finding myself able to see only two things, and two persons.

One is the darkness; the other is the light. One is Satan; the other is the Lord. It's when that's all you can see that priorities become crystal clear. Just as Job did, you will find yourself in worship. What you had learned as a Christian was good theology, though possibly confined pretty much to head knowledge. You never dreamed that you would be called on to undergo a test like this. But that teaching, that "head knowledge," now serves you in good stead because you are instantly aware of the fact that the Light is infinitely more powerful than the Darkness, and that the Lord has already defeated Satan. And that is worship.

Many believers throughout the United States experienced this the day or so after 9/11. Special church services were scheduled, and people by the thousands, in every community, gathered to pray, to hear God's word, to worship. Like Job, we needed to (and as believers we wanted to), because we knew we had no way to deal with the devastation on our own.

When this happens, we discover something happening in our hearts. There is an overwhelming sense of the presence of the Holy Spirit. It's unmistakable. It is as though there is no one else present. He is at work in you, and you know it. Because every other answer or remedy is absent, you have an awareness that the Lord is your only hope. But this is not a "last ditch" hope, because that kind of hope is a frantic one, a grasping at straws. This is a hope that is constituted of the "peace of God, which surpasses all understanding."[47] You wonder at such time why it was that you thought you could find help anywhere else.

---

47   Phil. 4:7.

THE SUBSTANCE OF JOB'S WORSHIP

This kind of worship is simultaneously mystical and substantive. Mystical, in that there is a general but inexplicable sense of peace and even joy that permeates the spirit. Substantive, because the Holy Spirit is already beginning to give you perspective in the very particular kind of trial you are being called upon to endure. For Job, this was loss of everything he possessed. But already he could see the Lord working in the devastation. He testified:

> Naked I came from my mother's womb,
>   and naked shall I return.
> The LORD gave, and the LORD has taken away;
>   blessed be the name of the LORD." (1:21).

If Job had ended what he said here after the first two lines, it would have been no testimony of his faith at all. Everybody says that, believer or not. I brought nothing into the world, and I can't take anything with me when I leave. Or simply, "you can't take it with you." And if that is all that a person sees, life is really depressing, because what's the point? Solomon, in the Book of Ecclesiastes, examines what our earthly existence would be like without God, and comes to the conclusion that it would be vanity, vapor, meaningless.

But the rest of Job's statement, "The LORD gave, and the LORD has taken away; blessed be the name of the LORD," changes everything. Job sees his birth, death, and entire existence in the context of God's providence. So I come into the world and leave the world with exactly nothing? That's okay, because the Lord did it. "Blessed be the name of the LORD."

But is it really possible, or even appropriate, to praise the name of the Lord when you have lost everything you had, including all your children? No one could do this in and of himself. The Holy Spirit alone is able to do it, and he *will* do it for every believer when the time comes.

STUDY THE WORD

Don't ever let anyone tell you that learning Biblical 'book' theology is spiritually second-rate or even crippling to Christian growth. The Bible is written for our study[48] so that we can store it away in our heads and hearts. We often hear scathing rebukes of 'head knowledge' from the pulpit. But what we have learned in our heads will prove to be essential in our experience.

Some of the great truths we learn as Christians are that God is Creator, that every good and perfect gift comes from him alone, and that he is sovereign. This "systematic" theology, since it arises from and is consistent with God's word, is invaluable. Here it anchors Job when he needs it most. In fact, he is really *discovering* that he was anchored all along. He knew that he had nothing when he was created, when he was born (not even clothes), that the Lord alone was the source of all that he had and was, and that it was that same sovereign Lord who, in his wisdom, had taken it all away from him. Job accepted that, hard as it was, and was able to say: "blessed be the name of the LORD."

Job knew where his estate and his children had come from in the first place. It was not a result of his works. He knew that God, for his own purposes, had blessed him by giving him a family and possessions, and that he, Job, was not the one to receive the credit. It was purely a gift: "The LORD *gave*..." What the Lord gave was by grace, and "[e]very good gift and every perfect gift is from above, coming down from the Father of lights with whom there is no variation or shadow due to change."[49] Since it was the Lord's to give, it was the Lord's to take away. Job had an understanding of God's grace in everything. This was the platform upon which his entire estate was built.

---

48 "But as for you, continue in what you have learned and have become convinced of, because you know those from whom you learned it, and how from infancy you have known the Holy Scriptures, which are able to make you wise for salvation through faith in Christ Jesus." (2 Tim. 3:14-15).

49 James 1:17.

JOB AND ROMANS 8:28

Christians rightly quote Romans 8:28 when trouble comes, but it is a verse that easily can be abused, as Sanderson notes:

> I remember reading just a few years ago of a young couple whose baby was not normal when born. They were comforted by Christian people in their sorrow. And yet they said that they counted up to 128 times when people said to them, in a kind of casual, pat way, "Oh well, Romans 8:28." And this couple said, "If I hear Romans 8:28 once more, I'm going to scream!"
>
> Now you know there's something wonderful about Romans 8:28, but Romans 8:28 wasn't made to make people scream. And something's wrong when the Word of God is used in such a way that it takes someone who is undergoing a very heavy burden, and makes their burden worse.[50]

So the verse must not be applied to Job in a casual, pat, or flip way. But Job clearly had an appreciation for the truth contained in it. He could bless the name of the Lord because he knew that the Lord is sovereign, and that the Lord loved him. Paul wrote:

> And we know that for those who love God all things work together for good, for those who are called according to his purpose. (Rom. 8:28)

When I was 9 years old, I remember sitting at the lunch table with our family on a summer day. We were eating leftovers, including some ham. My little brother Tim, then 2, choked on a piece of ham, and his face turned red. Dad and Mom grabbed him, pounded him on the back, and shook him, but the bit of ham had become lodged in his windpipe and his face began to

---

50   2 JWS 75-120A-B.

turn blue. Dad grabbed him up into his arms, raced to the car, threw Tim onto the front seat and drove at top speed toward Walker, Iowa, two miles south, to see the local doctor. As he flew out the door, he shouted back at us: *"Pray!"*

We did, fervently. Within a minute or two, Dad returned, got out of the car and walked into the house with a perfectly healthy 2-year-old in his arms, put him in his highchair, and sat down again at the table.

Dad told us that as he was nearing Walker, the car had hit a big pothole in the gravel road. Tim bounced up in the air, hit the floor of the car with a thud, and the bit of ham spurted out of his throat. Not exactly the Heimlich maneuver, but it had the same effect. The family's prayers had been answered by means of a pothole.

We actually had wished for some years that our road had been blacktop, not gravel. But the Iowa State Highway Commission had its priorities, and our road was well down on the list. I remember Mom's complaints about the constant white dust that blew into our house, requiring vacuuming and dusting way more than she would have liked. We also didn't like the muddy road when it rained; we didn't like the potholes. Potholes reduce the life expectancy of the cars having to negotiate them.

So gravel roads weren't "good." But God knew. He knew that on such and such a summer day in 1952, a gravel road with a pothole would save a child's life. He knew that on that day, a pothole would be an answer to a family's fervent prayers. Tim is now 66, practicing law, and in good health. All things—including potholes—work together for the good of those who love God.

WHAT ROMANS 8:28 DOESN'T SAY

In trying to wrap my head around this verse, I have found it helpful to analyze it from the standpoint of what it does not say, with the expectation that so doing will reveal what it does say.

First, it does not say some, or most, things. It says all. This is meant to be categorical. Paul usually spoke categorically in the Book of Romans, particularly in the use of such words as "all." "All have sinned and fall short of the glory of God."[51] "Therefore, just as sin entered the world through one man, and death through sin, and in this way death came to all people, because all sinned."[52] And here, in Romans 8:28, all means all—every detail, every event, small or large. If there were even the tiniest exception, this promise would be an empty one.

Second, the verse does not say that things just have a way of working out. Lots of people will tell you that, but it is wishful thinking at best. Without doubt it is an optimistic way to view events, and may make you bright and cheery for awhile, but it has no substance. What the verse says is that God, not things, is the one at work. Things have no direction or purpose in and of themselves. It is only because God is at work in every "thing" that the promise can be of comfort.

Third, the verse does not say that every event is good. There are events that are unspeakably evil, with nothing good about them at all. Not all clouds have silver linings. What Paul does say is that God works all things *together* for good—the bad and the good events of our existence.

Many years ago I attended the funeral of a good friend. He was a young father, and had died in an accident. There was joy in the service because he was a believer. But some of his friends took the pulpit exclaiming his death to be really a good thing. After all, it was his entrance to heaven. One by one, these well-meaning friends waxed increasingly eloquent. The testimonials reached a frenzied climax when one brother said that "this was actually the best day of Dave's life!"

---

51   Rom. 3:23.
52   Rom. 5:12.

Thankfully, a seasoned pastor then spoke. It's normally not acceptable to contradict anyone at a funeral, particularly when they're eulogizing the deceased, but he had heard enough. In a kindly but forceful way, he got up and explained that this was anything but the best day in Dave's life. Dave was young; he left a wife and children behind. His accident was a tragedy. His death left a gaping hole. What the Psalmist said is certainly true, that "precious in the sight of the Lord is the death of his saints,"[53] but the same psalm says:

> The snares of death encompassed me,
>   the pangs of Sheol laid hold on me.
> I suffered distress and anguish. (Psa. 116:3)

Paul wrote, "The last enemy to be destroyed is death."[54] No, Dave's death was not the greatest day of his life. It was, perhaps, the worst. The event itself was a tragedy, but God was "working for the good" through the tragedy and all other events. Ultimately, that's what matters, and God assures us that even tragedy will work for good.

Fourth, Romans 8:28 does not say that God is working all things for our good as we define the word "good." It is God's eternal and perfect plan that Paul speaks of. The verse is too often used to interpret events in our lives as good in our terms. But what we isolate as good may not be good or good for us at all, because our values are badly skewed, and because we have limited vision. For example, if a family member totals the car, the crash seems bad but the insurance settlement seems good. Maybe so, and maybe not. Time will tell. But what Paul is telling us here is this: we can be absolutely certain, in the end, that *God's* good for us will prevail—and in every detail.

Fifth, the verse does not say that God is working all things for the good of everyone. This is a special, limited promise made

---

53   Psa. 116:15.
54   1 Cor. 15:26.

only to his covenant children. It is for the good of those who love God, who have been called according to his purpose. The promise is neither universal nor utopian. Those whom God sovereignly calls, according to his purpose, are inextricably tied in with the events of their lives, every one of which God works together for their good. Thus we can have present confidence and comfort—not only that we are called to be his eternally, but that this calling is perfectly meshed, for our good, with every event in our lives. No one can claim that except the citizens of the Kingdom of Heaven.

JOB CLAIMED ROMANS 8:28

Though Job didn't have the benefit of Paul's letter to the Romans, he had faith. He trusted the Lord to do what was right, and what was right for him personally. Without the truth summarized in Romans 8:28, Job could not have blessed the name of the Lord. He could not have worshiped. If he thought that only some events were covered; if he thought that "things will just work out"; if he thought that all events must be interpreted as good in and of themselves (losing all his children was an unmitigated calamity); if he thought that his definition of the word 'good' was what controlled, then his response would have been to curse God to his face, just as Satan had predicted. But he didn't. Job blessed the name of the Lord.

SATAN LOSES ROUND ONE

In all this, Job did not sin or charge God with wrong (1:22). To charge God with wrongdoing is sin; it is to curse God. But Job had faith in God. He knew that God was sovereign, that God had done this to him (2:3), was responsible for the whole thing, and was good.

Satan lost this battle. He had been sure of himself, because he believed he knew what Job would prove to be under pressure—and 'pressure' is a trivial word to describe what Job had gone through. When God removed the hedge, Job would cave. Satan had bet that Job's reverence for God was based entirely on what things God gave him. He had no appreciation for the fact that Job's faith was not in his material possessions or children, but in God himself.

"I suppose," Sanderson says, "if we may use our sanctified imagination, we can detect a smile of satisfaction on God's face. And perhaps a bit of anger, and a look of defeat, on Satan's face, because it didn't work out the way he knew it would. Because Satan doesn't understand saving faith. He thinks we believe in God because God does good things to us, and that's all. He doesn't know that when we're brought to Christ, we love God. And our love for God is greater than our desire for any of the good things that God could possibly give to us."[55]

---

55   3 JWS 75-120B-B.

FOR REFLECTION

I.

Recognizing that Satan's earthly power far exceeds ours, what hope is there for a human being when the Lord has pitted Satan against the human race ("I will put enmity between thee and the woman, and between thy seed and her seed")? Is there any hope indicated in Genesis 3:15?

2.

What is your worst fear? If it were to happen, do you think you could worship God as Job did, knowing that God could have prevented it? If so, why do you think you could? If one of your worst fears has already happened to you, were you able to worship?

3.

Has your study of the Bible and biblical doctrine helped you in times of crisis? How, and in what specific ways?

4.

Can you give examples of where Romans 8:28 evidenced itself in your experience?

6.

SATAN'S SECOND ASSAULT

CHAPTER 2:1-10

"AGAIN THERE WAS ANOTHER DAY," the author writes, "when the sons of God came to present themselves before the LORD, and Satan also came among them to present himself before the LORD. And the LORD said to Satan, 'From where have you come?' " (2:1-2).

SATAN NEVER FACES FACTS

If you ever needed a clue about the devil's character, you have it here. He answered, "From going to and fro on the earth, and from walking up and down on it" (2:2). This was insolent. Since the last time he presented himself before the Lord he had been about the task of wreaking enormous devastation on the Lord's servant. But not a word of that.

Of course God knew what had happened, Satan knew, and Satan knew that God knew. It was all out there, and Satan's casual answer, making no mention of Job, was the answer of a smart-aleck punk. No embarrassment, no admission of defeat in Job's test just past. It's like Agur wrote:

This is the way of an adulteress:

She eats and wipes her mouth and says,
"I have done no wrong." (Prov. 30:20)

No conscience, no compass except for the one pointing to hell, and apparently no self-respect. Just roll on. "Whatever," and a shrug of the shoulders.

WE CAN DO THE SAME

I once knew a lawyer, who, as best she could, represented a client who was like this. The young man, as all clients do, deserved a vigorous defense, but it was challenging because he was forever in trouble with the law. He'd team up with other young men of like mind, all desperately in need of money to support their drug habits, enter homes (homes of the other guys' families) and burgle them. Whatever they took, they'd sell. Then the complicit homeowner would present a claim to his insurance company, which was typically honored. Because everybody in the picture was cooperating, and because insurance companies have a high duty under the law to pay up when a homeowner makes such a claim, the scoundrels collected that money too.

This happened twenty-one times in a row before enough evidence was collected to allow the prosecuting attorneys to file charges, even though they had more than a hunch about how these heists were being carried out. After conviction, our young client spent a good deal of time 'up the river.'

Between imprisonments, this client would come into the office looking a little bit penitent, but not much. It became clear after multiple convictions that his penitence was either fake or momentary. He was really helping to plan the next burglary and fraudulent collection of insurance proceeds. No concern about committing another crime, and no apparent concern as to consequences. There was no shame, no humility. Thankfully, the young man eventually came to Christ largely through the continuing testimony of the Christian woman who represented him.

We are all naturally like this, apart from the regenerative work of the Holy Spirit. But Satan is like this permanently. In his kingdom, there is no embarrassment or repentance. It was because of his nature that the devil answered the Lord flippantly, repeating the lie that he had told the Lord in Chapter 1: "[f]rom going to and fro on the earth, and from walking up and down on it." (2:2).

The Lord's response was sarcastic:

> Have you considered my servant Job, that there is none like him on the earth, a blameless and upright man, who fears God and turns away from evil? (2:3)

It's as though the Lord is saying, "Okay, I can play your game. We can pretend that this isn't the second go-round, that your devastation of Job never happened, and that you were proven wrong."

JOB HAD REMAINED FIRM; SATAN WAS WRONG

But God is reciting the same words used in 1:8 to remind us that even now, although Satan's calamity had struck Job full force, God could say of him what he had said before. He still is "blameless and upright"; he still fears God and turns away from evil. Job had not changed a bit. In fact, Satan's vicious, merciless blows had done nothing but drive Job more firmly into God's protective, loving hand. Satan's attack hadn't changed a thing.

Had Satan "considered" Job this time? Even more than at the first. He had a laser focus on him. He had done everything he could to destroy him, operating within the liberal boundaries God had set. He had attempted to get Job to curse God to his face, but his efforts had failed. This blameless and upright man who feared God and turned away from evil, though devastated, was intact. Since Satan didn't mention Job in his reply, the Lord, once again got right to the point. He confronts Satan with Job's reaction to what had happened: "He still holds fast his integrity,[56]

---

56 Though no person can trust his "integrity" for salvation, it is clearly some-

although you incited me against him to destroy him without reason" (2:3).

We need to deal with two questions raised by what the Lord said to Satan.

SATAN INCITED GOD

God says that Satan "incited" him to ruin Job. There is no clever way for us to avoid the subject, or to maneuver our way around it. God destroyed Job. The Lord is holding himself responsible for Job's calamity, and states that Satan incited him to bring it on.

Can God be incited? Does he react as we do, when somebody pushes one of our hot buttons? Did the Lord feel like he had had just about enough from the devil, reached his boiling point, and overreacted? Is the Lord saying that he was subject to a flash of temper, and then perhaps regretted what he has done after he had cooled off? Of course we know, from other Scripture, that these characterizations are impossible. The Apostle James wrote that "God cannot be tempted with evil,"[57] and in him "there is no variation or shadow due to change."[58]

No, the Lord is not subject to flashes of temper. Neither his words nor actions are "shifting shadows." He never does—he *cannot*—regret what he has done. He will not be manipulated by anyone. He is immutable:

> God is a spirit, infinite, eternal and *unchangeable*,
> in his being, wisdom, power, holiness, justice,
> goodness and truth.[59] (emphasis added)

---

thing that the Lord values highly in his servants.

57   James 1:13. See also 1 Ki. 15:29: "[T]he Glory of Israel will not lie or have regret, for he is not a man, that he should have regret."

58   James 1:16-17.

59   *Westminster Shorter Catechism*, Q. 4.

Yet he says here that Satan incited him to destroy Job. Can he be incited, yet not tempted, not unchanged? We could attempt to make answer, with Scripture proof, that God is beyond our understanding;[60] his thoughts are not our thoughts;[61] the clay does not question the potter[62]—and all this is unquestionably true. Yet many times in Scripture we are given seemingly inexplicable truths, even paradoxes, and God expects us to deal with the obvious tension with the aid of the Holy Spirit through Scripture. This is one of those times, and Scripture must interpret Scripture.

God cannot be tempted by evil. The Apostle James is saying something about the very nature of God: he cannot be tempted, and if he could be, he wouldn't be God. God did not ruin Job or allow him to be ruined because someone tempted him to do so. Certainly Satan tried. But the entire business was in God's hands. The only way to interpret the word "incite" here, it seems to me, is to understand that Satan challenged God, and God, in his wisdom, chose to let Satan have his way with Job. There is no question but that Satan was involved, and that the Lord responded to him by granting him his request to take Job on. God responds to man's requests as well. But no one can incite him to sin. It is enough to say, at this point, that Satan is always under God's control, and that God can and does use the beast to bring about his eternal will. In later chapters of the Book of Job this becomes clearer, and this truth will prove itself to be of inestimable comfort to Job, and therefore to us.

It is also helpful to remember the context of Satan's meetings with the Lord here. God called the meetings. The angels presented themselves before him—not him before them. No one, angel or man, can approach God without his permission or invitation. For "who would dare of himself to approach me? declares the Lord."[63] The Lord scheduled the meetings. He set the agendas.

---

60   36:26.

61   Isa. 55:8.

62   Rom. 9:20-21.

63   Jer. 30:21.

Everything said, everything done and decided, were within his eternal, perfect, sovereign design and control.

WITHOUT REASON

The Lord said not only that Satan incited him to ruin Job, but also that the ruination was *without reason*. What could he have meant by this? Very plainly, here he says that he himself did it, and that he did it without reason. Does God ever do anything without reason, or without justification?

There is a difference between the words "purpose" and "reason." What the Lord was telling Satan was that there was no reason known to Satan, angels or men for his ruination of Job. As we will see, the theology of the day was that when you see catastrophe strike a person, it always meant that the person was being punished for his sin. Such had to be the "reason." When God tells Satan that he did this to Job "without reason," he means that he wasn't punishing Job for any sin he had committed, or for any other matter.

But that is not to say that God had no *purpose* in ruining Job. I am sure that we, residing this side of heaven, cannot come close to comprehending what God's purpose was in devastating him. But we don't have to fully comprehend God's purposes. Ultimately, it's enough for us to know that he always has a purpose, and that it is always good. Every event, big or small, has divine purpose. The Westminster Catechism says that God's purposes are universal:

> *Q.* What are the decrees of God?
>
> *A.* The decrees of God are, his *eternal purpose,* according to the counsel of his will, whereby, for his own glory, he hath foreordained whatsoever comes to pass.[64] (emphasis added)

A friend of mine once told me that the phrase "God moves in a mysterious way" is overused and trite. Often it is, but not

---

64 *Westminster Shorter Catechism,* Q. 7.

here. The first stanza of William Cowper's great hymn, where the phrase originated, reads:

> God moves in a mysterious way
> His wonders to perform;
> He plants His footsteps in the sea
> And rides upon the storm.[65]

In Job chapters 37-41, Job and his friends will see that God "rides upon the storm"—literally. One of the great truths we can glean from the Book of Job is that God indeed moves in mysterious ways, but with the assurance that he has a purpose in it all: "his wonders to perform." The last two stanzas of Cowper's hymn read:

> His purposes will ripen fast,
> Unfolding every hour;
> The bud may have a bitter taste,
> But sweet will be the flow'r.
>
> Blind unbelief is sure to err
> And scan His work in vain;
> God is His own interpreter,
> And He will make it plain.

SATAN'S EXPLANATION

Satan had come up with an explanation for Job's holding fast to the Lord after he had lost everything. But he doesn't acknowledge that he was wrong in the first instance; not a whisper of that. He simply and blatantly claims that Job proved 'faithful' to the Lord only because he was trying to protect himself.

"Skin for skin!" he said.

Lovers of the game have assembled some great slang to describe baseball. One such term is "chin music." When a pitcher

---

65   William Cowper, "God Moves in a Mysterious Way" (1773).

sees that a batter is staking claim to too much of the plate, he will throw a high, inside fastball—a "brushback" pitch—to move the batter off the plate by the time the next pitch arrives. Instinctively, the batter' arm will fly up to protect his face and head. This is natural. Your body will protect a more important part with a less important part. You can lose an arm and live. But you can't live without a head. This skin for that skin. "All that a man has he will give for his life," Satan says (2:4).

JOB, SELFISH TO THE CORE

Satan, as mentioned previously, had already defamed Job before the Lord. Now, though his original slander had proven to be false, he intensifies his defamation of the man. Job, he says, is selfish to the very core of his being. Job knew that what his wife would say later was true—that if he cursed God, he would die. The reason he didn't curse God, Satan said, was because he didn't want to die.

The devil reasoned that Job was willing to give up everything he had, and was even willing to discount his children, if he could save his life in doing so. He would be willing to trade their skin for his skin. Satan was instructing the Lord that Job was worse than the Lord could even imagine. Job's apparent devotion to the Lord was irrefutable evidence not of his faith, but his selfish desire for personal protection.

Of course, Job hadn't actually given up his children or anything else; they had been taken from him. Satan is essentially saying that his children meant little or nothing to Job in comparison to his life. Job's body is what made Job tick. The Lord didn't understand this fact of life, Satan thought, so he would set him straight. Never mind that he was talking to the Creator of the universe, the one who had designed Job.

WHAT SATAN THINKS OF US

Satan's words here were baseline to him. He had adopted a false paradigm, and wouldn't let go of it. He had established in his warped mind an assumption about Job. He believed Job was selfish to the core (just as Satan himself is), and that everything must yield to that fact.

This calls to mind the story about a schizophrenic man who visited his psychiatrist. "I'm dead," he told his doctor.

"You're not dead," his doctor said. "Look at you. You are sitting there talking to me."

"That's just what it looks like to you," said the patient, "but seriously, I'm dead."

"OK," the psychiatrist said, "I'll prove to you that you're alive. Do dead people bleed?"

"No," the man answered. "I know that much." So his doctor pricked the man's finger, and a drop of blood oozed out.

"See," the doctor said. "You bleed, so you're alive!"

"Well, what do you know about that!" the paitent exclaimed. "I was wrong. I guess dead people do bleed!"

The man's baseline was that he was dead, and everything, including diametrically opposing, irrefutable evidence, had to conform to that paradigm.

So it was with Satan when he came in before the Lord. Job was selfish, and anything to the contrary had to yield to that. It thus actually became evidence supporting his original proposition! In truth, though, what Satan said was proof of his own insanity.

Satan is wrong about us—not just about Christians, but everyone. He does not want to accept the fact that we are made in God's image, that we are spiritual beings. He denies this truth and lies to everyone about it, including the Lord. It may also be that he is blinded from this fact, but if so, he is willfully blinded. But he's wrong about us. Parents *will* give up their lives for their children, and surely Job would have done so as well.

True enough, man in his fallen condition is unspeakably selfish. Except for common grace he would give up everything, including his children, to save his own flesh. But God's common grace, instilled in his creation, is a powerful countervailing shield. If it were not for that, humankind would have destroyed itself long ago.

My wife and I are good friends of a couple, our next-door neighbors, who lost their daughter, a toddler, to a rare form of blood cancer. No matter what the doctors did, the blood disease progressed. The ordeal lasted more than a year. Her father tearfully told me several times that what he ached for, as he stood by her bedside, was to go through the horrible experience for her. Nothing would give him more joy than to be able to take her pain, and if it came to it, die in her place. It would be a heartless father who would feel any other way, and such a person is rare.

But the devil refuses to understand that; he can't or won't take it for what it is. He thinks he knows what makes a father and mother tick, but he doesn't know the truth of the matter at all. "There is no truth in him."[66] He is not reluctant to deny the Word of God. In Satan's universe, man *does* live by bread alone.[67]

Satan's view stands in stark contradiction to the Creator's, whom he faced in Matthew 3. Jesus had just spent forty days without food, and being a man, was hungry. Satan appeared to him, and suggested that Jesus exercise his divine power and change the stones into bread. Tempting, when you haven't had anything to eat for more than a month. But Jesus declined, quoting Moses:

> Man shall not live by bread alone, but by every
> word that comes from the mouth of God.[68]

---

66 Jn. 8:44.
67 See Mt. 4:4.
68 Mt. 4:4, citing Deut. 8:3.

Jesus was answering Satan as a man, because Jesus was being tempted as a man. He's saying that Satan possessed only a small part of the picture of the nature of man. He's telling Satan, "You don't know what we men are like." True enough, man needs bread to live. But he needs something more: he need's God's Word. This isn't so much a requirement God imposes on man as it is a statement about the nature of man. Man *can't* live by bread alone. If he tries, he'll find it doesn't work.

Satan will never understand what makes us tick. He has no doubt but that if he's allowed to put Job to the test just once more, his theory will prove correct: "But stretch out your hand and touch his bone and his flesh, and he will curse you to your face" (2:5). Again, no apologies or embarrassment. This time, God, you'll see.

GOD'S PERMISSION (2)

In his inscrutable wisdom, God again gave Satan his wish: "Behold, he is in your hand; only spare his life" (2:6). You can strike his flesh and his bones. But spare his life; as in "here is where your proud waves halt" (38:11, NIV). God was again reminding the devil that he alone, the Lord of creation, was in control, and that Satan could not go beyond the word, the command, of the Lord.

Many times, in the history of his people, God set such limits. Take the case of the false prophet Balaam.[69] Balaam kept pushing, pushing, pushing the Lord to give him permission to curse Israel. At each 'push,' although the Lord made it clear that to go forward was sin, he nevertheless gave Balaam permission to speak to Israel. But it would be within the Lord's limits. When Balaam tried to curse Israel, the Lord intervened and turned his curses into blessings. The same was true where the Lord actually conscripted Nebuchadnezzar to attack Jerusalem. God permitted Nebuchadnezzar to do the wicked deed. He could go as far

---

69   Numbers 22-24.

as the Lord allowed, and no farther. He could go only so far as that permitted by the Lord's purposes.

So Satan got his admission ticket. He could attack Job physically. But he could not penetrate outside the parameters the Lord had set.

SATAN'S SECOND ASSAULT

Like a horse charging out of the gate at Churchill Downs, Satan left the presence of the Lord, eager to carry out his nefarious plan. And he meted out no minor injury, but one that he had custom designed to cause his human quarry horrifying pain day and night. He did not leave a millimeter of Job's body untouched. He "struck Job with loathsome sores from the sole of his foot to the crown of his head" (2:7). And it was apparently instant.

Think about Job's condition. There was no way he could escape the pain. If you have ever been in the hospital for a week or more, confined to a bed, you may have developed bed sores, what the doctors call "pressure" or "decubitous" ulcers. Even one of these bedsores can drive you crazy. If you have one on your heel, you can flip over in the bed but when you pull a sheet up over your feet you wince, because even a soft cotton sheet irritates the area and can cause unbearable pain.

That's just one bed sore. Job had boils,[70] staph infections that are worse than bed sores, and every inch of his body was covered with them. There was no morphine or other narcotic medication in his day—not even aspirin—to manage the pain. There were no anitbiotics to treat the infection. Because Job was a human being

---

70 The Lord had warned the Israelites, before they entered the Promised Land, that they would be afflicted with the "boils of Egypt" if they disobeyed the words of the law: "The LORD will strike you with the boils of Egypt, and with tumors and scabs and itch, of which you cannot be healed" (Deut. 28:27). Job was not afflicted with boils because of his sin, but like Jesus, he "suffered in the flesh" (1 Pet. 4:1), thus being sanctified.

subject to the law of gravity, he had to sit or lie down somewhere, sometime, with those boils.

JOB'S HEALTH ISSUES

Later in the Book of Job, the author records that Job suffered from these specific health issues:[71]

> disfigurement; a revolting appearance (2:12; 19:19)
> loss of appetite (3:24; 33:20)
> insomnia; tossing and turning all night (7:4)
> painful, festering sores over the entire body (7:5)
> nightmares (7:14)
> failing eyesight (17:7)
> excessive thinness; skeletal appearance (17:7;
>   19:20)
> halitosis (19:17)
> pain day and night (30:17)
> scabs that turned black and peeled (30:28, 30)
> fever (30:30)

Our daughter is a nurse, and on occasion I bother her with a visit when she's tending patients. She's really sweet about it, but lets me know by the expression on her face that I'm intruding. I've noticed a sign in the hospital hallway on her floor, "turn often," a reminder to the nursing staff to do what can be done to prevent bed sores. I handled a case once where the court ruled that failure to "turn often" constituted malpractice, so it's a must. But reading the above list of Job's medical issues makes it clear that turning often wouldn't help him. I think that a judge, in Job's case, might rule that "turning often" would *be* malpractice. Turning him over would only hurt: he needed a special sign on his door, saying "but don't turn this one." Even with all the advances in medicine over the past centuries, it's hard to come up with any protocol that would help our brother Job.

---

71   John W. Sanderson, Lectures (1981).

We don't know how someone afflicted with boils was treated in Job's day. Job, as he "sat among the ashes" (a sign of humility and deprivation), chose to "scrape" himself with a piece of broken pottery (2:8). The painful boils excreted pus, and it is most likely that Job scraped the sores so that the pus could be released. But whatever he did to give himself relief surely wasn't much of a remedy, and the unrelenting pain must have been intolerable. It would be so even in one of our spotless hospitals today, but on an ash heap?

JOB'S WIFE

Job wished at this point that the Lord had taken his life.[72] Living had become unbearable. His wife wished the same. Looking at him, she despised him. She couldn't imagine the burden it would be for her to continue life with her husband. Perhaps what she said to him arose partly out of pity (for Job or for herself), but whatever the reason, it was wrong: "Do you still hold fast your integrity? Curse God and die!" (2:9).

Job's wife, unwittingly, had become a messenger from hell. Do you want to end this nightmare? Don't let your 'integrity' stand in the way. Let go of it. It clearly hasn't done you any good up to this point. We've lost everything. God has taken our children away from us. You're a mess. You yourself wish you were dead. Curse God and die!

John Sanderson set out both the reasoning of Job's wife and the manner in which we may commit the same error.[73] As a logician, he did the first in syllogism form.

Her reasoning:

> if God is just, he must bless a just man
> Job is not blessed
> *ergo*, God is a sinner or God is unjust

---

72 3:1ff.
73 John W. Sanderson, Lectures (1981).

> she knows that Job is not a sinner
> *ergo*, God is unjust and unworthy of worship
> since death is approaching, you might as well
>   forsake God

and we commit her error when:

> we say "seeing is believing"[74]
> we make ignorance of facts a basis for dogmatism
> we discard a thing when we see no purpose
> we think God exists only to make us happy
> we think more of things than we do of God

You can see that though this woman was in error, Sanderson treats her with respect; he takes time to evaluate what she said. But she is often villified by commentators on the Book of Job. That's not really fair.

JOB'S WIFE DESERVES OUR CONSIDERATION

We must think of the context. Job's wife was the mother of ten children who had just been killed. She obviously joined her husband in understanding that the Lord had taken them, and that God alone was responsible. She was grief-stricken, just as her husband was. There is no evidence that she was hard-hearted or mean-spirited. She simply said something that was an awful thing to say, but it came from the depths of her own sorrow and bewilderment. She had, for the moment, unwittingly joined up with Satan, but that's not evidence that she ceased being a child of God. Sanderson steps in as her advocate, and takes those to task who belittle her:

> Now we need to take a close look at Job's wife.
> I think it's awfully easy for us to look back on
> her, and to sort of belittle her and say, "Well, you

---

74   Sanderson here cites "Doubting Thomas." (Jn. 20:24-25). John W. Sanderson, Lectures (1981).

know that woman was just a horrible, horrible wife. If we had been there, we certainly would have given better advice." And all that sort of rot.

I would like to make out a case for Mrs. Job. Apparently, she had lived with this man for quite a number of years. All of their children seemed to have grown up and matured. And she knows her husband. Her question betrays that: "Do you *still* hold fast your integrity?" You've been a good man all your life. I know you. I've lived with you. But now, the only advice I have for you is to curse God and die.

Notice, that without realizing it, she quotes Satan, and she also quotes God. She quotes God because she asks "Do you still hold fast your integrity?" And those are the very words which the Lord used in the third verse. She quotes Satan, because she says, "Curse God and die," and those are the very words that Satan had used twice before. Well, we will come back to her in just a moment, and try to analyze her reasoning, and why she might have said what she said, and what lessons we can learn from that.

But let's go on for just a moment. Job said to her, "You speak as one of the foolish women." Just the way he said that, it comes across to me that she didn't always talk that way. It seems to me he is saying, "Now, you're talking the way other women usually talk, but not you. And you've fallen into a trap. Shall we indeed accept good from God, and not accept adversity?" And Job's thought is that we ought to let God be God.[75]

---

75   5 JWS 75-120C-A.

All of us are weak like Job's wife. We say things, in the heat of the battle, that we later would like to retract.

Remember Peter, who uttered the "great confession." Jesus had asked his disciples "Who do people say that the Son of Man is?" and Peter answered "You are the Christ, the Son of the living God." Jesus's response to Peter could not have been more positive or affirming: "Blessed are you, Simon Bar-Jonah! For flesh and blood has not revealed this to you, but my Father who is in heaven. And I tell you, you are Peter, and on this rock I will build my church, and the gates of hell shall not prevail against it. I will give you the keys of the kingdom of heaven, and whatever you bind on earth shall be bound in heaven, and whatever you loose on earth shall be loosed in heaven."[76]

But then Jesus told his disciples about the fact that he was going to have to go to Jerusalem and die. Simon Peter, who had just been so powerfully affirmed, said: "Far be it from you, Lord! This shall never happen to you!" Jesus turned to Peter with stinging words: "Get behind me, Satan! You are a hindrance to me. For you are not setting your mind on the things of God, but on the things of man."[77] This turned out to be the great Apostle Peter. So let's give room to Job's wife. As the Lord did with Peter, we need to look past the person who said something terribly wrong, and see who it really is who's blaspheming *El Shaddai.*

Job and his wife apparently continued their marriage in some harmony, because the worst thing recorded that she said after this was that she couldn't stand her husband's breath (19:17), but that's not unheard of, not in my experience. At least that would indicate she was close enough to Job to tell.

JOB CAUTIONS HIS WIFE

Job didn't want to go on living. He fervently wanted to die (3:1ff). But he absolutely would not curse God; he refused (and

76   Mt. 16:16-19.

77   Mt. 16:23.

throughout the rest of the Book he will continue to refuse) to abandon his integrity. He answered his wife: "You speak as one of the foolish women would speak. Shall we receive good from God, and shall we not receive evil?" (2:10). Even in his abhorrent condition, his anchor was in the Lord. It was hard for him, but on the other hand it was a commitment he had made, and no matter what had happened to him, or what was still to come, his anchor, his only hope in life or death, was the Lord. Though written millenia later, Job was saying this to his wife:

> Whate're my God ordains is right
> His holy will abideth
> I will be still whate're he doth
> and follow where he guideth.
> He is my God; though dark my road,
> he holds me that I shall not fall:
> wherefore to him I leave it all.

> Whate'er my God ordains is right:
> Though now this cup, in drinking,
> May bitter seem to my faint heart,
> I take it, all unshrinking.
> My God is true; each morn anew
> Sweet comfort yet shall fill my heart,
> And pain and sorrow shall depart.[78]

JOB'S LONELINESS

Job prefigured Christ in many ways. One of those ways was in being cut off from those closest to him, those who should be expected to comfort, console and encourage him. He had already lost his children, who could have been an enormous source of help. His wife for a time was not keeping her marriage vow to stay close to Job "in sickness or in health." In the immediate aftermath of the calamities, she was more like Egypt was to the Israelites in

---

78   "Whate'er My God Ordains Is Right," Samuel Rodigast (1676), stanzas 1 and 5.

2 Kings 18:21, "that broken reed of a staff, which will pierce the hand of any man who leans on it." Job needed her to be a strong support, not someone who wounded him when he leaned on her.

Jesus' disciples did the same at his trial and crucifixion. King David had prophesied that the Lord Jesus "looked for pity, but there was none, and for comforters, but found none."[79] While Jesus was suffering, his friends were disappearing. Three of Job's best friends are coming to pay a visit, but as we will see, they turned out to be the worst deserters of all.

Job was going to find what Christians often find in the day of trial. Friends can desert us; it's too much for them to bear, and too much to be drawn into another's troubles. But even when others don't desert outright, a Christian often discovers a sense of aloneness in bearing the pain. Often he or she begins to realize that others *can't* help—there's really nothing they can do anyway (certainly this was the case with Job). Then true loneliness sets in, because it dawns on you that you are on your own, for real—even if others want to help.

But it is also just at such times that we are driven to Christ, and we begin to recognize the foundational truth that he is our only comfort in life and in death.[80] Surely Job, like all of us, had his doubts. But because the Holy Spirit was in him, working faith in his heart, he sensed that those clouds of doubt would eventually clear. He could not accept his wife's advice. He could not curse the very One in whom he believed. He was convinced by the Holy Spirit that God was able to guard what he had entrusted to him until that day.[81] He would not forsake that truth.

---

79 Psa. 69:20.
80 *Heidelberg Catechism*, Q. 1.
81 "But I am not ashamed, for I know whom I have believed, and I am convinced that he is able to guard until that Day what has been entrusted to me." (2 Tim. 1:12).

FOR REFLECTION

I.

Do you think Job's refusal to curse God after his first devastation was an "exception to the rule"? That is, do you think many believers would have done so? Have you ever witnessed a believer do so, or perhaps turn away from his or her faith, after catastrophe?

2.

Do you think Job was being treated fairly when God gave Satan permission to attack him a second time?

3.

Do you think Job's wife should be excused for her rash advice to Job to "curse God and die"? How did she "think more of things than she did of God," as Sanderson says?

7.

JOB'S FRIENDS

CHAPTER 2:11-13

IT'S A WONDERFUL LIFE

JUST ABOUT OUR FAVORITE Christmas movie, which we dredge up every year, is Frank Capra's 1946 "It's A Wonderful Life." Jimmy Stewart, in a career performance, played the part of Savings and Loan president George Bailey. George runs into serious trouble when his Uncle Billy mistakenly hands $8,000 to evil Mr. Potter instead of depositing it in the company bank account. The federal bank examiners are on his tail. He has no solution, and as most of us tend to do, isolates himself from everyone, and finds himself all alone. He then attempts suicide. He says that he wishes he had never been born, just as Job wished, in the strongest of terms.[82]

But not to worry. George's friends hear about his predicament, and know he can't handle it on his own. They criss-cross town and country with telephone and telegraph, seem to appear

---

82   3:1ff.

from nowhere, come to his home, and one by one pour currency, coins, jewelry and even I.O.U.'s into an overflowing bowl to
help him out. His boyhood friend Sam Wainwright calls and tells
George's wife that he is wiring more than enough money to cover
the shortfall. George turns out just fine, drops the suicide plan,
sticks with his beautiful wife (Donna Reed) and family, and in
the process learns something more important than the gifts in
the bowl: he has *friends*. The movie ends happily with all circled
around a twinkling Christmas tree. Everyone, including the federal bank examiner, is overjoyed, and George finds a book in the
money bowl inscribed with the encouraging words "No man is a
failure who has friends."

Job had friends too. Prior to his devastations, he had lots of
them, and they held him in high regard. They felt honored to have
Job as their friend. But later in the book, Job will testify that every
last one of them had deserted him and now despised the very sight
of him. Frank Capra would have to say that Job was a failure.

ELIPHAZ, BILDAD & ZOPHAR WERE JOB'S GOOD FRIENDS

Among Job's friends were some very special ones. Their
names were Eliphaz, Bildad, and Zophar. Throughout the centuries these three have been mocked and ridiculed because of what
they said to Job. Their names personify friends who turn out not
to be friends after all, as in "With friends like these, who needs
enemies?" When we refer to people as "Job's friends," everyone
understands that this is what we mean. And to a great extent, this
turns out to be true. The three will judge, criticize and even condemn Job because of their faulty theology.

But to leave it there is to give Eliphaz, Bildad and Zophar
short shrift. Sanderson has made out a case for Job's wife, and does
the same for Job's friends:

> Let's try to make out a case for the friends. And,
> incidentally, let's make out a case for you. Because
> the next time you go to the hospital, you want to

help. You may bawl them out for whatever they did, but these men didn't send word to each other and say, "Let's meet at such and such a place, and let's go and make life miserable for Job." They really wanted to comfort him. They were venerable men. They were obviously wise men. One of them came from Teman, which was proverbial for its wisdom. They came from the East; they were sons of the East. And one of the things that was said of Solomon, is that his wisdom was so great that he was "wiser than the sons of the East." So these are people who come from a place of erudition, a place of wisdom.[83]

As we consider their visit recorded in Scripture, how they approached their friend Job, and their overall purpose in coming to see him, it's clear that they were more than passingly concerned for him. Their good motives will persist through the end of the book, even though they turn against their friend.

You have visited friends and relatives when they were in the hospital. But how often did you plan ahead as Job's friends did here? The text says that the three men "came each from his own place," and "made an appointment together to come to show him sympathy and comfort him" (2:11). This is quite something. They had heard that Job had lost everything, including his children, and that he was a very sick man. He needed his friends to stand by him, sympathize with and comfort him. They thought Job deserved that. So the three of them met, for a planned, coordinated mission that they took very seriously. Later in the Book of Job, we are told what they discussed at this conclave.[84] They wanted to speak with one voice, united in their words of encouragement and godly advice. Few today take such care to plan for a hospital visit to a friend. I have never done anything close.

---

83   6 JWS 75-120C-B.
84   5:27.

JOB'S FRIENDS WEEP FOR HIM

So the three friends met, and having concluded their meeting, they came to Job, and

> [w]hen they saw him from a distance, they did not recognize him. And they raised their voices and wept, and they tore their robes and sprinkled dust on their heads toward heaven. And they sat with him on the ground seven days and seven nights, and no one spoke a word to him, for they saw that his suffering was very great. (2:12-13)

When I was in the law practice I found myself in the courtroom more than once facing a good lawyer on the other side whose name was Ken L—. He always came prepared, did stellar work in examination of witnesses, and had an outstanding reputation among members of the bar. We had mutual respect and became good friends.

I hadn't seen Ken in about a year, when my partner and I were having lunch at a local restaurant. Two other men sat down a table near us. My partner whispered, "Do you know who that is at that table?" I looked, and I didn't. My partner said, "that's Ken L—. He has cancer, you know." I hadn't known. I looked over at him again, and like Job's friends, I could hardly recognize him. I wasn't ready for this. I was shocked to see my friend in such awful shape. This man was not the lawyer I'd sat across from in the courtroom. He had no hair at all, and was emaciated and skeletal in appearance. The poor man looked like the walking dead. A few months later, he did die.

When Eliphaz, Bildad and Zophar saw this friend of theirs who was so sick they couldn't recognize him, they wept aloud, tore their robes, and sprinkled dust on their heads. I felt like doing something like that when I saw Ken, but refrained because of where we were. But you don't see that kind of sympathy unleashed in any venue today. These men were mighty friends of Job, and they empathized without restraint.

This was no Hallmark card visit, or an order for flowers, as helpful and appropriate as those gestures are. Any kind of encouragement is wonderful when someone is sick, and just to know they are thinking of you can work wonders. But I don't think mild gestures like that would be appropriate for Job. These men had "heard of all this evil that had come upon him" (2:11) and knew that it was not just a broken arm. Their friend had lost everything he had, all his children were dead, and he had been stricken with a dreadful and painful illness. And all of this had descended on Job at once. Probably there has been no man in recorded history who suffered more intense, personal and immediate loss. So it is not a surprise that his three good friends took him, his situation, and their visit to him seriously.

SILENCE

They wept, tore their clothes and threw dust on their heads, but Job's friends found it hard to speak. They came near him, sat down on the ground, probably in a semicircle around their friend, and didn't utter a word. They sat there for a week in silence. But every moment of silence meant that they were concerned about Job. Sanderson, speaking to ministerial students, observes:

> You know that often when we get together, all we do is jabber, jabber, jabber. But isn't it nice, every now and then, just to sit, to enjoy one another's company, and not talk? We seem to feel something's wrong if no one's saying anything. Maybe something's right. Maybe we underestimate the value of silence.
>
> And for those of you who are in pastoral counseling, when you're calling on people, don't feel that you just have to jabber all the time. Just sit and let words and thoughts take their course. And sometimes, silence means considerably more than a whole lot of empty words.

And so these men, for seven days and seven nights, were not wasting their time. Good things can happen with silence.

I have gone into homes that have been struck by disaster, and I haven't even known what to say. On some occasions, I haven't said anything. And people have said later, "You know, just the fact that you were there, that counted."[85]

This is quite a picture. One almost unrecognizable and deathly ill man, sitting on a pile of ashes, scraping himself once and awhile with a shard of pottery. That eerie scraping noise day and night, and his moans of pain, were the only sounds for a week. Three other men, sitting around him on the ground, with their arms folded across their upright knees and chins resting on their arms. Just watching and listening. They couldn't even begin to start up a conversation. No word in the spoken language would be appropriate. Anything they might say would seem trite.

So what can they do for Job? What would you be able to do, if you were sitting there? All they had was themselves and their words. But what words? How to start? Who should speak first? What to say after they start? Did Job even want to hear them say something?

THE PRE-VISIT MEETING

Actually, these three men did have a pretty good idea as to what they were going to say to Job, because they had met beforehand to discuss the matter.[86] In the rest of the Book of Job, beginning in Chapter 4 and running through Chapter 25, this message becomes increasingly clear. They considered their words to Job would be just the medicine he needed for a cure, and deliverance from his suffering. But those words (and they knew this) would

---

85   6 JWS 75-120C-B.
86   5:27.

be hard to say, and they were concerned that Job might take them to be unloving and unsympathetic.

They weren't going to mean it that way, of course, any more than a doctor who comes into the room and tells a patient that a tumor has been found and surgery is essential. It's bad news, it's painful news, but the doctor who does her duty must speak out because she knows that it's for the ultimate welfare of her patient. Carrying bad news to someone in any situation, even when you believe the bad news will prove helpful, is hard to do and takes courage.

The men had met so they could speak to Job with one voice about the origin of his troubles, and as his friends, help him get through them. They wanted him to know that he was not helpless in the situation, but could *do* something about it, that there was a remedy and a cure available to him. They were there for him. Genuine love was going to be tough medicine, both for them to administer and for Job to receive, but they were determined not to leave Job in his pathetic condition.

I'm not sure what Job expected them to say or do. What they were going to tell him that he was being punished for his sin. They were absolutely convinced of it, and were also convinced that Job was continuing to suffer because he refused to acknowledge it. But they were not going to tell him this because they disliked him. They didn't shun him. Quite the opposite; they had Job's welfare in mind.

So there the four men sat, for seven days and seven nights, without uttering a syllable. Silence may be golden, but someone had to speak pretty soon. Job needed help, and he wasn't getting any this way.

FOR REFLECTION

I.

Do you see any evidence that Eliphaz, Bildad and Zophar had any reservations in their concern for Job? Do you think their expressions of grief and sympathy were genuine?

2.

Have you had any acquaintance who got so sick that he or she didn't look the same, maybe even hard to identify? Were you shocked? Did you experience any difficulty in approaching that person, or in knowing what to say? If so, why did you feel that way?

3.

Have you ever visited a sick friend and sat in silence? Do you think any help can be given if you are silent? What?

8.

JOB'S LAMENT

CHAPTER 3

L ET'S LOOK at Chapter 3. Sanderson says to us: "The thing I want you to recognize is that here we have Job in the depths of despair. But it's important to notice that his despair does not come from the fact that he is a sick man. He is not in despair because he is in pain. He is in despair because God is playing a significant part in his troubles. He is, if I may say so, enough of a Calvinist to see that God is in his problems. And that's what bothers him. Then we need to see that this is one of the clues to the interpretation of the book. This is not a book about 'Why do people suffer?' This is a book about 'What is the relationship between man and God?' And *how does the revelation of God's glory reflect on man's response to that glory, that faith which binds man back to God?* So let's keep this in mind as we proceed."[87]

The first two chapters of the Book of Job covered the events in Job's life leading up to what may be described as a "debate"

---

87   7 JWS 75-120D-A. The italicized portion is Sanderson's stated theme for the

between Job and his three friends. This debate continues through Chapter 31. But it did not start as a debate. When it did develop into the to-and-fro argument we see in Chapters 4-31 between Job and his friends, even there Job's primary argument was with the Lord.

JOB FORCED TO LOOK IN TWO DIRECTIONS

Poor Job! On the one side, he will be facing a trio of adversaries, and on the other he faces the Lord, whom he oftentimes sees as his true adversary. The Lord didn't enter the debate while the friends were talking, but Job continually addressed the Lord as though his real argument was with him. History shows that it's difficult to win the war if you have to fight on more than one front.

Just a few days before, everything in Job's relationships with his friends and with God seemed positive and healthy. Now, through no fault of his own, Job finds or will find himself in conflict with everybody: his wife, his friends, and God. The Lord was testing him, in every aspect of his life, and he wasn't going to administer the test piecemeal.

Apparently his friends weren't going to say anything, because they'd already been silent for a week. So Job cleared his throat, and began to speak.

JOB WADES IN

Job spoke, but could not have imagined that he was touching off the firestorm that resulted. Unbeknownst to him, he would be bucking the theology his friends had settled on. But after more than a week of stifling silence, he had to speak. No doubt his three friends, who had not yet come up with exactly how to begin, were relieved. And even in his pain, Job was probably thankful he had someone to talk with even if he had to do the talking. His friends

---

Book of Job.

couldn't think of what to say, but it wasn't the easiest thing in the world for him to start the conversation either, because as will become immediately evident, his first soliloquy demonstrates his bewilderment. He doesn't have any explanation for why he is sitting on top of an ash heap,[88] covered with boils. He's not going to be able to tell them why.

JOB WISHES HE HADN'T BEEN BORN

Job had been considering his plight for all this time, while his feelings fermented inside. Boils on the outside, boiling on the inside. Sooner or later, those feelings had to erupt into words. And they did.

It was not a positive start, nor did he ease into the subject at hand. He didn't begin by thanking his three friends for their visit. The text reads, bluntly: "After this, Job opened his mouth and *cursed the day of his birth*" (3:1). He began:

> Let the day perish on which I was born,
>   and the night that said,
> "A man is conceived."
> Let that day be darkness!
> May God above not seek it,
>   nor light shine upon it (3:3-4)

After long days and nights of tormented consideration, this was Job's wish: that he had never existed.

HAVE YOU WISHED TO BE DEAD?

Many people wish they were dead. I have had that wish. In the second semester of my first year of college, when everything seemed hopelessly bleak—grades, girlfriends, money (to a fresh-

---

88 Of possible significance here is the fact that under Levitical law the ash heap was located outside the camp, the site where the intestines, skin, head and dung from animal sacrifice were to be burned up and disposed of (see Lev. 4:11-12). It was not a place of honor.

man in college, that's pretty much everything)—I was driving down a street in St. Louis one night and looked at a light pole on the side of the road. It looked inviting. I wanted to swerve straight into it. But Someone inside me told me that it wouldn't be a good idea, and I didn't.

When everything comes crashing down around and on top of you, or seems to be, you can reach the point where to go on living seems intolerable. You are in a spot where you can't even see why God would want you to keep living. You feel like you're a burden to him and to everyone else; that everybody would be better off if you could just depart the scene, or if you just weren't there in the first place. This doesn't necessarily mean that you are ready to commit suicide, though sometimes it does. But it does mean that you are sick and tired of being sick and tired, that you can't do anything about it, and that you want your life to end as soon as possible. Lord, just take me! Let's be done with it!

One of the major restraints in such a mindset is family. You think of your spouse and children, and realize that they may need to have you around even though you may be a burden to them. This is a powerful countervailing influence. Many people have recanted their death wish just because of family.

But Job didn't have a family any more, except for his wife who talked to him as the heathen women do (2:9-10). And in her exclamation "Curse God and die!" she made it clear that she didn't want him around either. In this one respect Job was in agreement with his wife—not that he should curse God, but that he would be better off dead.

And Job went far beyond wishing for death. He wished he had never been born. He cursed the day of his birth. He wished he had never *been*. Perhaps, from his point of view, sitting atop an ash heap scraping his unrelentingly painful boils, we couldn't blame him. For the moment, his perspective was limited and skewed. Nevertheless, his view was not his Creator's view.

JOB'S TROUBLES WEREN'T IMAGINARY

My troubles as a freshman in college, when I wanted to run into a light pole, proved to be a product of my skewed view of how things really were. My grades could be improved, I could earn enough money, and hopefully something could be done about girlfriends too. A great part of it was that I was simply depressed.

But Job's situation was different. He was depressed, but it wasn't a chemical issue. He needed something much different from antidepressants. When people are depressed and seek treatment, before drugs come into play, a good psychiatrist will first ask questions regarding the patient's life story and current situation. Are there some things in the patient's life that are going badly, like maybe a traumatic event? If so, it may not be an organic or chemical problem at all, and perhaps the best thing to do is to obtain counseling, or take other steps in an effort to manage the crisis.

I would love to have sat in on a discussion between Job and his psychiatrist. Somebody throw you a curve ball? Life going badly? A traumatic event, maybe? Job's 'traumatic event' was off the charts. It was not medication that he needed. He did have counselors available—three of them, sitting around the ash heap. The next twenty-eight chapters of the book constitute a transcript of their counseling sessions with him. Counseling can be a great help to a person attempting to manage a life crisis, but in this case, as we shall see, the counselors only made things worse.

JOB CAME CLOSE TO CURSING GOD

To curse the day of your birth is not to curse God, but it comes perilously close. Saying it regarding someone else is to damn that person. Moments before Judas carried out his plan to turn coat on Jesus, and after he had left the Lord's presence, Jesus said that "It would have been better for that man if he had not been born."[89] Job said the same, but with regard to himself.

Job, after Satan's second onslaught, crossed a line he had not crossed after the first devastation, when he lost everything. After that episode, the writer says that "[i]n all this, Job did not sin or charge God with wrong" (1:22). We could argue, and would have the rules of logic on our side, that Job is *now* charging God with wrongdoing because God is the one who brought about Job's birthday. Because Job curses the day of his birth (we could argue) he is charging God with wrongdoing.

We've already given space to Job's wife and his three friends. We need to do the same for Job, because he needs it. He also deserves it.

JOB WAS A VERY SICK MAN

My father was always buoyantly thankful for food. No matter what was served, he delighted in it. This was a good quality, and spoke volumes to us kids, to be thankful for everything we had. But occasionally he carried it too far.

Once, after Sunday dinner, he lingered at the table for the whole afternoon, talking do-or-die theological issues with a fellow clergyman who had been invited over. Dad was Presbyterian and his friend a Baptist, so it took awhile to sort out infant baptism, sprinkling or immersion, predestination, free will and the like. I'm not sure they ever did get those things settled.

The table had long since been cleared when the two men began to feel hunger pangs again. Conveniently, they were still at the table. Dad went into the kitchen, saw what he thought was salad (lettuce, tomatoes, onions, fresh garden radishes, turnips and such, all piled on a newspaper) and filled two plates. The men ate the 'salad' as the discussion continued into the evening. Mom came down after a nap, and to her horror found that they had

---

89   Mt. 26:24.

partaken of what she had earlier designated as garbage. That was Dad when he was in good health.

Many years later, when he was on his deathbed in a hospital with cancer, I witnessed something quite different. I was in his room when food service brought him a wonderful meatloaf dinner, with all the fixings. Dad took a quick look at it, shoved it away in disgust, and said "Is that what they call food around here?" In his good days, he would have thought it a feast fit for royalty. Someone who is deathly ill should not be held to the strictest of standards.

So we shouldn't parse Job's curse, directed at the day of his birth, too carefully. But even if we do, Job did not curse his Maker, nor did he exactly charge God with wrong. The direct object of Job's lament in Chapter 3 was his birthday. He was not so bold as to claim that God erred. He just states, in the strongest of terms, that he wishes his birthday had never, never happened.

SICK OR WELL, WE ARE MADE IN THE IMAGE OF GOD

Job was speaking from the flesh when he cursed his birthday. There was nothing of the Holy Spirit in his wish; the Lord was not up in the air on the subject. As is every human being, Job was made in the image of God. We are not our own, and the Holy Spirit lives in our bodies:

> Do you not know that your body is a temple of the Holy Spirit within you, whom you have from God? You are not your own, for you were bought with a price. (1 Cor. 6:19-20)

Job was taking serious issue with the providence of God, and in this he was taking the wrong path. For the moment, he lost sight of the fact that his body was not his own. He was beginning to lose sight of a fact that he surely knew quite well, enunciated later by the Apostle Paul when he was on Mars Hill in Athens:

The God who made the world and everything in it, being Lord of heaven and earth, does not live in temples made by man, nor is he served by human hands, as though he needed anything, since he himself gives to all mankind life and breath and everything. And he made from one man every nation of mankind to live on all the face of the earth, having determined allotted periods and the boundaries of their dwelling place, that they should seek God, and perhaps feel their way toward him and find him. Yet he is actually not far from each one of us, for "In him we live and move and have our being[.]" (Acts 17:24-28)

REMEMBER YOUR CREATOR

The gospel begins and ends with the Creator God. Genesis reveals the creation itself, and Revelation reveals just a bit of God's new creation. These are the gospel's bookends, because everything from A to Z arises out of, and is in the context of, the created order—or more to the point, the Creator. For Job, the fact that God created everything will prove to be the key to an ultimate understanding of his own existence, including his troubles, and will give him unshakable assurance of his safe, favored standing in the sovereign One who made him and everything else.

At the end of the Book of Job, in chapters 38 through 41, God will have the final word. (Not surprisingly, his speech ends the book.) When God speaks, he is answering Job and his friends, so it is relevant to all the issues they had raised. What the Lord will say there will bring all the other talk in the book to an end; it will put everything in right perspective. In the Lord's answer, he speaks of nothing other than his creation. In this he makes explicit what Paul later said in summary: "[t]he God who made the world and everything in it is the Lord of heaven and earth."

So a fruitful way to exegete the Book of Job is by analyzing everything that is said in light of the fact that God alone made everything that exists:

> It pleased God the Father, Son, and Holy Ghost, for the manifestation of the glory of His eternal power, wisdom, and goodness, in the beginning, to create, or make of nothing, the world, and all things therein whether visible or invisible, in the space of six days; and all very good.[90]

CREATION MATTERS

It is sad that the church today often treats the subject of creation as little more than an appendage to the Good News—in some cases, almost an inconsequential matter. But it is absolutely central. How can we miss it? All the way through both the Old and New Testaments, the Holy Spirit (who, in the Creation record, is the very one who "hovered over the waters")[91] presents the Creator God center stage. It has everything to do with the Good News, including the final judgment, because it is creation that will condemn men and women who have denied their Creator:

> For the wrath of God is revealed from heaven against all ungodliness and unrighteousness of men, who by their unrighteousness suppress the truth. For what can be known about God is plain to them, because God has shown it to them. For his invisible attributes, namely, his eternal power and divine nature, have been clearly perceived, ever since the creation of the world, in the things that have been made. So they are without excuse. (Rom. 1:18-20)

---

90   *Westminster Confession of Faith*, Ch. 4, Section I.
91   Gen. 1:2.

I DESPISE MY BIRTHDAY

Job was a precious soul and body, made in the image of God. But sitting on the ash heap, he laments his existence:

> That night—let thick darkness seize it!
> Let it not rejoice among the days of the year;
> let it not come into the number of the
> months. (3:6)

He beckons those who "curse the day" to curse *that* day, those who "are ready to rouse up Leviathan" (3:8). He means those who have such brash and foolish courage as to employ the devil in the curse; those who are not worried about touching the evil one.

If the day of his birth can't be done away with, Job wishes that he had been stillborn, because then he wouldn't be covered with boils, sitting on an ash heap. He also wouldn't be bereaved of his children, because there wouldn't have been any children. Job would now be at rest, at peace, asleep in his grave (3:11-16). He would be the same as kings, counselors, and rulers, lying beside them. There *everyone* is at rest—the wicked, the weary and captives. Slaves are there at rest, freed at last from their masters. Every dead person, Job thinks, is better off than he is.

Why am I, who *wishes* to be dead, not given the mercy these people were given? "Why is life given to a man whose way is hidden, whom God has hedged in?" (3:23).

WHY ME?

Job ends this opening lament with a nightmarish statement:

> What I feared has come upon me;
> What I dreaded has happened to me.
> I have no peace, no quietness;
> I have no rest, but only turmoil. (3:25-26, NIV)

What human being, what parent, cannot feel the depth of Job's grinding heartache? Possibly you have had such feelings. What do you fear the most? Your child killed in an accident? Kidnapped? Dying in an overheated car, sitting forgotten and alone in the sun? We have frightening dreams about such things, making us sit up in bed with a start, awaking only to find that those things didn't really happen.

But with Job, they really *did* happen. Those very things that he feared the most were now reality. He couldn't wake up, relieved, from a dream. The devastation was real; there was no way out. He had no peace, quietness or rest. All he had when he woke up from whatever sleep he got was more turmoil. There was no way out of this living hell.

Maybe his friends had some answers.

FOR REFLECTION

1.

What does Sanderson mean when he says that Job's "despair does not come from the fact that he is a sick man"? If Sanderson is right, then where did Job's despair originate?

2.

Have you ever wished that you hadn't been born? Have you ever considered suicide? If so, what factors in your life brought you to that point? What made you change your mind?

3.

When contemplating suicide, or just entertaining the thought that it would have been better if you hadn't been born, how does the fact that God created you factor in?

9.

THE ELIPHAZ FORMULA

CHAPTERS 4-5

ELIPHAZ AND HIS TWO FRIENDS may well have been taking notes as Job spoke. They could not have predicted what Job was going to say, even though they had discussed their approach beforehand (5:27). They had a game plan, as will become evident, but they had to be flexible, depending on what Job would say.

TOUGH LOVE

From Job's lament, they could see that he was despondent. That was to be expected; they knew that before they came to visit, and surely his discouragement with life played a big part in their decision to make the trip. But now that Job had spoken, they knew something else about Job they hadn't been sure of, and it gave them some traction. In all of Chapter 3, Job had not mentioned any wrongdoing. He had bemoaned his awful plight; he had cursed his birthday. But he had not attributed his condition to anything or anyone other than the Lord. In short, Job had not assumed personal responsibility for his trouble.

Eliphaz, Zophar and Bildad believed they would have to bring Job to an understanding of his own accountability for what had happened to him if they were to be of any help. They didn't mean to inflict further sorrow on the man, but they knew that merely soothing his feelings with something less than the truth (as they saw the truth) would do Job no good. They had to exercise tough love, because they wanted only the best for Job.

JOB MUST OWN HIS TROUBLE

However they were to broach the subject, Job had to be brought to the point where he personally owned his plight. He could not point fingers, because there was no one at whom to point them, particularly not God. Job, they will argue, needed to be pointing his finger at Job. They thought this was a necessary first step for him to take, if he truly wanted to recover from the disasters that had come upon him.

The three will stick to this theme for the rest what they have to say, all the way through Chapter 25. Though it might here sound like good counsel, down the line it will get them into serious trouble, and will injure their friend, which was not at all what they had in mind.

PIETY COUNTS

Eliphaz began in a kindly way: "If someone ventures a word with you, will you be impatient?" (4:2). Or, "do you mind if I say a few words, Job?"—and he then immediately tries to encourage and support his friend.

Right now, Job, I agree with you: things do seem terribly dark. But remember your past: you have upheld those who stumbled, and made firm faltering knees (4:4). That's your history. You've got the worst kind of trouble right now, and though you're discouraged, you should remember your past: "your *piety* should be your confidence, and your *blameless ways* your hope" (4:6, NIV)[92] You've been a support for those who stumbled, and "you have strengthened faltering knees" (4:4). This was meant to give Job

---

92   In this, Eliphaz was on solid ground, because it is what God said about his servant Job immediately before Job's catastrophes (1:8; 2:3).

perspective, and it is right to encourage discouraged folks with such reminders. But in this case, Eliphaz was steering the ship in the wrong direction.

HOPE THROUGH PIETY

Eliphaz is only six verses into it, but has just launched a badly flawed theology. The last two words in 4:6 are "your hope." His foundational principle, which will remain the cornerstone of his theology, and afflict all three friends throughout the rest of the book, was that "piety," or righteous living, was Job's only real hope. Those who are innocent and upright *never* perish, he claims (4:7). Really, Eliphaz? What about Abel, for example? He was murdered.

But if Eliphaz had considered Abel, he must have thought him to be exception to the rule. Eliphaz tells Job, "As I have seen, those who plow iniquity and sow trouble reap the same" (4:8)—not those who lead righteous lives.

What was Job to think of that? He had surely "reaped trouble"—that was not even open to debate. So had he plowed iniquity? Was that what Eliphaz thought?

ELIPHAZ DOES HAVE SOME PROOF TEXTS

As mentioned previously, the Book of Job is one of the earliest in the Bible. Eliphaz probably didn't have much of the written word for reference. But if he had, he could have mentioned Psalm 1, where David said that

> [The righteous person] is like a tree
>> planted by streams of water,
>> that yields its fruit in its season
>> and its leaf does not wither.
> In all that he does, he prospers.
> The wicked are not so,
> But are like chaff
>> that the wind drives away. (Psa. 1:3-4)

So Eliphaz had some biblical support for what he said. But he had bought into some really bad theology, and as in all bad theology, it was truth mixed with error. The faulty line of thinking expands in scope, too. For the next three verses Eliphaz claims to have witnessed the here-and-now destruction of the wicked. They might roar like lions for awhile, but they are all destroyed.

AN ETERNAL PERSPECTIVE

David, in Psalm 1, spoke from an eternal perspective. Eliphaz had just part of the picture—temporal, not eternal—and even that part was wrong, because there were and are plenty of examples of the righteous suffering even to the point of death. As mentioned, consider Abel. He was first on Jesus' list of these martyrs, in his scathing rebuke of the Pharisees:

> [O]n you [will] come all the righteous blood shed on earth, from the blood of righteous Abel to the blood of Zechariah the son of Barachiah, whom you murdered between the sanctuary and the altar. (Mt. 23:35)

And the author of Hebrews, speaking of the righteous, said:

> Others suffered mocking and flogging, and even chains and imprisonment. They were stoned, they were sawn in two, they were killed with the sword. They went about in skins of sheep and goats, destitute, afflicted, mistreated—of whom the world was not worthy—wandering about in deserts and mountains, and in dens and caves of the earth. (Heb. 11:36-38)

Eliphaz's observation was contrary to the facts.

A SCARY VISION

In the rest of Chapter 4, Eliphaz relates a vision that he had in the nighttime, and reading it reminds one of Scrooge's nightmare in Dickens' *A Christmas Carol*. There's no reason to doubt what Eliphaz experienced. But it doesn't sound like divine revelation. Maybe it was just "an undigested bit of beef," as Scrooge surmised. The message conveyed in the vision was this: God has little time for human beings. He says that our foundations are in the dust; that we are more easily crushed than a moth (4:19). And there's no way out, for in 5:1 he continues:

> Call now; is there anyone will answer you?
> To which of the holy ones will you turn?

APPEAL TO GOD'S GRACE

And *that* was supposed to encourage poor Job? Yet Eliphaz apparently had not given up on prayer, on crying out to the Lord, because in 5:8-9 he encourages Job to appeal to God, to lay his cause before him, because God works wonders and miracles. But something was prerequisite, before Job could expect the Lord to answer his cry: Job needed to repent of his sin that brought about his downfall. Eliphaz saw Job's suffering, and it was rockbed truth to him that suffering comes only from as a direct result of sin. So he tells Job to "despise not the discipline of the Almighty" (5:17).

If Job will just humble himself and accept his plight for what it is—a consequence of yet unconfessed sin—wonderful things await. In 5:18-26, Eliphaz describes where Job could be if he would just yield and confess. He will "laugh at destruction" (5:22); enjoy perfect harmony with nature (5:23); have a house that can't be touched by tornadoes or other catastrophic agents (5:24); regain and retain all of his property (5:24); have many children and grandchildren (5:25); and come to the end of his life in "full vigor" (5:26).

ELIPHAZ'S ARGUMENT WAS TAILORED TO JOB

Eliphaz was well-prepared; he had done his homework. In all these things he was targeting exactly what Job had gone through. Job had no harmony with nature because the wind had destroyed his children. His house had come crashing down. He had retained none of his property. Because he had lost all of his many children, he would have no grandchildren. He may come to the end of his life in full vigor, but only after he had confessed his sin.

The three friends had discussed this before they came to visit Job:

> We have examined this, and it is true.
> *So hear it and apply it to yourself.* (5:27, NIV)

Eliphaz, as though Job hadn't caught his drift, advises him to simply take what was "true," and "apply it to yourself." Simple as that. It's your way out, Job, your only way out.

LOGICAL ANALYSIS: VENN DIAGRAMS

John Venn (1834-1923), was a brilliant logician. He is best known for his use of diagrams to probe propositions graphically. It's helpful, at least to the author, to use these "Venn Diagrams" to analyze what Eliphaz has said in Chapters 4-5, to see how his propositions look graphically.

Here, Eliphaz has made two propositions: (1) all sin causes trouble, and (2) all trouble is caused by sin. So Professor Venn would draw two circles: No. 1, "sin." No. 2, "trouble."

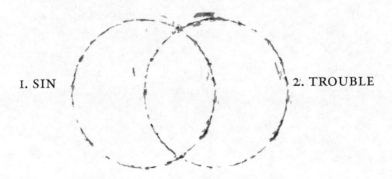

1. SIN   2. TROUBLE

Then, as to the first proposition ("all sin causes trouble"), he would say that you have to cross out all the sin outside of trouble, because the proposition means that there is *no* sin that does not cause trouble. Eliphaz says that sin always causes trouble. So I've crossed out the portion of circle 1 that had left open the possibility that there could be sin without trouble.

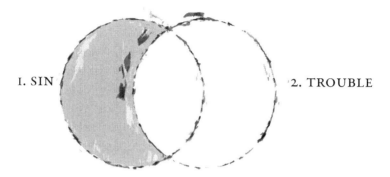

However, this leaves open the part of Circle 2 that would allow for some trouble to be caused by something other than sin. But Eliphaz has said that whenever you see trouble, it means sin. Always. So Venn would continue his analysis this way:

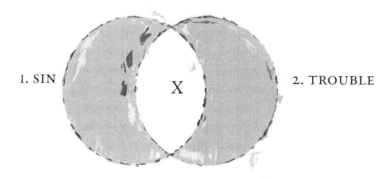

Thus, whenever you see sin, you'll see trouble (always). Whenever you see trouble, you'll see sin (always). The two worlds are mutually *in*clusive; what's left of circle 1 means circle 2, and what's left of circle 2 means circle 1.[93] So we put an "x" in what's left, and we have a kind of logical equivalence.

This is exactly what the Pharisees taught. Take, for example, the story of the man born blind (Jn. 9). To them, it was clear that his sin (they claimed he was "steeped in sin" from birth) was why he was blind.[94] And they also believed his blindness was proof positive of his sin. You don't see sin without trouble, and you don't see trouble without sin.[95]

IN A LONELY BOX

If this were true, we'd be in a box, all by ourselves and lonely. This is the theology that Eliphaz espoused. It was formulaic, and left no wiggle-room. Eliphaz's two friends were in lockstep with him (5:27). It will prove to be the sum of their sledgehammer advice to Job. And they had wide support for their theology: it was conventional wisdom, a paradigm that was generally accepted in their day.

This theology fails for two major reasons. First, it leaves a man or a woman in complete control of his destiny, because the only way out is to confess sin, even that which has not been committed, as in Job's case. Second, it leaves no room at all for the grace of God. There are just two categories. Eliphaz apparently doesn't

---

93   For the first segment of Job's speeches, he indicates his agreement with the first half of the Eliphaz Formula. For a time, Job applies this theology to himself, as Eliphaz had advised in 5:27. However, while Job will admit to some truth in Eliphaz's theology, his position throughout is that it was not his sin that had caused his trouble, and thus the Eliphaz Formula was inapplicable. Sanderson says, "Beginning at the 20th verse [3:20], we see that the conflict is brought on by the fact that Job has a clear conscience. And he seems to have the idea that the suffering that he is going through can only be due to sin. In this, he's not going to be entirely different from his wife, and he's not going to be different from the three friends when they begin to expound their doctrine." (7 JWS 75-120D-A).

94   Jn. 9:34.

95   The three friends had limited knowledge, and perhaps we should be cautious about being too critical of them. But the Pharisees had the entire Old Testament, including the Book of Job.

recognize at least two additional circles that should be there: one labeled "grace" and another "the sovereignty of God." Then there would be hope, but otherwise, we would be eternally boxed in with no way out.

Eliphaz ends his speech arrogantly when he says that he and his friends "have searched it out, and it is true." He's telling Job that his thoughts aren't needed, wouldn't make any difference anyway, and aren't worthy of further discussion. Nope, Job, no reason for more research. We've already decided, and we're the experts. All you need to do is "apply it to yourself"—then we can all go home.

But from Job's response to follow, it becomes evident that he has no intention of bowing to Eliphaz's advice.

FOR REFLECTION

I.

Was Eliphaz right, in whole or in part, in telling Job that "your piety should be your confidence, and your blameless ways your hope?" If a fellow-believer were to say that to you, would or should it encourage you? Why or why not? Should you be encouraged by those times in your life when you have been obedient to the Lord's revealed will?

2.

Do you agree or disagree with Eliphaz when he told Job to "despise not the discipline of the Almighty"? Do you believe Job was being disciplined, and if so, why or what for?

3.

When you have sinned, has it always resulted in trouble for you? When you have had trouble, have you always been able to trace it to some particular sin you have committed?

10.

JOB RESPONDS TO ELIPHAZ

CHAPTERS 6-7

J OB ANSWERS ELIPHAZ indirectly. He will argue, he will
make his points; but so far as Job is concerned, it will be as if
Eliphaz had wasted his time. It may seem to be somewhat of
an insult to Eliphaz, because it's insulting to ignore what someone
has just said to you. But then, Eliphaz had just insulted Job, so fair
is fair.

JOB NEEDS A SYMPATHETIC EAR

Though indirect, Job does answer Eliphaz. "Oh that my vex-
ation were weighed, and all my calamity laid in the balances," he
laments (6:2). I want someone to sympathize with me, to mea-
sure, to quantify my suffering. Right now, I don't need somebody
telling me what needs to be fixed in my life. What I need is someone who can appreciate this awful *suffering*. Then you could understand why my words seem hotheaded, or "rash" (6:3). Don't
just tell me to calm down. Calming down isn't appropriate here.

JOB'S PATIENCE

Job doesn't charge God with wrong—he never does—but he
has already come to the conclusion that God alone is responsible

for his plight. *El Shaddai's*[96] arrows are in him and God has poisoned him (6:4). At this point he wants God not to heal him, but take him (6:8-9). He has no prospects, certainly none that are any good (6:11), and therefore has no reason to be *patient* for things to work out—"what is my end, that I should be patient?" (6:11). Just take my life, Lord, and please don't delay. I'm not interested in persevering. I just can't hold on and what's more, I don't want to. My suffering is too much for me to bear.

This is the first mention of "patience," and it's in the negative. Yet the Apostle James commends Job for his patience, his "steadfastness":

> Behold, we consider those blessed who remained
> steadfast. You have heard of the steadfastness of
> Job, and you have seen the purpose of the Lord,
> how the Lord is compassionate and merciful.
> (James 5:11)

This is curious. Can a man be commended for patience when he has no choice in the matter? If Job was patient, it seems involuntary at best.

Actually, there were choices open to Job. He could commit suicide, of course, and that is the negative opposite of patience. Or he could curse God and die, as his wife had earlier advised (2:9). But it is obvious that both of those choices were odious to him. Perhaps he didn't see any compelling reasons why he should be, but he nevertheless was, steadfast, as the Apostle James said.

In the James passage just quoted, the Greek word is translated "perseverance" in the New International Version; in the King James it is rendered "patience"; in the English Standard Version "steadfastness." Greek dictionaries assure us that "endurance" would work just as well, because that word carries both active and

---

96   The Hebrew name *El Shaddai* means "God Almighty," or "The All-Sufficient One."

passive meanings, and seems to be what James is commending Job for. What Job went through was cast upon him, and there was no choice in the matter. What did matter is how Job would respond to his plight. He responded by choosing to endure it, and that is why James commended him.

TRUE FRIENDSHIP

Now Job addresses his friends, and it isn't pretty. If you are my friends, you should act like it. I should be able to expect your kindness toward me, but you've withheld it (6:14). I can't depend on you.

Have you had friends like that? Undependable? Who, when the rubber hits the road prove weak and wobbly? I have. Sometimes, when I've been in the moment of deepest need, they have run away from my trouble, or even accused me for bringing on my trouble. They were there when times were good, but when things got sticky, they were gone with the wind. You have likely experienced the same.

Or, more directly, have you been such a friend? I have, and more often than I've had such friends. When friends of mine have been in a hot and dry season (6:17), I've often failed them miserably. I've proven that I'm nothing more than a "splintered staff" when someone tries to lean on me.[97] My friends needed my support, but when they leaned on me they got hurt worse than if they hadn't leaned on me in the first place. I was out of there when trouble came. I shudder when I think of how I failed some friends. I wish I could go back and do it right. Lord, have mercy.

And that's really what Job's three friends were doing. They were there in the flesh, but they were separating themselves from his spirit. This is common. When we see someone in trouble, we instinctively want to assure ourselves that it couldn't happen to us. We seek personal safety and peace, because in the flesh, apart from God's grace, this is our top priority. So we adjust reality to

---

97 2 Ki. 18:21.

convince ourselves that we are different from those who have had the world collapse on them.

THE FRIENDS DISTANCE THEMSELVES FROM JOB

When I was growing up, I remember a saying used by some adults when they drove by an automobile accident: "two fools met." Of course that's ridiculous, first because it would take only one fool to cause an accident. Or no fool at all. But the motivation and purpose for quoting that silly proverb is to gain a manufactured, false assurance that I am not in danger of a car accident, because I am no fool.

All I'm doing when I quote that proverb is separating myself from the suffering victim, by putting myself in a different class of people—those wise folks who know how to drive. That way I can breathe easier, cruising right past the accident and going on my way, feeling safe and secure. In fact, having adopted this skewed view, the accident can even serve as a kind of warped encouragement to me, because it increases my confidence in my personal safety.

WE'RE SAFE

Here Eliphaz is doing that. Job, he says, you have done something bad (I haven't) to bring trouble on (couldn't happen to me, because I haven't). He wants to escape even the possibility that Job's calamities could be his. In Eliphaz's theology, he finds consolation because he's in a different, safe, category. He's conjuring up this categorical distinction so he can breathe a sigh of relief, and cruise by this accident consigned to an ash heap. But we all do it.

We do it when we watch the late night TV news. A toddler is shot on an open porch in a drive-by shooting and dies on the way to the hospital. Our first thoughts: Where did it happen? When did it happen? Then (if we live in the burbs) we begin to feel relief, because it's reported that it happened in a poor, dying part of the city, where windows are boarded up. But we are wise enough to live where we don't have drive-by-drug-related shootings. Whew! Then we feel even better when we find that it happened at 1 am. Why in the world would parents allow their child to be out on the porch at that unearthly hour? Couldn't happen to us because we don't live there, and we keep our kids in the house after dark. A bigger sigh of relief, and off to bed.

JESUS NEVER DISTANCED HIMSELF FROM US

This "safe haven" attitude is diametrically opposed to Jesus' teaching, by word and by deed. When he sees us by the side of the road, he intentionally pours himself into our category, whatever it might be. We are commanded, and empowered by the Holy Spirit, to do the same. The Apostle Paul said:

> Have this mind among yourselves, which is yours in Christ Jesus, who, though he was in the form of God, did not count equality with God a thing to be grasped, but emptied himself, by *taking the form of a servant*, being born in the likeness of men. (Phil. 2:5-7)

Jesus knows what we need because he became exactly like us in all of our weaknesses. But Eliphaz wasn't like Jesus in this instance. He didn't want to become like Job. Job hoped that his friends would put themselves in his shoes, on his pile of ashes. He hoped that they would thus know the hell he was going through. But they didn't want to. Jesus intentionally entered in; Eliphaz and his friends intentionally kept a safe distance away.

THE WEE HOURS

Up to this point in his life, Job had been the master of his house and affairs. He was an entrepreneur; he hired folks to work for him. He had looked at life from the top down, but now, all of a sudden, everything is from the bottom up. I'm like a slave, he says, and now, looking in the rear view mirror, I can see that it has all been for nothing. It's been utterly futile (7:1-3).[98] All that I've accomplished—our wonderful home, our children, property, reputation—it's come to nothing. And on top of that, I'm deathly sick. And it's worst at night:

> When I lie down I say, "When shall I arise?"
> But the night is long,
> and I am full of tossing till the dawn. (7:4)

I suspect it's true of most of us: night time, the wee hours, can be excruciatingly lonely and painful. Like Job, we look for comfort when we go to bed, and when comfort isn't there—but nightmares—we are boxed in with horror. Job felt so boxed in with terror that he wanted to die. (7:13-16).

Though I've never come close to suffering as Job did, I've been through some awfully black nights. Everything in my life seems hopeless, and I'm all alone—unless you count my ticking clock. If I could just get to sleep, and be delivered by a few hours of blissful unconsciousness, maybe things will look better in the morning.

Job's nights, though, were worse than anything I've been through. The light of dawn usually brings a brighter perspective for me. But when Job's sun came up, it didn't do anything but confirm the fact that he really *was* deathly ill and in a terrible state, from every standpoint. It wasn't merely a wee hours perspective. It was just like when we all woke up on 9/12, hoping the previous day had been a bad dream. But things were just as bleak and dark as they had been when we went to bed the night before.

PLEASE STOP CONCENTRATING ON ME, LORD!

Eliphaz, committee chairman, had blamed Job's sin for his condition, and Job could have just argued that point with Elip-

---

98   Sanderson notes that Job's reference to "months of emptiness" in 7:3 implies that at this point he had been suffering for a very long time. John W. Sanderson, Lectures (1981).

haz. He will do so later, as Eliphaz persists, but Job already understands that his primary dispute is with the Lord. His life, he says, passes by swiftly like a breath, a cloud, a runner, a skiff, an eagle (7:7; 7:9; 9:25-26). So why does God pay so much attention to him? Man is nothing to write home about. Does the Lord have no sense of proportion? Job complains:

> I loathe my life; I would not live forever.
> Leave me alone, for my days are a breath.
> What is man, that you make so much of him,
>   and that you set your heart on him,
>   visit him every morning
>   and test him every moment? (7:16-18)

Please, just forgive me if I sin, and then stop focusing on me. Before you know it, I'll be dead anyway. Then you will look for me, but I won't be around (7:20-21).

In other words, "Lord, I just don't deserve all this attention!"

FOR REFLECTION

I.

Was Job right in claiming that God was responsible for his plight? If so, was he in effect charging God with wrong?

2.

Have you had times where you perhaps subconsciously distanced yourself from others who were having trouble? If so, in what ways?

3.

Have you, like Job, had sleepless nights? What caused them? How did you deal with the problem?

4.

Do you sometimes feel that all that you have accomplished in life has come to nothing? If you have, who or what helped you to change your feelings?

II.

THE REST OF ROUND ONE

CHAPTERS 8-14

THERE ARE THREE rounds of argument between Job and his friends. Chapters 4-14 constitute the first, 15-21 the second, and 22-31 the third. In the rounds, Eliphaz, Bildad and Zophar, in that order,[99] set forth their arguments, and Job responds to each in turn. For the reader's ready reference, here's the plan:

Job: Chapter 3
Eliphaz: Chapters 4-5
Job: Chapters 6-7
Bildad: Chapter 8
Job: Chapters 9-10
Zophar: Chapter 11
Job: Chapters 12-14
Eliphaz: Chapter 15
Job: Chapters 16-17
Bildad: Chapter 18

---

99   Zophar speaks in the first two rounds only.

We are midway through Round One. Eliphaz has spoken and has set the stage. He and his two friends will continue to expound their theology, and consequent advice, to Job. Their theory will always be that Job has to look no further than his own sin if he is serious about wanting to find relief.

Job never buys it.

BILDAD THINKS HE SPEAKS FOR THE LORD

Batting second is Bildad. He swings at the first pitch, wasting no time in insulting Job: "Your words are a blustering wind" (8:2, NIV). Not the preferred way to speak to your friend when he's deathly ill.

But Bildad is confident that he is speaking for God. Job, it sounds to me that you are saying that by striking your children dead God has perverted justice. But God is never unjust. Understand that it is because your children had sinned that they were killed (8:3-4). Remember the Eliphaz Formula. Your children's deaths prove their sin. (In this, Bildad is not only defaming the children, but denying the efficacy of Job's prayers for them).

Repent of your sin, Job. Ask God for mercy, and then start living right, like you used to. Because if you "are pure and upright," the Lord will rouse himself and restore you, making you richer than ever (8:5-7). That's how God operates: when you sin he heaps trouble on you, but if you turn from your sin, he restores you and makes you rich.

THE ANCIENTS ARE OFTEN WRONG

Bildad speaks not just from what the committee of three had agreed upon. He speaks from human tradition, from the wise fathers of "bygone ages." This isn't something new, he says. If you won't listen to us, listen to your forefathers, and learn from them. They will teach you (8:8-10). It was conventional wisdom. But conventional wisdom is often wrong. The Lord Jesus himself spent much of his ministry confronting and condemning the conventional wisdom of the day.

Once I heard a great preacher take on the subject of proverbs—not the proverbs of Solomon, but worldly-wise sayings like "Children are to be seen and not heard," and "Honesty is the best policy." He dissected these two proverbs from a Scriptural perspective. "Children," he said, "are to be heard. The Bible encourages children to praise the Lord, for example, and not once warns us to keep them quiet." Isaac Watts wrote:

> And infant voices shall proclaim
> Their early blessings on His name.[100]

I'll never forget what this seasoned preacher said about "Honesty is the best policy." "Sounds air-tight, doesn't it?" he asked the congregation. "But honesty is not a 'policy' at all, because that implies that we are honest only so long as it will result in something useful to us, and if it stops being useful, we stop being honest. And it's not 'best,' as though there are other alternatives. Rather, honesty is an absolute, good and necessary because of the ninth commandment. Dishonesty is sin, and honesty is obedience, not a policy." Since I heard this preacher, I've never again quoted this proverb.

Maybe Bildad was quoting these kinds of worldly proverbs from bygone ages as he continued his argument. Plants die when it doesn't rain and the ground dries up. Meaning, you are like those plants, dying because your water has dried up. And the

---

100 "Jesus Shall Reign Where'er the Sun," Isaac Watts (1674-1748), stanza 3.

water you need to restore yourself is your uprightness, righteousness, and piety, which you formerly had but have lost. This is what happens to everyone who is evil, who forgets God. Their hope is gone. They have nothing to lean on to support themselves. You have forgotten God, Job. You are leaning on a spider's web (8:13-19).

BILDAD'S 'ENCOURAGEMENT' CONTRADICTS THE LORD

Bildad finishes his argument genuinely trying to encourage Job to see what blessings lay before him if he'd just take his advice. "God," he says, "will not reject a blameless man"—of course meaning that God had rejected Job because he was not blameless. But in saying this, Bildad flat contradicts (albeit unwittingly) what the Lord had already said about Job immediately before Job was struck with calamity, where three times the Lord called his servant "blameless" (1:1, 1:8, 2:3). Bildad agreed with his forefathers, but in doing so, wound up differing with the Lord. He would have been wise to have left out this part of his speech. When you take issue with the Lord, while claiming to speak by his authority, it undermines your argument substantially.

JOB AGREES WITH BILDAD—IN PART

You might think that Job would respond to Bildad's insults about him and his children by insulting him back. I think I would have, but Job ignores the insults.

Job does concede that there is some truth in what Bildad has said. "Truly I know that it is so" (9:2), he begins. Considering the context of the whole Book of Job, I think he here speaks of the truth set forth by David in Psalm 1. It is true that the way of the righteous will flourish and prosper, and it is the wicked who are like "chaff that the wind drives away."[101,102] But David does not at all say that trouble is proof of sin.

---

101   Psa. 1:3-4.
102   Later, in 21:18, Job retreats from this by asking why it is that the wicked

Bildad was also right about the fact that God is *El Shaddai*, the "Almighty" (8:4), transcendent and above all. This is so, of course, and that truth concerns Job greatly. One cannot "contend" with God; a man cannot answer him. He moves mountains, shakes the earth, commands the sun to rise or to stay put.[103] He is the Creator God who made the heavens, the earth, the sea, and the constellations. (Job names some of them: the Bear, Orion and Pleiades in 9:9). A man cannot question what the Creator does (9:3-12); it would be to no avail. In all of this, Job unwittingly foretells what the Lord will say to him at the end of the book.

JOB DOESN'T BELIEVE GOD HEARS HIS COMPLAINTS

So Job quickly turns from Bildad to his deep concerns about the Lord. "If I summoned him, and he answered me, I would not believe that he was listening to my voice" (9:16). God is the one who has crushed me, and I haven't even had time to catch my breath.[104] He's way up there; I'm way down here. Job doesn't take comfort in God's transcendence; he worries about it. He is sure that the Lord "passes by me," not stopping to listen to my complaint. And no one can stop him, or question what he is doing (9:11-12).

GOD DOESN'T ALWAYS SEEM CLOSE AT HAND

I suspect that every one of us has felt this way during hard seasons. Of course there are those times in our lives when we have a keen sense of the nearness, intimacy and care of the Lord, when we are confident that he is hearing our cries and is working in our lives, when it is crystal clear to us that there is

---

don't seem to be like chaff that the wind drives away.

103   The Lord says the same when he speaks: "Have you commanded the morning since your days began, and caused the dawn to know its place, that it might take hold of the skirts of the earth, and the wicked be shaken out of it?" (38:12-13).

104   1:13-19.

Peace, when trouble blows,
Jehovah sees, Jehovah knows;
He is my peace, when sorrow nears,
Jehovah sees, Jehovah hears.[105]

But there are many other times when we must candidly admit that we don't have peace, when it seems like Jehovah doesn't see or know, when the heavens seem like bronze.[106] God seems utterly, intentionally detached. Prayers bounce right back to where they came from; we are in an echo chamber. No answers. And it goes on, and on, and on. The only thing we hear is our own voice, and that's not the voice we want to hear. Pain and trouble not only continue, but intensify.

Then, because I know that God is sovereign (he has total control over my situation), I know he could fix it in a blink. But he is intentionally *not* fixing it, and I can easily begin to think of him as my adversary. That's right where Job is at this point. He doesn't know why, but God, he thinks, is his enemy, the one with whom he must contend.

So what to do when you are convinced that God has turned against you? It doesn't seem there is anything you can do, but you still look for answers. Job is looking, and can't find any. He has become convinced that God's judgment against him is final, irreversible, and unappealable. Even if, as Job says, I were to "wash myself with snow, and cleanse my hands with lye"—get all cleaned up—God would "plunge me into a pit" (9:30-31). No hope.

JOB WANTS AN ARBITER

The problem, Job says, is that God is unapproachable. I can't argue with him; I can't set forth my case before him. God is not a man, so we can't meet in court to decide the case (9:32). If I could

---

105 "Peace, When Trouble Blows," Lionel Peterson, 1999 (used by permission).
106 Deut. 28:23.

only engage the Lord, talk with him, perhaps there would be some hope.

Job needs help.

When I practiced law, clients would often present with the same difficulty on a human scale. They would have a grievance against another—often, an employee against a giant corporate employer. In one case, our client was a woman who had high qualifications for her job. She had received the highest marks from her supervisors in their quarterly evaluations, had an impeccable resumé, and yet had been replaced by a man clearly less qualified.

She was demoted, for no apparent reason. She had filed a grievance with her employer, but to no avail. She felt she had been wronged, and the employer just wasn't listening. She was nothing to the international corporation, she thought. She needed someone to help, someone to bring the giant corporate employer into the courtroom, someone who could compel her employer to listen, someone who could arbitrate her case. But Job says about God:

> For he is not a man, as I am, that I might answer
> him, that we should come to trial together.
> There is no arbiter between us,
> who might lay his hand on us both. (9:32-33)

Job wants, and badly needs, a hearing, and a mediator at the hearing. Whatever charges God may have against him, whatever divine reasons there are for his landing on the ash heap, he wants to confront those issues and somehow get them resolved. He knows he can't do that by himself. He needs an intermediary, someone who is able and qualified to lay one hand on the Lord, and the other hand on Job. "Then," he says, "I would speak without fear of him" (9:35). But without such a mediator, I'm helpless. Sanderson illustrates:

> One of the advantages that you and I have is,
> that if we have a difference of opinion, you and I

can sit down, we can talk. If we can't work it out that way, we can bring somebody else in. If worse comes to worse, I could sue you, and take you to court. There are things we can do.

But what can you do with God? Nothing. Nothing. Kind of frustrating, isn't it, when you think about it. What do I need? I need an intermediary. And, Job says, that's my problem. There's no umpire between us, who can lay his hand upon us both.

Have you ever seen two children who were fighting, and did you ever come up to them and lay one hand on one of them, and the other hand on the other, and say, "Now, let's be friends; let's talk this thing over"?

But Job says, "God and I are on the outs, and we don't have anybody who can put one hand on God, and one hand on me, and say 'Let's talk this thing over.' I wish I had an umpire. I wish I had an intermediary."[107]

JOB NEEDS JESUS

Job's cry for an arbiter, an intermediary, is, in fact, a cry for Jesus. Job knows that he is in a horrible dilemma because he is a man, who has an issue to settle with God. He knows that he is no match for God. God doesn't deal with men as equals. We are not God's peers. A man does not have the right, or even the capacity, to approach the Living God by himself. But we see Jesus[108]:

Since then we have a great high priest who has passed through the heavens, Jesus, the Son of God, let us hold fast our confession. For we do

---

107   9 JWS 75-122A-A.
108   Heb. 2:9.

not have a high priest who is unable to sympathize with our weaknesses, but one who in every respect has been tempted as we are, yet without sin. Let us then with confidence draw near to the throne of grace, that we may receive mercy and find grace to help in time of need. (Heb. 4:14-16)

Who is Job's adversary? God! Who is Job's mediator? God! Who is the judge? God! That's unheard of in human parlance; it seems to be a perfect example of 'the fox guarding the chicken coop.' We can't have that. The mediator would have to recuse himself, because he'd have what's called a "conflict of interest." But in the matter of reconciliation with *El Shaddai*, it can be no other way,[109] and—praise God—Jesus will never recuse himself.

Job didn't yet know any specifics about Jesus, but he did know that he had urgent need of just such a person, and he actually described him. But that person was in fact already there for him. He had, and we have, someone greater than an arbiter: we have an *advocate*.[110] Children of the Kingdom are assured of that advocacy "since he always lives to make intercession for them."[111] But for Job, and for us, that's hard to remember in the deep, dark swirl of despondency. You know he is there for you, pleading for you and making your case. But you just can't feel it. It doesn't seem real.

JOB'S PATHÉTIQUE

Chapter 10 is an eloquent, deep lament.

The last music that Tchaikovsky composed was his Sixth Symphony, the *Pathétique*. It is the musical utterance of a discouraged, despondent man. The last movement of the *Pathétique* is sorrowful, mournful, and tragic. As you listen to it, you are taken to the depths of a hopeless human existence. It ends quietly, as

---

109   10 JWS 75-122A-B.
110   1 Jn. 2:1.
111   Heb. 7:25.

life ebbs away. Tchaikovsky composed the symphony in the last year of his life. He conducted it only once, and died nine days later, perhaps a suicide. The composition is powerful and beautiful, and every time the St. Louis Symphony performs it, I buy tickets.

Tchaikovsky wrote the score, but millenia previous, Job had written the lyrics. "I loathe my life," Job says, and I "will speak in the bitterness of my soul" (10:1). His bitterness is directed upward, to his Creator:

> Does it seem good to you to oppress,
>> to despise the work of your hands? (10:3)

You created me!—but only to oppress and despise me? Why would you do that? Remember, Lord. Remember that *you* are the one who formed me as a potter molds clay; *you* are the one who "clothed me with skin and flesh, and knit me together with bones and sinews" (10:11). Job is saying what David later said:

> For you formed my inward parts;
>> you knitted me together in my mother's
>> womb.
> I praise you, for I am fearfully and wonderfully
>> made. (Psa. 139:13-14)

But unlike David, Job is not praising the Lord. At this point he is bitter, and not a little bewildered. So he reminds the Lord of the truth about his own creation.

Of course it isn't really necessary for us to 'remind' the Lord of anything. He hasn't forgotten. But we can, and must, wrestle with God, as Jacob did,[112] and as Job does here. Job has a plausible argument. Would God make something, particularly in his own image, the crown jewel of his creation, just to despise and destroy it? But Lord, that's what you're doing with me.

Further, "[y]ou bring fresh troops against me," Job complains. Job had experienced the first waves of attack in Chapters 1

---

112 Gen. 32:22-32.

and 2, when God allowed Satan to bring catastrophe on him. But now, in Job's utter desolation, God has marshaled up the reserves. They are Job's three friends, who, Job says, are "your witnesses against me" (10:17). These "fresh troops" are prepared and apparently eager to finish the job.

THE LAND OF GLOOM AND DARKNESS

Job reiterates his wish that he had never been born (10:18-19; 3:1ff), that he had been taken directly from womb to grave. But given the unfortunate fact that he was born, and is where he is, he implores God for some respite. He wants the Lord to let up, to "leave me alone, that I may find a little cheer" (10:20) before he dies.

We don't get the impression here that Job fears death. God had removed that fear.[113] But death is still a mystery. We really don't understand it, mainly because, by definition, no living person has experienced it in order to report back what it's like. We are left to speculate. Job's educated guess is that death is:

> the land of gloom like thick darkness,
> like deep shadow without any order,
> where light is as thick darkness. (10:22)

DEATH AND THE NEW CREATION

I recently watched a cosmologist on the Science channel predicting the future of the universe, based on the 'Big Bang' theory. He said that since the whole universe came from a single particle that (for whatever reason) exploded, expanding into a universe of stars and planets now some 14 billion light years in diameter, the universe is destined at some point to collapse and return to a single particle. This he described as the "death" of the universe, and this grim prospect has to be so because gravity ultimately will pull everything back together. One particle again, a "singularity." He

---

113   Heb. 2:15.

described this future particle as having no dimensions, no laws, and no order.

That is essentially how Job describes death, too. No order. No laws of nature. Light becomes darkness—the two are indistinguishable—reversing the work done on the first day of creation when God "separated the light from the darkness."[114]

I have never viewed a body in a casket without thinking "this isn't right." Not that death isn't natural or to be expected, but that a corpse just looks like something went very wrong. That incredible body, with all its systems and senses, its emotions, verve, smiles, tears, wits, laughter, hopes—it could *never* have been made to come just to this. And if no consideration is given to the resurrection, it doesn't make sense. The human body, from birth to death, is wonderfully composed, fully integrated in all its amazing, complex systems. But at the moment of death it becomes *dis*ordered, *dis*integrated and begins to *de*compose. Death is, indeed, a reversal of creation.

But death is not the final state. Scripture promises the children of God that "the creation itself will be set free from its bondage to corruption and obtain the freedom of the glory of the children of God."[115] Our bodies will be recreated, reintegrated, but this time, incorruptibly. God will '*re*order' and '*re*compose' his creation from top to bottom. There will be no caskets; no graves of maggots chewing on rotting flesh.

Job later will affirm sure confidence in the bodily resurrection. But like us all, his confidence will flag. Moses had those moments, and so did Abraham. Every forthright believer will admit to them.

Right now, though, all Job wants is a little interval, a little cheer "before I go—and I shall not return" (10:21).

---

114   Gen. 1:3.
115   Rom 8:21.

ZOPHAR PERSISTS WITH INSULTS

If Job thought he'd get that little 'cheer' from Zophar he was wrong. Zophar insults Job as nothing more than "a man full of talk." Hot air. As has been said of the Texas farmer making bids at an auction, with nothing to back them up, Job is "all hat, no cattle." A pretender. Zophar self-confidently scuttles Job's words as "babble" and "mocking" (11:2-3). These guys were sure of themselves—we have to give them that.

Like Eliphaz and Bildad before, Zophar believes that he speaks for God, and that if God himself would only speak to Job he would set Job straight, and show Job that he was getting off easy—that God "exacts of you less than your guilt deserves" (11:4-6). God will show you that you deserve worse. Zophar will get his wish in the last chapters of the Book of Job when the Lord speaks to Job, but it's not going to be exactly what he here predicts. We all must think things through carefully before we ask the Lord to speak.

In 11:7-12, Zophar parades before Job something that Job really didn't need to be reminded of (as we have just seen): the utter transcendence of God. God is higher than heaven, and deeper than the grave. Longer than the earth, broader than the sea. You can't begin to understand God's work, Job, any more than a "donkey's colt is born a man," because you are a stupid man.

But if you will just repent of your iniquity—just do it, Job!—then you'll forget your misery, your life will be brighter than noonday, you will feel secure, and you will again have hope. But in your present state of wickedness you will fail, and your only hope will be to breathe your last (11:13-20).

Zophar really knows how to visit someone in the hospital, doesn't he?[116]

---

116   Sanderson comments: "You might read [the friends'] speeches, and learn how not to do hospital counseling—and how not to do a few other things too!" (1 JWS 75-120A-A).

JOB'S DISPUTE IS WITH GOD

At this point, Job has had just about enough from his three friends. He begins his response with cutting sarcasm, and ridicules their arguments: "No doubt you are the people, and wisdom will die with you!" (12:2); "Oh that you would keep silent, and it would be your wisdom!"[117] (13:5); and "Your maxims are proverbs of ashes; your defenses are defenses of clay." (13:12).

These men needed to be put in their place, and though Job was a sick man, weakened and wearied, he was up to the task. You three think you are speaking for God, he says, but your words are false. You are not "pleading" (as in a legal document) for God as you think you are. And when he searches you out, he will rebuke you. Job proved to be right about this. In the last chapter of the book, God does rebuke Eliphaz and his two friends: "[y]ou have not spoken of me what is right" (42:7). It's one thing for Job to put his friends in their place, but quite another for God to do so.

But as Job does throughout all his arguments, he makes it clear that his fundamental dispute is with the Lord and not with the three.

WHY DO THE WICKED PROSPER? (I)[118]

Job doesn't charge God with injustice, but he wonders about it. He doesn't understand. Neither did Asaph the Psalmist, at first. They both wondered about the prosperity of the wicked, while the righteous are afflicted. Asaph was mystified as to why

[the wicked] have no pangs until death;
their bodies are fat and sleek.

---

117   Job here expresses, sarcastically, the wish that his friends would return to their mode of silence that they had exercised for the first week when they came to visit him, because he received more wisdom from them when they were silent than now, when they are speaking. (2:13).

118   Job asks the same question later in 24:1-12.

> They are not in trouble as others are;
>> they are not stricken like the rest of mankind.
>>> (Psa. 73:4-5)

The Psalmist didn't understand until he entered "the sanctuary of God,"[119] and we will see that Job later finds answers there as well. But not yet. Job says that he has become a laughingstock to his friends (12:4), while robbers have peace and security (12:6). "Lord," Job is saying, "this doesn't seem at all right to me; does it to you?"

It is a good question, but when we feel the way Job and Asaph did, and speak of the wicked *categorically* as living a life free of trouble, there is just a tiny bit of exaggeration going on. In ordered society, the robber is usually sent to jail. But I can testify that when I have been in the slough of despond, I've felt exactly as Job and Asaph did. It seems that everybody is getting along just fine except for me.

DESPAIR, YET HOPE

Job hasn't given up. He hasn't revised his estate plan that we discussed earlier. He had told his wife that God was just; that they must accept "evil" from God as well as good (2:10). Though he is being shaken to the core, and despairs of life, he has not lost his foundational hope in God.

This side-by-side state of despair and hope is not untypical for believers who go through great troubles. Think of the Apostle Paul, writing to the Christians at Corinth regarding his troubles in Asia:

> [W]e were so utterly burdened beyond our strength that we despaired of life itself. Indeed, we felt that we had received the sentence of death. But that was to make us rely not on ourselves but on God who raises the dead. He delivered us

---

119   Psa. 73:17.

from such a deadly peril, and he will deliver us.
On him we have set our hope that he will deliver
us again. (2 Cor. 1:8-10)

It is perfectly possible for us to have grave doubts about our lives, to be utterly confused at what's happening to us, and to feel so threatened that, like Paul, we think we have received the death sentence. Yet, at the very same time, we can claim solid hope that God will ultimately deliver us. In fact, believers who have been through the nightmares of life will testify that it is exactly at their lowest point, when they are forced to fall on their knees and scream to God for help, that hope somehow arises, well before the troubles are visibly conquered. The trouble may persist thereafter, but there is now an awareness—a *present* awareness—of the fact that, as Paul says, this is happening to us "to make us rely not on ourselves but on God who raises the dead." This has happened to me more than once. Paul's hope, and Job's hope, is there for our encouragement.

Job testifies of such hope here at the perigee of his anguish. He claims this foundational confidence:

Though he slay me, I will hope in him;
yet I will argue my ways to his face. (13:15)

DEATH ISN'T THE END

The natural man sees death, the end of this natural life, as the limit, the defining terminus. Solomon described this worldly view as "under the sun,"[120] but also noted that God "has put eternity into man's heart."[121]

---

120   Eccl. 1:3ff.
121   Eccl. 3:11. Reference was made earlier to the feeling that "something has gone wrong" when we view a corpse—that there must be something more. Surely this 'feeling,' a sense that "there has to be something more than this," comes from the Holy Spirit's implantation of eternity in the hearts of men and women, as Solomon here states.

Job possesses not merely a general sense of eternity—that there is something beyond this temporal life—but a knowledge of and faith in his Eternal God. Death may come ("though he slay me"), but he will still be there, above and beyond it all, and "*I will hope in him.*"

This is the great confession of faith, the confession of Abraham and everyone who is Abraham's child through the Promise.[122] God told Abraham that, by the way, there's going to be a funeral for you, but four hundred years later your children will take possession of Canaan.[123] That will actually be you, Abraham, taking possession of it as I have promised. It isn't recorded whether or not Abraham blinked when God said this (probably not, because he was sound asleep),[124] but it is recorded that he believed God when God told him something, and that his faith "was counted to him as righteousness."[125] Both Job and Abraham believed in the One who would be there for them after death.

A COMPOSITE IS STRONG MATERIAL

American interstate highways are built to last. They are built of composite materials—crushed rock, pebbles, sand, water and a cement bonding agent. Sand, rocks, pebbles, water or cement in isolation wouldn't work at all, but mixed together they support millions of heavy cars and trucks for years.

God is in the business of building us to last like I-80. Our lives, in his careful providence, are mixtures of joy, grief, trouble, success, and even sin. These never come in isolation. In his hand, they appear together, always and categorically working for our good.[126]

So it is not surprising that Job testifies of his experience in composite form. He says that a tree has more hope than he does

---

122   Rom. 4.
123   Gen. 15:13.
124   Gen. 15:12.
125   Gen. 15:6; Rom. 4:3.
126   Rom. 8:28.

because even after it's cut down, it can sprout again (14:7). Man dies; his body sends out no shoots. A man just breathes his last, and that's the end for him (14:10-12).

Simultaneously, though, Job has hope—hope where there is no hope. Reference Abraham again, to whom God had promised a son. But, unfortunately, his body was about 100 years old. Paul records that Abraham "[i]n hope believed against hope" *even though* his body was about a hundred years old.[127] That was how, Paul says, Abraham became the father of many nations. We can capture this best by seeing it not in the disjunctive but in the conjunctive: I have no hope *and* I have hope. Both and, at the same time. His testimony becomes: "my body is 100 years old *and* I'm going to have a son!" I-80 is open for traffic.

MY CHANGE IS COMING

So it's not only possible, but typical, for a believer to express lack of faith while professing faith. Though Job says that trees are better off than a man, in the next breath he says:

> If a man dies, shall he live again?
> All the days of my service I would wait,
>   *till my renewal* should *come.* (14:14)

The American black slaves set this to music. The slaves teach us much. Their lives were without hope, yet they had hope. An old black spiritual we often sing at our church in St. Louis goes like this:

> My way may not be easy
> You did not say that it would be
> But when it gets dark
>   and I can't see my way
> You told me to put my trust in thee.
> Lord, help me to hold out
> Lord, help me to hold out

---

127 Rom. 4:18.

> Lord, help me to hold out
> *Until my change comes.*

Whoever wrote these words must have memorized Job 14:14, because the literal translation of the last phrase in that verse is "until my change comes" (NASB, KJV). I think that the English word "change" is best here. As Job sat on the ash heap, a near-skeleton[128] scraping its sores, this man could nevertheless claim the glorious truth that a change was on its way. And, he said, I own it already: it is *my* change.

If you would take a moment to reflect on where you are today in your life, and what you want to improve, the word "change" will be the word that immediately pops into your head. A human being can never be perfectly happy with the *status quo*. Change is a desire planted in a person's heart. It is a good desire. When is the last time you prayed, and didn't ask God for some kind of change? And it is not trite for us to say that "prayer *changes* things." God does change things because of prayer, and the 'things' he is going to change most is us.

Whenever we are in trouble, whenever we suffer, we are on a kind of ash heap. Yet it is a very good place to be, because it is there that we will find God's construction project going on. We will find his "both/and." He is mixing all kinds of things together in us, to form a perfect aggregate composite that will endure for eternity. The Creator God, the God who "calls into existence the things that do not exist"[129] is at work. We have hope where there is no hope.

---

128 When the Lord took the prophet Ezekiel into the valley of dry bones, he told him to "[p]rophesy over these bones, and say to them, O dry bones, hear the word of the LORD. Thus says the LORD God to these bones: Behold, I will cause breath to enter you, and you shall live." (Eze. 37:4-5).

129 Rom. 4:17.

FOR REFLECTION

1.

Bildad thought he spoke for the Lord. Is it always wrong to do so? If, when you are counseling someone, you make that claim, how can you be sure that you're speaking for God? Is there any basis in any situation where you could show that to be true?

2.

Does God's transcendence ever bother you? In what ways, and why?

3.

Does God's sovereignty ever bother you? Since you know that he is able to remedy any problem you face because he is sovereign, when he doesn't do so, have you questioned his love for you?

4.

Have there been times when you could see no hope in your present circumstances, and yet did not give up? Have you experienced what Abraham did when Paul said that "in hope [Abraham] believed against hope"? At such times, what is it that gave you hope?

12.

ROUND TWO

CHAPTERS 15-21

JOB'S FAITH is evidenced by particular glimpses of hope. We have already seen a couple of these: "Though he slay me, I will hope in him" (13:15), and his confidence that "my change" will come (14:14). We will see more particulars as we continue through the book.

EVIDENCE OF JOB'S FAITH

But I am convinced that the most poignant testimony of Job's faith is not to be found in these discrete statements. Job's faith is best evidenced in his insistence on continuing to argue with the Lord. He does this throughout the book. He rightly believes that it was God who brought disaster upon him and his family (2:30), so he believes his argument is with God. He believes God is there, that God hears and changes outcomes. The late Francis Schaeffer explicated this truth powerfully for us who live in the modern era.[130]

---

130   Francis A. Schaeffer, *He is There and He is Not Silent* (Tyndale House Publishers, 1972).

That is why Job persists in seeking an audience with God, and when you seek an audience with God, you are making a profound statement of faith. While concerned about his transcendence, Job's incessant pleas to the Lord demonstrate his confidence that Schaeffer was right, that "he is there and he is not silent."

Obviously, he also believes that God is just, because Job's arguments are made altogether on that basis. He believes God can be moved by appeal to his revealed attributes. So he continues to cry out to *El Shaddai*.

This exercise, or discipline, was not new to Job. He was a man who prayed, and not just occasionally. He prayed "continually" for his children long before disaster struck (1:5). Men and women who do that learn something about the intimate nature of their God. Deep inside, Job knew that God was listening to him. This was not new territory for Job. Indeed, that's why he is confused by God's silence when he needs help more than he ever has in his life. God was listening, but not yet speaking.

Meanwhile, though, he has other matters to deal with, such as putting up with his three friends.

YOU ARE ALL MISERABLE COMFORTERS

The chairman of the board of deacons, Eliphaz, doubles down on Job in Chapter 15. It seems inconceivable, but he proceeds to ridicule the sick man he had initially come to comfort:

> Are you the first man who was born?
> Or were you brought forth before the hills?
> Have you listened in the council of God?
> And do you limit wisdom to yourself? (15:7-8)

It's important to pause along the way here and ask: Where did all this vitriol come from? Why are Eliphaz and his two companions so angry at Job?[131] Are they just really bad (I mean *really*

131　Job himself asks this question of his friends: "[W]hat provokes you that you answer?" (16:3).

bad) at interpersonal relationships? Is it that they haven't had proper training in counseling? Did they need some counseling themselves in how to develop a good bedside manner? There is evidently something more going on.

LISTEN TO THE COUNSELEE

We've already seen that the three convened before meeting up with Job and had settled on what they were going to say to him (5:27). They had formulated their theology before they spoke to Job; they had established a kind of mini confession of faith in the Job matter and they didn't intend to swerve from it.

It is always a mistake to arrive at conclusions about what you are going to say to people who need counsel before you listen to them. It's not that we must approach the visit bereft of settled truth. But how to apply that truth, and indeed, to determine if it is even applicable to that person in his or her situation cannot be done properly without hearing them out. The suffering person's story is an indispensable part of the equation. With regard to the three friends, in speaking to future pastors in his lectures at Covenant Seminary, Sanderson says:

> They substituted their opinions for the facts. How do you get the facts? You're a pastor. How do you get the facts? Well, apart from some special revelation, as in the case of, say, Nathan with respect to David, you and I have to depend upon the honesty of the individual that we are dealing with, and the conviction that the Holy Spirit brings to bear on him. We can't make up facts. And that's why it often takes a long time of patient counseling to really get to the facts.

> But, you see, these guys didn't have time for that sort of thing. They've got it all worked out; it's all

neat; it's all clear. They just hit Job over the head
with their doctrine.[132]

I received my undergraduate degree in philosophy from
Covenant College in 1965. It was a wonderful education. I graduated, degree in hand, with Reformed, Biblical theology coming
out my ears. Things were pretty well nailed down as far as I was
concerned. I graduated law school five years later, and felt ready
to face and answer any questions thrown at me. This confidence
lasted right up until I met with one of my first clients, a Christian
woman who reluctantly believed she should pursue a divorce.
When I heard her story, I began to realize that meaningful answers were not to be obtained merely through theological or philosophical charts and outlines. Those foundational truths were
indispensable as she and I began to decide what to do, but her life
story was indispensable too. It was a mistake to prejudge her. It
was a mistake not to listen to her story.

DON'T PREJUDGE

Eliphaz, Zophar and Bildad had prejudged Job, and his suffering. They were self-confident theologians, and they had dia-
grammed the answers before listening to the facts. Furthermore,
their doctrine was superglued by a pre-visit meeting, and they were
wary of even considering an amendment. That's the way it is when
you nail everything down before listening, because you're scared
to abandon conclusions already reached. Consequently, they were
frustrated, because what they were advocating wasn't working.
Frustration can lead to anger. Anger often leads to sin. You start
using a sledgehammer on your computer and throwing things at
the wall. You may even wind up murdering your brother. [133]

---

132   8 JWS 75-120D-B.

133   When the Lord accepted Abel's sacrifice but rejected Cain's, Scripture records: "Cain was very angry, and his face fell. The LORD said to Cain, 'Why are
you angry, and why has your face fallen? If you do well, will you not be accepted?
And if you do not do well, sin is crouching at the door. Its desire is for you, but
you must rule over it.' " Cain wouldn't let go, and as a consequence, murdered

DON'T STICK WITH BAD THEOLOGY

You "are doing away with the fear of God," Eliphaz tells Job. Your own mouth condemns you; your iniquity teaches your mouth (15:4-6).

What is the "iniquity" that Eliphaz cites? He doesn't have any particulars because there aren't any. The "sin" he's talking about is generated entirely by his bad theolgy: if Job is sufffering, it is a result of his sin because there isn't any suffering without sin. The Eliphaz formula. And Eliphaz is arrogant: "I will show you; hear me!" he shouts (15:17). As my father often said of an overly self-confident person, "He thinks he knows everything, and if you don't believe him, just ask him."

So Eliphaz spends the rest of the time describing the wicked, and though he does so in the third person, he's clearly talking about Job. Thus he accuses Job of defying *El Shaddai*, "running stubbornly against him" (15:25-26).

Well, of course this doesn't comfort Job. "Miserable comforters are you all," he responds (16:2). I could accuse you too if you were in my place. I could do as you do. I could "join words together against you." But I wouldn't. I would do what you should be doing for me. I would "strengthen you with my mouth, and the solace of my lips would assuage your pain" (16:5). That's what a true friend should, and would, do.

GOD HATES ME

However, my issue is with God, Job says. He has worn me out, made me desolate, shriveled me up, torn me in his anger and *hated* me (16:7-9). Men who once treated me with honor now make fun of me; they strike me on the cheek. Everywhere I look, whether to the public, my friends, or the Lord himself—everyone despises me.[134] Therefore,

---

his brother Abel. (Gen. 4:5-7).

134   In this passage Job is seen as a type of Christ. On the night of the betrayal,

My spirit is broken; my days are extinct;
>   the graveyard is ready for me.
Surely there are mockers about me,
>   and my eye dwells on their provocation.

(17:1-2)

Have you ever been so dismayed that you have thought God actually hated you? We may be reluctant to say so outright, but that's often the way we feel. We know theoretically that God is love,[135] but there are times when he sends so much pain and suffering our way that he seems to be the negative opposite of love. It is as though he has us cornered, and is beating us without mercy. Would anyone do that to someone he truly loved? Yet we know that "his steadfast love endures forever."[136] We can't reconcile the two.

But we are not called upon to reconcile the two, nor are we capable of doing so. We must pray for wisdom, and God has promised to give us such without reservation,[137] but fundamentally it is an article of faith. We learn to take God at his word when he says that his love for us is absolute and forever. That is where we rest; it is the sole ground of our comfort.

The distresses of our lives are swallowed up in the confidence we have in his word (he does love us) and his character (he never changes). Christians who have experienced Job-like catastrophe will testify that comfort does not appear so much when the here-and-now trial ends, but before that, in the vortex of the trial, when the Holy Spirit gives sweet and unshaking assurance that God sees, hears and delivers his own—that is, that God is love.

---

one of the Jewish officials slapped Jesus on the cheek (Jn. 18:22), and like Jesus, Job was "despised and rejected" by men (Isa. 53:3).

135   1 Jn. 4:8.
136   Psa. 136:1.
137   James 1: 5-8.

MY WITNESS IS IN HEAVEN

Through it all, Job does not give up. He has just said that God hates him, but he continues to cry out to him. Whatever he thinks God's disposition toward him might be at present, he still has hope:

> O earth, cover not my blood,
> and let my cry find no resting place.
> Even now, behold, my witness is in heaven,
> and he who testifies for me is on high.
>
> (16:18-19)

Even now! Let my cry find no resting place (my cry must continue), because I know God will eventually answer it. Why? Because there is someone who is in God's presence, right now, pleading my case. I have a representative there, not just in the future, but as we speak. I have no hope in myself, but I have hope in my arbiter.

Verse 19 is evidence of the Holy Spirit's progressive work in Job. God does not usually change our hearts and thoughts (that is, he does not sanctify us) in a sudden flash, but as we go along.[138] In 9:33 Job had said that "[t]here is no arbiter between us," but he has moved forward. He now expresses confidence in just such a person. And that person is not merely a human priest. This is someone "on high," in the seat of authority and power. He is Job's arbiter, mediator, advocate, and Savior. Job couldn't say it yet, "But we see Jesus..."[139]

The Holy Spirit, the Comforter,[140] is progressively drawing Job closer to Christ. And that is the place—the only place—where Job or any of us will find real comfort. The Heidelberg Cate-

---

138 *Westminster Shorter Catechism* states that while justification is an "act" of God's free grace (Q. 33), sanctification is the "work" of God's free grace (Q. 35), positing that it is an ongoing process rather than a sudden act.

139 Heb. 2:9 (KJV).

140 "But the Comforter, which is the Holy Ghost, whom the Father will send in my name, he shall teach you all things, and bring all things to your remembrance, whatsoever I have said unto you." (Jn. 14:26, KJV)

chism's first question is: "What is your only comfort in life and death?" The answer:

> That I am not my own, but belong with body and soul, both in life and in death, to my faithful Savior Jesus Christ. He has fully paid for all my sins with His precious blood, and has set me free from all the power of the devil. He also preserves me in such a way that without the will of my heavenly Father not a hair can fall from my head; indeed, all things must work together for my salvation. Therefore, by His Holy Spirit He also assures me of eternal life and makes me heartily willing and ready from now on to live for Him.

Job had properly hoped for comfort from his three friends, but found them to be "miserable" comforters (16:2). They failed. But the Holy Spirit cannot fail; he will not leave Job, nor will he leave any of us who name the name of Christ in the lurch. In fact, God will use even failing comforters, maintaining a false theology, to drive Job to trust in him alone. And the process is not gentle.

BILDAD TO JOB: YOU DON'T EVEN KNOW GOD

Bildad berates Job: It's a whole lot worse than you think, Job. You don't even know God (18:21). You are Exhibit A of the wicked man. Your suffering is altogether your fault. Your evil plans have caught up with you, and you are hoisted on your own petard.[141] We all know what happens to a wicked man: traps seize him by the heel, terrors frighten him, he has no strength, he suffers calamities, his skin and flesh are consumed, he has no posterity[142] (18:9-21). Just take a good look at yourself, Job! This describes you perfectly. Such is the one who "knows not God" (18:21). You need blame and look at none other than yourself.

---

141 "[H]is own schemes throw him down." (18:7).

142 A direct reference to the premature deaths of Job's children: "He has no posterity or progeny among his people, and no survivor where he used to live." (18:19).

Satan has us just where he wants us when we adopt Bildad's advice. Self-examination is important, without doubt. But to leave a person where Bildad leaves Job is to tell that person that he has no hope at all.

It is telling that in Bildad's invective contained in Chapter 18, he nowhere acknowledges the *affectionate* sovereignty of God in Job's life. Bildad doesn't seem to be interested in that. He just scrutinizes Job, and instructs Job to look only at Job for why this happened to Job and that he look only to Job for a solution for Job. As Job later claims, the friends are falsely saying that "[t]he root of the matter is found in me" (19:28). Whenever we reach that point, whenever we believe that we must straighten ourselves up, by ourselves, before God will hear us, and that answers will be found only through introspection, we are in Satan's grip, and we have lost hope. Many counselors, including Christian ones, depend almost exclusively on self-reflection, or introspection. Such dependence is misplaced. Bildad is giving Job bad advice.

IT'S NOT MY FAULT

Job's response, however, is clear: I'm not looking at myself, or to myself, for an answer. I'm looking solely at, and to, the Lord. Job was still right on track.

You three are looking in the wrong place because you're looking at me. You are tormenting me, crushing me with your words (19:2). You have cast reproach on me ten times already (Job was exaggerating here—it had only been five so far, but it seemed like ten to him).

When Job says that "*God* has put me in the wrong, and closed his net about me" (19:6) he is specifically refuting Bildad, because Bildad had said that Job's own schemes had thrown him down (18:7). No, Job says, it is God who had thrown him down. God is the one who has walled up my way, stripped from me my glory, and taken the crown from my head (19:8-9). I had nothing to do with it. *It's not my fault.*

Job is not claiming that he's attained sinless perfection, and no longer in need of redemption. He never says such, and in fact recognizes his need of a redeemer (19:25). What he is saying here is that he is neither the problem nor the solution.

The "problem" is immense, because God has turned adversary (19:11). My family (he mentions only brothers and other kin, being bereaved of his children) are estranged from me; my relatives have failed me; guests in my house and my maidservants count me as a stranger; even children despise me (19:13-18).

Why was this so? It isn't natural or typical for family and friends to forsake, or disown, a man when he is sick and has lost everything. You wouldn't expect the poor man would have to plead with his own servants for mercy (19:16). Why was everyone treating Job like the plague? The answer has to be that the three friends' theology was conventional wisdom of that day, as mentioned in chapter 9 of this book, The Eliphaz Formula again. Under that schematic, those who suffer are rightly despised because their suffering is incontrovertible evidence of their wickedness.

But Job adamantly refuses to go down that path, because he knows that though he is a sinner, his sin is not the cause of his trouble. So he cries out to his friends: "Have mercy on me, have mercy on me, O you my friends, for the hand of God has touched me!" (19:21). I haven't brought this disaster upon myself. It's God. Why can't you accept that?

BRING IN THE COURT REPORTER

Because of my training and background, I like to think of the Book of Job as a legal proceeding. The facts of the case are set out in the first two Chapters. The trial, during which the facts and applicable law are hashed out, is between Job as plaintiff, and God as defendant.[143] It takes place before a panel of three judges, Eliphaz,

---

143   While Job debates the three, he makes it clear throughout that his dispute is not with them, but with God.

Bildad and Zophar (who are his adversaries), and is contained in Chapters 3-29, a transcript of the proceedings. Job loses at trial; the panel of three rules against him. But Job, beginning in Chapter 30, takes his case up on appeal. His appeal is to the Lord, who, while being the defendant at trial, is also the final judge. The Lord announces his ruling on appeal in Chapters 38-42. Of course no more appeals could then be taken. We'll get to the Lord's appellate decision later, but right now let's return to the county courthouse in the midst of the trial.

In such trials, the judge often takes a short recess to discuss legal issues with the attorneys. For example, a lawyer may have objected to certain evidence, but the judge may not be sure what the law is on the matter, and wants to be sure before he rules. The jury stays in their seats while the judge and lawyers retire to the judge's chambers to resolve the legal issue. Typically, such discussions "outside the hearing of the jury" begin informally, as the judge asks counsel to present authority and arguments supporting their respective positions. Soon it becomes evident that the judge is about to make up his or her mind, and the lawyer who feels that the judge is about to rule against him will often say "I want this to be a part of the record, Judge." The lawyer has an absolute right to "make a record." The judge can't say no. So the judge calls out to the clerk, "Bring in the court reporter!"

The lawyer wants a record to be made so that the issue will be preserved for appeal. This is just what Job is doing when he says, "Oh that my words were written! Oh that they were inscribed in a book!" (19:23). He is asking for a court reporter. He can see that he's losing his argument before his three friends. He wants to make a record for appeal. Like a lawyer in the judge's chambers, he wants a certified court reporter to nail down every word, so that there is no later doubt about what he's about to say. He wants his words to be engraved with an iron pen, in a rock, forever (19:24).[144] It is Job's unshaken confession of faith:

---

144 The Lord gave Job his request, but on a medium more permanent than

I KNOW THAT MY REDEEMER LIVES

> For I know that my Redeemer lives,
>> and at the last he will stand upon the earth.
> And after my skin has been thus destroyed,
>> yet in my flesh I shall see God,
>> whom I shall see for myself,
>> and my eyes shall behold, and not another.
> My heart faints within me. (19:25-27)

In the blackest darkness of his trial, feeling that death was imminent, Job sets forth the sole ground of his argument. It is his anchor, and if it fails, all else fails.[145] The Holy Spirit had placed it in Job's mind and heart, and moved Job to request that it be written down for future reference. God did the same thing with the prophet Habakkuk. He told Habakkuk to "write the vision, make it plain on tablets."[146]

Some scholars wonder if Job here speaks of the Resurrection at the last day, when those who believe will be brought back to life, or if Job is saying that, before he dies, he will actually see God (which Job did in fact experience, in the theophany recorded in Chapters 38-41).

There are three reasons for concluding Job is describing the Resurrection. First, the context for this event is "at the last" when God "will stand upon the earth" (19:25). Second, Job says this will occur "after my skin has thus been destroyed" (19:26). In other

---

rock. Job's argument, or great confession, contained in 19:25-27 became a part of Scripture, the very Word of God. Job's words were, as he requested, "inscribed in a book" (19:23), a book that lasts like no others. "The grass withers, the flower fades, but the word of our God will stand forever." (Isa. 40:8).

145 "For if the dead are not raised, not even Christ has been raised. And if Christ has not been raised, your faith is futile and you are still in your sins. Then those also who have fallen asleep in Christ have perished. If in Christ we have hope in this life only, we are of all people most to be pitied." (1 Cor. 15:16-19).

146 Hab. 2:2. What the Lord wanted to have recorded there was that "the just shall live by his faith." (Hab. 2:4, KJV).

words, Job believed that he would see God after his life on earth had ended.

AN IRON PEN

The third and most compelling reason for understanding these lines as speaking of the Resurrection is that Job requested an iron pen. There isn't any record of Job's having been informed that he would "see God" in this lifetime, even though he did (38:1ff). In these lines, Job isn't talking about that kind of interim epiphany, similar to the Transfiguration.[147] Rather, he is talking about seeing God on that great Last Day. No other day can be called the ground of a person's faith. But this Day, unmistakably at the core of Job's faith, when Job would see his Redeemer face to face, was Job's ultimate assurance.[148] That's why he wanted it recorded for eternity. That's why he called for an iron pen.

Job had serious doubts about his earthly life, but none about eternity.

RESURRECTION IN THE OLD TESTAMENT

It isn't as though people before Christ knew nothing of the resurrection at the last day. Their knowledge was sketchy,[149] but they had more than an inkling of it.

The Jews of the Old Testament believed that a person possesses a fleshly body, and a spirit, or soul. At death, the body returns to dust, but the soul lives on, and the body remains in the grave until Resurrection Day.[150]

---

147 Mk. 9:2ff.

148 The resurrection is the essential hope of believers. The Apostle Peter wrote: "According to his great mercy, he has caused us to be born again to a living hope through the resurrection of Jesus Christ from the dead, to an inheritance that is imperishable, undefiled, and unfading, kept in heaven for you." (1 Pet. 1:3-4).

149 1 Pet. 1:10-12.c

150 Orthodox theology is essentially consonant with this understanding. In the *Westminster Shorter Catechism* the divines wrote: "Q. 37. What benefits do believers receive from Christ at death? A. The souls of believers are at their death made perfect in holiness, and do immediately pass into glory; and their bodies,

Hannah prayed for years that the Lord would give her a son. When her prayers were answered, moved by the Holy Spirit, she sang for joy. She saw the newborn Samuel not only as an answer to her prayers, nor just as a mortal who would live out his days and die. By faith, she also saw the resurrection. She sang:

> The LORD kills and brings to life
>> he brings down to Sheol and raises up.
>>> (1 Sam. 2:6)

David testified to the resurrection as well:

> Therefore my heart is glad, and my whole being
>> rejoices; my flesh also dwells secure.
> For you will not abandon my soul to Sheol,
>> or let your holy one see corruption.
>>> (Psa. 16:9-10)[151]

Isaiah confirmed it:

> He will swallow up death forever;
>> and the LORD God will wipe away tears from
>>> all faces,
>> and the reproach of his people he will take
>>> away from all the earth,
> For the LORD has spoken. (Isa. 25:8)

The prophet Ezekiel witnessed, in a vision, the Lord's promise of the Resurrection. In the "valley of dry bones," the Lord said: "Thus says the Lord God: Behold, I will open your graves and raise you from your graves, O my people."[152]

---

being still united to Christ, do rest in their graves till the resurrection."

151 David's testimony is certified by the Apostle Paul as referring to the resurrection of Christ, thus incorporating the resurrection of believers. (Acts 13:35; 1 Cor. 15:20).

152 Eze. 37:12.

IN MY FLESH

Job also believed that the Resurrection will be in the flesh. You three friends, he says, have an unending appetite for my flesh (19:22), but it is in my flesh that I will see God (19:26). Job may not have known exactly what the Apostle Paul knew regarding the body, that "[w]hat is sown is perishable; what is raised is imperishable."[153] But Job knew that it was in the flesh that he would be resurrected and see God, with real, physical eyeballs.

This truth is great comfort to us. God has given us bodies. We love our bodies, when they work. We are physical. We can't imagine it any other way. We can taste, see, smell, feel, hear, walk, get hungry and eat, run, sleep, laugh out loud. So could Jesus, before and after his resurrection. In our resurrected, incorruptible bodies we will actually sit down with him at the banquet table and eat real food. We might ask for seconds, and so might Jesus, because just like us, he gets hungry.[154]

That's what Job was looking forward to.

A REBUKE AND A WARNING

Job thought of the Resurrection very personally. It would be in his own body; he said he would see God "for myself" and "not another" (19:27). He knew that for such to happen he would have to be pure, or righteous. So he wants his three friends to know that he is now, and on that day will be, righteous in God's sight.

Eliphaz, Bildad and Zophar have hammered away at Job, telling him that he cannot stand before the Lord because of his wickedness. They have tried to shame Job into confession of a non-existent sin. But in the face of his friends, Job is like the Apostle Paul, who wrote:

> I am not ashamed, for I know whom I have believed, and I am convinced that he is able to guard

---

153 1 Cor 15:42.
154 Mk. 11:20; Mt. 25:35.

until that Day what has been entrusted to me. (2
Tim. 1:12)

Job trusted God for his righteousness. And by professing faith
that he would see God on that Day, Job is not merely express-
ing his convictions concerning the Last Day, but repudiating the
friends' charges. Job tells them that they are erring greatly, and
there are consequences.

"Be careful!" Job warns. I will stand before God, dressed in
his righteousness. My three friends, if you persist in denying that
righteousness, God will judge you. You are judging me wrongfully. You are sinning against me and against the Lord. You should
"be afraid of the sword, for wrath brings the punishment of the
sword, that you may know there is a judgment" (19:29). Had the
book of James existed in his day, Job could have cited these two
verses:

> Do not speak evil against one another, brothers.
> The one who speaks against a brother or judges
> his brother, speaks evil against the law and judg-
> es the law. But if you judge the law, you are not
> a doer of the law but a judge. There is only one
> lawgiver and judge, he who is able to save and to
> destroy. But who are you to judge your neighbor?
> (James 4:11-12)

ZOPHAR IGNORES JOB'S WARNING

Job's friends just can't seem to heed his caution. It's frustrating, just reading about it. They're too entrenched, and their
collaboration has emboldened them beyond reason. They aren't
consigned to an ash heap, and they aren't a bit concerned about a
warning from someone who is.

It's Zophar's turn, and he rolls on. He does so with disdain:
"I hear censure that insults me" (20:3). He's essentially saying, "I
believe I just heard my name mentioned?" Kind of smart-aleck.

I'll tell you who is going to be judged, Job, and it's not me. It's the wicked whom God brings to nothing, and it's pretty obvious who *that* has happened to. The "exulting of the wicked is short, and the joy of the godless but for a moment" (20:5).

Zophar's words in Chapter 20 are nothing other than another insult aimed indirectly at Job. Zophar doesn't mention Job as such; it's more effective to let Job figure that out. He wants Job to understand that that's assumed, that his wickedness is a settled fact, not up for debate. The third person description of the wicked is intended as an indictment of the man sitting before him on the ash heap.

CROSS-EXAMINATION

Zophar is skilled. He calls up some of Job's own words to buttress his assault. He uses a technique familiar to trial lawyers, when, in the course of preparation for trial, witnesses are examined, under oath, by means of deposition. Though these proceedings aren't in front of a judge and jury, the testimony taken is every bit as important, and serves as a guide for the trial itself. A lawyer must read and index the depositions carefully before trial, so that when the witness testifies before the judge and jury he will be able to spot any inconsistencies between what the witness said at deposition and now, at trial.

While examining the witness at trial, a favorite and effective technique attorneys use is to remind the witness of what he said previously, catching him in his own words. Zophar attempts to do that here. In 20:6-7 he says:

> Though his height mount up to the heavens,
> and his head reach to the clouds,
> he will perish forever like his own dung;
> Those who have seen him will say, "Where is he?"

and in doing so he is taking Job back to what Job himself had said previously: "But a man dies and is laid low; man breathes his last, and where is he?" (14:10). Zophar also says:

> The eye that saw him will see him no more,
> nor will his place any more behold him. (20:9)

reminding Job of his own previous testimony: "The eye of him who sees me will behold me no more; while your eyes are on me, I shall be gone" (7:8). Zophar continues:

> He will flee from an iron weapon;
> a bronze arrow will strike him through.
> It is drawn forth and comes out of his body;
> the glittering point comes out of his
> gallbladder;
> terrors come upon him. (20:24-25)

reminding Job of what Job said earlier: "[H]is his archers surround me. He slashes open my kidneys and does not spare; he pours out my gall on the ground. He breaks me with breach upon breach; he runs upon me like a warrior" (16:13-14).

BEGGING THE QUESTION

Zophar is clever, in his attempt to show Job that he has already admitted his wickedness. But not clever enough. He and his buddies, at the outset, came up with the Eliphaz Formula, a logical proposition, and they should stick with the rules of logic. One logical "fallacy" is that of "begging the question,"[155] that is, assuming a conclusion that is really a premise of the argument.[156] Zophar does that here. He assumes the major premise of the Eliphaz Formula, that suffering is always a direct result of a particular

---

155   The term "begging the question" has morphed in recent years to mean something like "this statement that you just made raises an issue that must be answered," or "begs" an additional question. This was not the original meaning of the term. It originally meant "circular reasoning," or "assuming the premise."
156   As in, "Have you *stopped* beating your wife?" where the primary issue is whether the husband had beaten his wife in the first place.

sin of the sufferer. That's what is up for debate. Thus he has committed a logical fallacy, and hasn't proved a thing. His reasoning is circular.

Job hadn't admitted his wickedness in his previous statements. Rather, he was describing his pathetic condition, and in fact wondering how this could happen to a righteous man. Zophar's errant gloss, once again, is a result of his errant theology, that the wicked—and only the wicked—suffer the way Job is suffering.

SMOKING JOB OUT

Zophar is so sure of himself in his conviction that Job has sinned that he takes a wild stab at what the particular sin might be. But before he does, he prefaces his unfounded accusation with the charge that Job has not been forthcoming[157]:

> Though evil is sweet in his mouth,
>> though he hides it under his tongue,
>> though he is loath to let it go
>> and holds it in his mouth... (20:12-13)

We know you're hiding your sin, Job, but (for your own good, of course) we are going to ferret it out of you. The way we're going to do it is by flushing you out of your deceitful thicket.

In the practice of law, I've seen this "technique," if it deserves such an elegant term, used by police detectives. They've nabbed a "person of interest," against whom they have little or no evidence. Like Zophar with Job, they choose or pretend to think the person isn't being forthcoming as they interview him. They just have a very strong hunch that he did the deed. They think their suspect "hides it under his tongue," and is "loath to let it go" (though I've not read any police reports where those exact terms were used). So they resort to scare tactics, telling the poor suspect that they have

---

157 Job later pleads with the Lord to examine him carefully to see if he has been dishonest, to see "if I have concealed my transgressions as others do, by hiding my iniquity in my heart."(31:33).

evidence to prove that he did it, and he might as well 'fess up.'
When, of course, they have no evidence at all. They're just trying
a shortcut to a finding of guilt by means of confession.

That's what Zophar is doing here. He implies that he has adequate evidence to convict Job on this ridiculous charge:

> For he has crushed and abandoned the poor;
> he has seized a house that he did not build.
>
> (20:19)

That's pretty damnable, all right, if it had happened. But it
hadn't happened. Zophar, the police detective, is the one lying
here, not Job, the person of interest. He's shooting in the dark, trying to shake loose whatever secrets are in the suspect's head.

In a way this might have been somewhat reassuring to Job,
because he could sense that his accusers were running low on am-
munition. Zophar was resorting to scare tactics,[158] and when that
stage is reached, the innocent accused can sense that the prosecu-
tors really don't have anything to go on.

I love Job's bitterly sarcastic response to Zophar. Presumably,
Zophar had come to comfort Job, but Job now says to him, "let
this be *your* comfort": that if you will just bear with me a little,
and let me speak, then I'll let you speak, and you can "mock on"
(21:1-3). Zophar had that one coming.

WHY DO THE WICKED PROSPER? (II)

To an extent, a worn-out Job takes the bait. His rejoinder to
Zophar takes a bit of a detour from the real issue. Job touched on
this in Chapter 12, but he again attempts to prove to the three that
the evil man does not necessarily suffer because of his wickedness,
and that the Eliphaz Formula is defective from the get-go.

Job argues, as he did in Chapter 12, that though he doesn't
understand why it's so, the wicked seem to get along pretty well in

---

158   Eliphaz will do the same, only on steroids, in Chapter 22.

life. He's seen it. They live to a ripe old age, are powerful, establish great families, have beautiful, safe homes, and possess burgeoning herds of cattle that never miscarry. The wicked sing and dance, and are buried in peace and honor (21:6-13). And even though they say to God "Depart from us! We do not desire the knowledge of your ways" (21:14), yet "no rod of God is upon them" (21:9). Job shudders at the thought of this apparently gross injustice (21:6).

SEE THE WORLD, MEN!

Job here questions how this squares with the truth that David stated about the righteous man being like a tree that flourishes, but that

> [t]he wicked are not so,
> but are like chaff that the wind drives away.
> (Psa. 1:4)

Job wonders about that, and asks, how often is it

> [t]hat [the wicked] are like straw before the wind,
> and like chaff that the storm carries away[?] (21:18)

Job can't fathom why his friends haven't seen what he has seen. Maybe it's because they don't know much about the world. Maybe they hadn't taken enough trips to different parts of the country, and had become parochial.

When my wife and I lived in Muscatine, a beautiful city in Iowa, located on the west bank of the Mississippi, we knew a woman in her thirties who grew up there and had never traveled out of Iowa. I too was raised in Iowa, and it's a beautiful state, but really. Can't a person get away once in awhile? The Father of Waters is wide, but my goodness, we could see Illinois from our house. And this woman lived where we did, right on the border. True enough, the bridge across the river into Illinois was kind of rickety (she said she was afraid to cross it, and her fear was not altogether unreasonable). But it was worth the risk, just to expand horizons.

It doesn't hurt a bit to venture out and look around occasion-ally. Job didn't think his friends had done enough of it. Apparent-ly, they hadn't even attended travelogues to learn from those who *had* been out and around:

> Have you not asked those who travel the roads,
>   and do you not accept their testimony
>   that the evil man is spared in the day of
>   calamity,
>   that he is rescued in the day of wrath?
>
> (21:29-30)

No, Job says, it isn't any comfort to me when you say that only the wicked suffer, and if I'd only repent, God would restore me. You're trying to "comfort me with empty nothings," and "there is nothing left of your answers but falsehood" (21:34). Your Eliphaz Formula is dead wrong.

This is the end of Round Two. Thankfully, the four parties to this debate will have just one more bout in their attempts to convince one another. And I predict they won't be able to do so, if the first two bouts are any indication of what's to come.

FOR REFLECTION

I.

How did Job's habit of praying for his children, recorded in Job 1, help him now that he wasn't hearing from God? What are the benefits of a life of regular prayer?

2.

Have you ever received counsel or advice from a person who gave you advice before listening to your story? How did it make you feel? Did their counsel help you? What can you learn from such an experience as you are asked to give counsel to others?

3.

Does the prospect of the Resurrection encourage you in practical ways? Does it seem remote to you, or real? In what ways is it relevant for you in your daily life, and in your troubles?

13.

FINAL ARGUMENTS

CHAPTERS 22-25

WHEN A CASE is tried to a jury, the concluding stage of the trial is called the "summation" or the "final arguments." It is then that the lawyers are given the opportunity to try to convince the jury that the evidence requires a verdict in favor of their client. Often the arguments get loud and hot. Even good lawyers can lose their composure, and when they do, the jury can tell, and their argument suffers.

We are at the summation stage in Job. As you read through these arguments, beginning with Eliphaz's speech (his last, Chapter 22) you'll notice a level of anger and contempt not evident in what has been said before. Eliphaz seems to have lost his composure. He says some things that are at best intemperate, but worse, most of them are false. This sort of thing began with Zophar's final speech in Chapter 20, but Eliphaz dials it up several notches.

SO WHAT IF YOU WERE RIGHTEOUS?

Eliphaz first informs Job, in a kind of "by the way" manner, that no matter if Job is righteous or not, it makes no difference to God:

> Can a man be profitable to God?
> Surely he who is wise is profitable to himself.
> Is it any pleasure to the Almighty[159] if you are in
> the right,
> Or is it gain to him if you make your
> ways blameless? (22:2-3)

"Job," Eliphaz is saying, "don't think that God is impressed by your claims to righteousness. It might make a big difference to you ['surely he who is wise is profitable to himself'], but it makes no difference to *El Shaddai*. It wouldn't please God even if you were in the right."

Now this is wrong, particularly by "Eliphaz" standards. The Eliphaz Formula holds that God is *very* impressed by righteousness, because the righteous man never has trouble. But as mentioned, lawyers get mad and lose their composure. If Eliphaz hadn't, he probably wouldn't have said this. But he did, so let's process it.

True enough, God doesn't need our obedience to make him happy; he is complete in himself. Eliphaz was right in saying that God doesn't "gain" anything from man's conformity to his law. But Scripture is replete with the truth that God takes great delight in the faithful obedience of his servants. One example will suffice. Samuel, by the Holy Spirit, told Saul that God took delight in the obedience of his servants more than in sacrifices and burnt offerings.[160] Eliphaz's summation doesn't require a labored rebuttal with Scripture proofs, because it's on nearly every page.

It is appropriate, however, to look at another reference, and that is 40:7, where the Lord tells Eliphaz that "[m]y anger burns against you and against your two friends, for you have not spoken of me what is right, as my servant Job has." There are other examples of the friends' false statements about the Lord, but surely

---

159 *El Shaddai*. Eliphaz uses this name to emphasize God's transcendence.
160 1 Sam. 15:22.

this was one that the Lord had in mind when he rebuked Eliphaz later. God does take pleasure in our obedience.

But this is merely Eliphaz's intro. Next he tells Job what he really thinks.

ELIPHAZ CHARGES JOB WITH PARTICULAR, HEINOUS SINS

Eliphaz addresses the one who, by the way, God had declared to be "blameless and upright," unlike any other man on the face of the earth (1:8, 2:3), and accuses him by way of this laundry list of evildoings:

> Is not your evil abundant?
> There is no end to your iniquities.
> For you have *exacted pledges of your brothers for nothing,*
> and *stripped the naked of their clothing.*
> You have *given no water to the weary to drink,*
> and you have *withheld bread from the hungry.*
> The man with power possessed the land,
> and the favored man lived in it.
> You have *sent widows away empty,*
> and *the arms of the fatherless were crushed.*
> (22:5-9)

Where in the world did Eliphaz come up with this list?[161] Did he click one of those teasers on the internet, akin to "You Won't Believe These Ten Celebrities Went Bankrupt," only labeled "The Six Worst Sins of All Time"? Job hadn't done these things, and if he had, it isn't likely that his three friends would have been his friends in the first place.

---

161 A possible explanation lies in the fact that the offenses listed have primarily to do with economic wrongdoing and oppression. Eliphaz and his two friends had likely become convinced that because Job had been a wealthy man before God struck him, and since God took away everything he had, his sin must have been that he put his estate together by nefarious means, particularly injustice to others.

Then, as Zophar did in 20:12-13, Eliphaz charges Job with dishonesty. You know in your heart, Job, that you're guilty of these sins,

> [b]ut you say, "What does God know?
> Can he judge through the deep darkness?
> Thick clouds veil him, so that he does not see,
>   and he walks on the vault of heaven."
>   (22:13-14)

The reason Eliphaz charges Job with such heinous acts and dishonesty is, once again, the wrong-headed theology adopted by him and his friends at the outset. They have no question whatever but that Job's sin caused Job's trouble. But they think Job is stonewalling them. And because Job is *so* determined to keep his sin from being known, Eliphaz reasons, it must have been a monstrous series of sins. In Eliphaz's mind, the level of Job's resistance to the friends' charges is a barometer indicating the level of seriousness of the sin Job had committed. That's why Eliphaz picked the worst sins he could think of.

I wonder if Job, at this point, was tempted to cross his fingers behind his back, admit to some bogus sin, and tell the three to go on home. Just to get rid of them.

"AGREE WITH GOD"

"Agree with God, and be at peace" (22:21), Eliphaz tells Job. Listen to him and "lay up his words in your heart." Pray to him, and he will hear you. You will once again delight yourself in the Almighty and lift up your face to God. (22:22-27). This sounds good, and relatively mild. Further, there are all kinds of cross references to Scripture supporting this kind of counsel.

But on this day, and in this context, what Eliphaz is saying to his friend borders on the abusive. It amounts to a slur. It was an affront to Job for two reasons.

First, it discounted virtually everything Job had said, and was therefore demeaning. It assumed what Job has persistently denied: that his sin was the cause of his suffering. The problem was that Job *had* "laid up God's words in his heart." That was one of the primary issues he faced, because the truths Job had laid up in his heart about God didn't seem to square with what God was taking him through. That's why Job was wrestling with God, and Eliphaz was utterly dismissive about Job's intense struggles and legitimate concerns. Job's concerns didn't concern Eliphaz. Eliphaz wasn't 'there' for his friend. He gave no weight to what Job had been saying.

Second, it was haughty. When Eliphaz says "agree with God," in this context it can be interpreted only to mean, "agree with me." That's so because Eliphaz has just laid out *his* list of six specific transgressions that he claimed Job has committed. The clear implication is that Job must repent of Eliphaz's list, thus being reconciled to, or brought into agreement with, God. It's an awful thing that Eliphaz is doing: he knows that this list is pulp fiction, but implies that it came from God! That's taking God's name in vain in the worst possible way. Specific repentance for the specific sins is the term Eliphaz mandates for reconciliation. But the "sins" were made up out of the whole cloth, solely the product of Eliphaz's imagination, and he knew it.

IF I COULD LOCATE GOD, HE WOULD VINDICATE ME

Eliphaz's charges were so outlandish that Job doesn't bother to answer them. That was wise, for Solomon said: "Answer not a fool according to his folly, lest you be like him yourself."[162] Job wasn't going to get further mired down in a foolish argument. Rather, he was on an all-out mission to locate the Lord.

When we seek the Lord, Jesus told us to

> [a]sk, and it will be given to you; seek, and you will find; knock, and it will be opened to you.

---

162 Prov. 26:4.

> For everyone who asks receives, and the one who
> seeks finds, and to the one who knocks it will be
> opened. (Mt. 7:7-8)

However, it's evident that Job was already doing these things with fervor, even desperation. He was asking, but getting no answers; he was seeking, but wasn't finding; he was pounding his fist against heaven's door with all his might, but so far as he could tell, no one was coming to the door. To Job, it seemed soundproofed and double-locked.

"Oh, that I knew where I might find him, that I might come even to his seat!" Job cries (23:3). I *know* that if I could only find him, he would pay attention to me and give an answer. He would deal fairly with me, and would "acquit me forever" (23:4-7).[163] Job believed what the author of the Book of Hebrews believed, that "whoever would draw near to God must believe that he exists and that he *rewards* those who seek him."[164] He was confident of the final result. Even with all his questions and doubts, in his heart Job believed this, and was trying with all his might to draw near to God. But so far, he couldn't locate him.

DO I NEED TO TRY HARDER?

Have you ever been like Job? When encountering turbulence in your life, have you sometimes started off with a basic confidence that

> you will call upon me and come and pray to me,
> and I will hear you. You will seek me and find me,

---

163 As mentioned previously, the friends had bludgeoned Job with the (true) doctrine of God's utter transcendence. Job does not dispute God's transcendence, but here expresses confidence that his transcendence does not preclude dialogue with him: "Would he contend with me in the greatness of his power? No; he would pay attention to me." (23:6).

164 Heb. 11:6.

> when you seek me with all your heart. I will be
> found by you, declares the LORD. (Jer. 29:12-14)[165]

—but as you call on him, the Lord just isn't visible? Do doubts then arise that maybe you are not seeking God with all your heart? Do you feel like you just need to try harder? Is it a failure on your part? Is that why God isn't "showing up"?

I have felt like that many times, and it is a lonely and hopeless state because God's presence seems to be altogether dependent on my effort. But though God honors the fervent prayers of the righteous,[166] the believer's confidence does not come from fervency. You know that, if you have prayed passionately. Confidence comes from God's immutable promise: "*I will be found by you.*"[167] His assurances are absolute and forever, though our efforts are weak and momentary.

God doesn't promise that he will be found on our timetable, or exactly where we want him to meet us, or on what terms. In his sovereign wisdom, he chooses all of the times and circumstances. Our angst is in the waiting for him to make himself visible and real in our lives, and during that time we can become downcast because we can't see God at all.

We shouldn't forget that Job had faith that he would see God in the future, for he earlier testified:

> [A]fter my skin has been thus destroyed,
>> yet in my flesh I shall see God,
>> whom I shall see for myself,
>> and my eyes shall behold, and not another.
>
> (19:26-27)

This is confidence in an infinitely superior vision of God than is possible in this life. Job doesn't say that he had lost that confidence. It is just that "now we see in a mirror dimly, but then face

---

165   See also Jer. 4:29.

166   James 5:16.

167   Jer. 29:14

to face."[168] And for Job, it was worse than "dimly." It was the darkness of the Ninth Plague of Egypt,[169] so thick you could feel it.

I DON'T SEE GOD, BUT HE SEES ME

Though Job says that he doesn't see God—God isn't visible to the front, the rear, the left or the right (23:8-9)—he does have confidence that *God sees him*.[170] He testifies: "But he knows the way I take" (23:10). It is as the Psalmist said:

> You know when I sit down and when I rise up;
> you discern my thoughts from afar.
> You search out my path and my lying down
> and are acquainted with all my ways.
> (Psa. 139:2-3)

It is an unspeakable comfort to know that while we await that Great Day when "we shall see him as he is,"[171] we have the present assurance that God sees us every second of the day.

AMENIONA

Some years ago, one of our elders at New City Fellowship in St. Louis, Steve St. Pierre, visited the Congo on a short-term mission trip. After spending a long, hot day in Kinshasa, Congo's capital city, he was to participate in an evening worship service. He recalls his experience:[172]

---

168 1 Cor. 13:12.

169 Ex. 10:21-23.

170 Job's utterance here, "[b]ut he knows the way I take," is positive and re-assuring. It was not a positive thought to Job previously, where he complained that the Lord paid too much attention to him: "[h]ow long will you not look away from me, nor leave me alone till I swallow my spit?" (7:19). Perhaps his testimony here in 23:10 is additional evidence of Job's progressive sanctification. Job humbly recognizes here that he may not know his own ways, but God does. Another episode of God's "seeing" care takes place in Gen. 16:1-14.

171 1 Jn. 3:2.

172 Steve St. Pierre, letter to the author (6/10/2016).

The American pastors I was with had the usual crowd of people around them, listening to them, taking care of their needs and making plans for the evening. I, on the other hand, had a headache, felt tired, hot, sticky, and utterly alone. Lord, why am I here? What do I have to offer you, these people or even those back home?"

As I stood complaining to the Lord, feeling small and unwanted, I noticed out of the backside of the church, down a steep hill, there was a small living area with a few plywood dwellings. The closest dwelling had three women cooking over an open fire just outside their hut. The sun was going down, not quite dark, but shadows falling. On top of it all, bloodthirsty mosquitoes began to bite me, and I, in my selfish misery added it to the list of complaints to the Lord. As I swatted at a mosquito, jerking my head back, my eye was distracted by something moving in the shadows, maybe 10 yards from the women at the fire. My eyes strained in the light to make sense of what I was seeing, but then she came into view.

The movement I had seen was arms and hands waving above the head of a young woman sitting in a crude wheelchair in the mud. She was clearly afflicted, trapped in her chair with some sort of palsy, a captive to the mosquitoes. But she was waving her hands above her head as if she was celebrating something. I then noticed that all of the women cooking at the fire were now up and dancing around—they too were waving their hands over their heads.

"What's this?" I wondered. What do these women have to celebrate, especially this young woman? I mean, I only had to deal with this one day: the mosquitoes, dirt, feelings of being lost and alone in a city of fifteen million people, poverty. All of it, this was just daily life for them! What were they celebrating?

The scene had so distracted me that I had become unaware of the music and singing coming from the worship band. As I began to focus on the music, I realized this was the first song in seven days that I actually knew the words to and the meaning of those words. Nitamwimbia Bwana, Nitamrukia Bwana, Nitamchezea Bwana, Kwa kuwa yeye ameniona, *ameniona, ameniona, ameniona!*

These women were singing, jumping and dancing because they understood something I had missed. They were living the words blaring from the speakers, I will sing...I will jump...I will dance...for Jesus, because *he sees me! He sees me! He sees me! He sees me!*

I stood there, tears streaming down my face, no longer aware of the day or mosquitoes, no longer aware of my complaints, no longer alone. Just stood there weeping and understanding again that the Lord is good, he is on the throne, and we have the power to push back the brokenness, pain and death that seem to saturate life. These women, who arguably suffer more in a day than I have suffered in my whole life, were exercising that power and were pushing back brokenness, pain and death with weapons of joy. *Ameniona! He sees me!*

That word, in any language, calls for the joyful dance of King David.[173]

As Job said, "he knows the way I take." This was a profound statement of faith, because God was silent. But a glance from the Lord in our direction means everything. When the Children of Israel were under the merciless rod of Pharaoh in Egypt, Moses records:

> The Israelites groaned in their slavery and cried out, and their cry for help because of their slavery went up to God. God heard their groaning and he remembered his covenant with Abraham, with Isaac and with Jacob. *So God looked on the Israelites and was concerned about them.* (Ex. 2:23-25, NIV)

Job had lost sight of the Lord for the present. God was hidden in impenetrable, dark clouds. But Job was nevertheless persuaded that the Lord had not lost sight of him. Our eyesight is impaired. God's is perfect. And isn't his seeing us all that really matters? The great Biblical expositor A.W. Pink wrote: "But [Job] consoled himself with this blessed fact—though I cannot see God, what is a thousand times better, He can see me!"[174] *Ameniona.*

I SHALL COME OUT AS GOLD

What Job has to say next is another evidence of his fundamental faith in God, but it is different from his previous statements. We have already seen his testimony that "my change will come" (14:14), "my witness is in heaven" (19:25), "my Redeemer lives" (19:26), "in my flesh I shall see God" (19:26), and "he knows the way I take" (23:10).

But when he testifies to his confidence that "I shall come out as gold," in the last half of 23:10, there is a dimension of faith not

---

173   As in 2 Sam. 6:14.

174   Pink, Arthur W. (2012-06-17). *Comfort for Christians* (Arthur Pink Collection Book 5) (Kindle Locations 420-421). Prisbrary Publishing. Kindle Edition.

evident in his previous statements. When a person says that he "shall come out" of something, of course it means that he "is presently in" something. And the something that Job was presently "in" was unmitigated ruin. So far there is no evidence of recovery, restoration, or healing. Yet somehow Job is able to tell his friends that "I shall come out as gold."

That is a confidence that every believer needs deep in his or her heart, because when we look at our shabby, dirty existence, nothing looks like it could possibly come out as gold. That looks impossible. But it's God's promise.

Job is talking about the same thing that the Apostle Peter discussed in his first letter. Peter even went a step further. He said that Kingdom children will come out "*more* precious than gold"! But how is this to be realized? It comes through trials. For a little while, Peter says, "you have been grieved by various trials," whose purpose is to test "the genuineness of your faith." And during those trials the child of God is able to understand exactly what Peter means when he says "[t]hough you do not now see him, you believe in him and rejoice with joy that is inexpressible and filled with glory, obtaining the outcome of your faith, the salvation of your souls."[175]

When Job testified that "I shall come out as gold," he was speaking from a joyful heart. It is very possible to be horribly discouraged and yet have a heart of joy. It often comes as a surprise, when we see it in ourselves. Surprising, because it is not of ourselves.

Though Job's mortal state was in ruins, his soul was "filled with glory." Christians who have been through trouble understand what this means. It is there when your life is being ripped to shreds. It is not a superficial or giddy joy, but a deep, abiding joy that the Holy Spirit has installed, and is continually installing, deep in our beings. It is not so much a confidence that "I shall come out as gold" *in spite* of my trial, but *because* of my trial. It

---

175   1 Pet. 1:3-9.

gives our trouble significance, because we know that the trouble itself will yield indescribably wonderful, eternal consequences.

Think of what a far cry this is from the Eliphaz Formula. There, trouble is nothing other than evidence of sin. But Peter is saying that trouble for believers is a *gift from God*, a gift that results in our transformation into something more precious than gold.

Isn't it true, from a personal standpoint, that what you want most is to come out as gold? At bottom, everyone wants to—those who confess the name of Jesus, and those who don't. The problem is that we want that to happen in ways that we approve of, ways where our comforts and earthly joys will be not just accommodated, but enhanced. We want it to happen easily, on our terms. But that's not how God does it. He accomplishes it through trial, by enduring very hard things—past, present, and future.

Even Jesus, though he is the Son of God, "learned obedience through what he suffered."[176] He did it "for the joy that was set before him," and thus he "endured the cross, despising the shame."[177] His future during his earthly ministry seemed terribly bleak to his disciples, so much so that they couldn't bear the thought of his death, and urged him to take a different path.[178] But he knew what the future held; he knew what would result from his suffering, and it was glory.

JOB WILL CONTINUE HIS ARGUMENT

It is because Job has faith that in the end he will "come out as gold," and because he understands that God's transcendence will not bar his speaking to him, that he has the courage to persist in his debate with the Lord.

---

176 Heb. 5:8.
177 Heb. 12:2.
178 Mt. 16:21-23.

Job doesn't deny, but affirms, God's transcendence. "I am terrified at his presence; when I consider, I am in dread of him," he says (23:15). "God has made my heart faint; the Almighty has terrified me" (23:16). Nevertheless, Job says, "I am not silenced because of the darkness, nor because thick darkness covers my face" (23:16-17).

It is an amazing and precious truth that Job here expresses. Though he lived before the cross, he already knew something about what the work of Christ would mean, the magnificent fact that we know, on this side:

> For you have not come to what may be touched, a blazing fire and darkness and gloom and a tempest and the sound of a trumpet and a voice whose words made the hearers beg that no further messages be spoken to them. For they could not endure the order that was given, "If even a beast touches the mountain, it shall be stoned." Indeed, so terrifying was the sight that Moses said, "I tremble with fear." But you have come to Mount Zion and to the city of the living God, the heavenly Jerusalem, and to innumerable angels in festal gathering, and to the assembly of the firstborn who are enrolled in heaven, and to God, the judge of all, and to the spirits of the righteous made perfect, and to Jesus, the mediator of a new covenant, and to the sprinkled blood that speaks a better word than the blood of Abel. (Heb. 12:18-24)

Moses trembled before the awesome display of the Sinai fire of Jehovah God. Yet "the LORD used to speak to Moses face to face, as a man speaks to his friend."[179] Abraham did the same.[180] And both of them even had the courage to *argue* with the Lord, and

179 Ex. 33:11.
180 Gen. 18:22-33.

the Lord, in each case, "yielded" to their advocacy—Abraham's for Lot, and Moses's for the nation of Israel.

By the Holy Spirit, Job knew that he too had such a privilege. This right, this incredible privilege, has been accomplished once for all by our Great High Priest, Jesus. It was available to every believer before the cross, and it is available to every believer afterwards. It is an eternal right that transcends the Old and New Testaments. It is a right forever preserved and guaranteed by the finished work of Christ, who ripped the veil of the temple in two.[181]

Thus Job is *enabled* to continue.

THE WICKED ARE NOT JUDGED

Whenever we begin to compare ourselves to others, we wander from the truth.[182] In Chapter 24, although Job doesn't explicitly say that he's comparing himself to others, that is, in fact, what he's doing.

We can't blame Job for believing that God was judging him. He wasn't informed of the 'behind the scenes' meetings in Chapters 1 and 2, where God called him "blameless and upright" (1:8; 2:3). Nor did he know that the Lord said that Satan had incited him to "destroy [Job] *without reason*" (2:3). Job apparently was left in the dark on these matters. All he knew was that God had smitten him. Job believed that he was being judged. And he didn't understand it, in view of the fact that others who had led anything but righteous lives were not being judged. Something had gone awry; it just didn't add up.[183]

It often appears to us that it doesn't add up either. Headlines daily announce injustice throughout the world, but we, more of-

---

181   Mt. 27:51; Heb. 10:19-22.

182   2 Cor 10:12.

183   Yet Job did not charge God with wrong. (1:22).

ten than not, cannot see God's intervention, either in halting the injustices themselves, or in judging the sinners who commit them.

Richard John Neuhaus, in *The Naked Public Square*, begins with the story of a preacher who commenced his pastoral prayer with the words: "O Lord, haven't you read this morning's *New York Times?*"[184] Often it seems to us that the Lord is not reading the headlines because he doesn't seem to be engaged in our bloody human mess. We read of the wickedness of mankind and yearn for God's intervention and judgment. The headlines bother us.

Job had seen plenty of these kinds of headlines too. Men had moved landmarks, dishonestly increasing their property. They took what wasn't theirs; they oppressed the widow, the poor, the orphan. They had no concern about the destitute, who "lie all night naked, without clothing, and have no covering in the cold" (24:7). They murder, pillage, and steal. They have made an alliance with "the terrors of deep darkness" (24:17).

Remember that Eliphaz had just told Job that he was guilty of sin—terrible sin—mainly having to do with the oppression and abuse of the poor, the widow and the orphan (22:5-9). Examination of the nature of the sins listed by Job here in Chapter 24 shows a remarkable similarity to those Eliphaz had accused Job of. "They drive away the donkey of the fatherless; they take the widow's ox for a pledge. They thrust the poor off the road; the poor of the earth all hide themselves" (24:3-4). But Job means to make a distinction between him and them. "There *are* those who snatch the fatherless child from the breast, and *they* take a pledge against the poor" (24:9). But, he implies, I am not one of them. Yet I am being judged, and they are not.

Job recites his understanding as to what ought to happen to such people. "*You say*," he says to the Lord, that "their portion

---

184 Neuhaus, Richard John, *The Naked Public Square* (William B. Eerdmans Publishing Company, 1986, Second Edition), p. 3.

is cursed in the land." *You say* that Sheol will gobble them up, so that "they are no longer remembered, so wickedness is broken like a tree" (24:18-20).

But that's not what Job sees happening at all, not in real life. In fact, far from seeing God's judgment at work, what Job sees is that

> God prolongs the life of the mighty by his power;
>> they rise up when they despair of life.
> He gives them security, and they are supported.
>> (24:22-23)

Job does not err in longing for God's judgment on wickedness and on wicked men. Saints rightly desire judgment. The Apostle John, speaking of those who are "made perfect in holiness,"[185] records in his vision:

> When he opened the fifth seal, I saw under the altar the souls of those who had been slain for the word of God and for the witness they had borne. They cried out with a loud voice, "O Sovereign Lord, holy and true, how long before you will judge and avenge our blood on those who dwell on the earth?" (Rev. 6:9-10)

MYSTERY AND TENSION

If it is so, as the Apostle John records, that those who have gone on before us and are now without sin, express a kind of "holy frustration" with regard to God's evident delay in bringing judgment upon sin and sinners, it's not surprising that it should bother us as well. As mentioned in chapter 10, in Psalm 73, the psalmist Asaph struggled mightily with the fact that God very often seemed to bless, not judge, the wicked.

But both the Psalmist and Job, while confessing their worry and frustration, arrive at the same conclusion, though neither

---

185 *Westminster Shorter Catechism*, Q. 37.

claims to have the answers. Asaph says that he couldn't figure it out "until I went into the sanctuary of God; then I discerned their end." Job, without even so much as an "until"—he provides no transition whatever between his frustration and ultimate relief—states the same:

> They are exalted a little while, and then are gone;
>> they are brought low and gathered up like all others;
>> they are cut off like the heads of grain.
> If it is not so, who will prove me a liar
>> and show that there is nothing in what I say?
>
> (24:24-25)

The chasm between God's wisdom and man's understanding is vast. It will not be bridged by man's reasoning or reflection. So it is with Job in Chapter 24. God prolongs the life of the wicked by his power (24:22); with that same power God cuts off the wicked like heads of grain at time of harvest (24:24).

Job would like to be able to understand exactly what is going on, and exactly what God is like. We would too. But it is neither our role nor do we have the capacity:

> Who has measured the Spirit of the LORD,
>> or what man shows him his counsel?
> Whom did he consult,
>> and who made him understand?
>
> (Isa. 40:13-14)

None of this is to say, however, that we are unable to obtain peace in such matters. God has provided that for us. The mystery and tension may remain, but they need not produce ulcers. Trying to put it all together on his own was to Asaph a "wearisome task"—but the wearisome task ended when he "went into the sanctuary of God."[186] When we enter the Lord's presence, we

---

186 Psa. 73:16-17.

have something far superior to our attempts to figure it all out. We have *him*.

BILDAD THROWS UP HIS HANDS

My eight-year-old granddaughter and I took a trip north from our home in St. Louis to Iowa one October afternoon, arriving in the evening. The city lights of the St. Louis area don't often permit you to get a view of the stars, even when it's clear. But the dark Iowa countryside does.

The sky was crystal clear that night, and it was frosty cold. When we stepped out of the car, we could see forever. It was a moonless night, and the otherwise black sky was blazing with stars. The Milky Way stretched over us like an arch. We could see the constellations my granddaughter had seen before only in bedtime books—Pleiades, the Big Dipper, the Little Dipper—all magnificently displayed above and around us. It was too much to take in. No bedtime book had come close. We were awestruck, and felt very, very small and insignificant.

That's how King David felt too, when he looked up at the night sky from Israel's dark countryside:

> When I look at your heavens, the work of your fingers, the moon and the stars, which you have set in place, what is man that you are mindful of him, and the son of man that you care for him?
>
> (Psa. 8:3-4)

Most Old Testament scholars consider the Book of Job to be the oldest book in the Bible,[187] and thus it is possible that the Psalmist drew on what Bildad said in Chapter 25:

> Dominion and fear are with God;
> he makes peace in his high heaven.
> Is there any number to his armies?

---

187 Clines, David J.A., *World Biblical Commentary, Volume 17, Job 1-20* (Word Books, 1989), p. LVII.

Upon whom does his light not arise?
How then can man be in the right before God?
How can he who is born of woman be pure?
Behold, even the moon is not bright,
    and the stars are not pure in his eyes;
    how much less man, who is a maggot,
    and the son of man, who is a worm! (25:2-6)

So now Job is a maggot, a worm. Bildad should run for Congress. If you can't win the argument, just insult your opponent. Sanderson comments sarcastically:

> Now this is just a sort of a nice, cheery thought, directed at a man who is suffering like Job is. It really speaks right to his problems, and it's just tremendous burden bearing. You can just hear Job saying, "Man, this just really makes my itches stop!"[188]

But the first four lines of what Bildad said here are true. Dominion and fear are with God; the moon is not bright, and the stars are not pure in his eyes. God is immense; man is tiny. David and Bildad are saying the same thing.

So did the late cosmologist Carl Sagan, who in 1990 requested that NASA turn the camera on *Voyager One* back toward Earth as the spacecraft exited the solar system. The earth appeared to Sagan as a "pale blue dot" on the photos taken, a "mere pixel against the vast dark canvass of space." Sagan was deeply moved by what he saw, and what he saw was hopelessness and terror:

> Our posturings, our imagined self-importance, the delusion that we have some privileged position in the Universe, are challenged by this point of pale light. Our planet is a lonely speck in the great enveloping cosmic dark. In our obscurity,

---

188 II JWS 75-122B-A.

in all this vastness, there is no hint that help will
come from elsewhere to save us from ourselves.[189]

So are we left to utter insignificance? Is Sagan right, that we
are delusional if we believe that we have some privileged position
in the universe? That we are foolish to think that help will come
from somewhere else? Is Bildad right, that man is a maggot, that
the son of man is nothing more than a worm? Was Job insane by
persisting in his claim that he could reason with the Creator? Was
Job, as Sagan says, just "posturing"? Is that where we are to leave
it?

Where we leave it is, in fact, what makes all the difference. Or
more importantly, where God leaves it. Because if as Sagan says,
our importance is merely a product of our imagination, we are
indeed delusional.

Bildad and Sagan both leave it there. Bildad's speech, the final
words recorded from the three friends, takes up just five verses,
the whole of Chapter 25. His conclusion is a fitting end to the
arguments advanced by the three: There's no hope for you, Job.
In God's sight, you are a maggot, a worm. Bad theology injures
people badly, particularly those you love.

THE IMMENSITY OF MAN

David, however, does not leave it there. True enough, in
Psalm 8 he first wonders how an infinite God could have any concern for a creature of dust. That God does, though, is what truly
amazes him:

> Yet you have made him a little lower than the
> heavenly beings and crowned him with glory
> and honor.

---

189 Sagan, Carl; Druyan, Ann (2011-07-06). *Pale Blue Dot: A Vision of the Human Future in Space,* (Kindle Locations 318-320). Random House Publishing
Group. Kindle Edition.

You have given him dominion over the works of
    your hands;
    you have put all things under his feet,
    all sheep and oxen,
    and also the beasts of the field,
    the birds of the heavens, and the fish of the
        sea,
    whatever passes along the paths of the seas.
O LORD, our Lord,
    how majestic is your name in all the earth!
                      (Psa. 8:5-9)

Job was made in the image of God. All human beings are, and though we are fallen beings, we bear his image. We are not worms or maggots. We have been given dominion over all of creation. We are immense in God's sight, because he made us in his image. Sagan was wrong. Man does have a "privileged position" in the universe. It's not a position that we've constructed, nor is it something we've attained. It isn't a symptom of our arrogance. It is altogether God's design, his gift, his doing, and to deny it is to deny the Creator himself.

Bildad didn't see that. Thus his final words to Job were black, utterly devoid of hope. When he looked at Job on the ash heap, he didn't see someone who had dominion over anything. He didn't see someone crowned with glory and honor. He didn't see someone made in the image of God. He didn't see someone who could encounter God.

Eliphaz, Zophar and Bildad are through arguing. They haven't made any headway, and they certainly haven't been of any help to Job. But they have done a pretty effective job of discouraging him, as if his calamities weren't enough. Sadly, what Job has to say from here on out, is evidence that their discouraging words have had some effect.

FOR REFLECTION

1.

Do you believe that God takes pleasure in your obedience? Does it make any difference to him? Does the fact that your only hope is in the righteousness of Christ make your righteousness irrelevant?

2.

Have you ever felt that your prayers weren't being answered because you weren't trying hard enough, or that your prayers weren't fervent enough? If you then tried to pray more fervently, did it make a difference? Did it make you more confident?

3.

Have you had times when although you couldn't see the Lord in your life, you sensed that he still had his eye on you? If so, on what basis could you say that? What difference did it make?

4.

How do you deal with apparent injustice in the world? Does it often seem to you that God isn't judging sin, and alleviating the oppression and suffering of the innocent? How do you resolve that tension?

14.

JOB'S RETORT

CHAPTERS 26-28

I F BILDAD THOUGHT that his short finalé would shush
Job up, he miscalculated by a long shot. Job wasn't through.
He will continue, this time uninterrupted by his friends. He's
going to speak for six chapters yet.

Though Job isn't through, he's through with his friends.
Sanderson says that he "had had enough of his friends, of their
wisdom. They have not comforted him; they have not solved
his problems. The only person who can solve his problems isn't
talking. God still remains silent. And God has his wisdom in remaining silent."[190]

NO HELP FROM HIS FRIENDS

As he did earlier, Job begins this, his final statement, with ac-
rid sarcasm,[191] aimed at his three friends:

How you have helped him who has no power!

---

190   11 JWS 75-122B-A.
191   Job had already showed a penchant for sarcastic remarks: "No doubt you
are the people, and wisdom will die with you!" (12:2).

How you have saved the arm that has no strength!
How you have counseled him who has no
    wisdom, and plentifully declared sound
    knowledge!
With whose help have you uttered words,
    and whose breath has come out from you?
                    (26:2-4)

Eliphaz, Zophar and Bildad, just preaching away. But their words have been light wooden mallets pounding away on a steel anvil. Job hasn't abandoned his faith. The only response they get from him is scorn. "You three have been such an enormous help to a man without strength!" Job mocks. "There is no way you could have come up with this brilliant material on your own. Who helped you put it all together?"

Job could have expected better from his friends, and they were indeed his friends. Remember that they sat silently with him for a week, fully engaged in his suffering. They surely meant the best for him. But a physician's best intentions, where the wrong treatment is administered, is at best a waste of valuable time, and sometimes proves lethal.

We must admit, once again, that we have an advantage over the three. They had not heard the conversation between the Lord and Satan recorded in Chapters 1 and 2, where the Lord declared Job "blameless," and where he said that Job had been destroyed "without reason" (2:3). They thought that Job was anything but blameless, and that he was being punished for good reason. And although we have the information, they had no way of predicting what the Lord would say to Eliphaz at the end of the book.[192]

Put yourself in the shoes of the three friends. When I do that, it's painful. I realize that I am prone to do what they did. I can remember too clearly an instance where a friend of ours died

---

192 "My anger burns against you and against your two friends, for you have not spoken of me what is right, as my servant Job has" (42:7).

young, and it immediately crossed my mind that the Lord probably ended his life because he was such a problem in our church (as it seemed to me). In another case, when a contemporary died of cancer at age 41, I remember saying to myself: "Well, I'm not surprised, because he was so arrogant." If that were the case, I would have died before age 21. Lord, have mercy.

Job didn't know what caused his suffering, but he knew it wasn't particular sin that he had committed. Thus he and his friends had never really joined the issue; they assumed his trouble to be from sin, and he knew it was not.

Not having received any help or comfort from the three, Job thinks, erroneously, that he is now strictly on his own, right where his friends wanted him in the first place. Job probes for an explanation, but is now convinced that it's not forthcoming, that he is going to be left hanging.

GOD'S WAYS ARE BEYOND UNDERSTANDING

In the balance of Chapter 26, Job gives us a foretaste of what the Lord himself will say in the final chapters of the book. God, the creator and sustainer of the universe, is inscrutable. We see him in what he has made,[193] but we aren't capable of understanding him. He "hangs the earth on nothing"[194] (26:7); "[h]e has inscribed a circle on the face of the waters"[195] (26:10); "[b]y his power he stilled the sea."[196] God also has absolute authority over his creatures: he "shattered Rahab," and "his hand pierced the fleeing serpent" (26:12-13).

---

193 In particular, through creation man sees God's "invisible attributes, namely, his eternal power and divine nature" (Rom. 1:20).

194 Job apparently did not buy into what the ancient Greeks believed (whether Job lived before or after them), that Titan Atlas cradled the earth on his shoulders.

195 The reference here is probably to the horizon, which appeared as a segment of an arc, indicating the curvature of the earth.

196 See Mk. 4:35-41, where Jesus spoke and calmed the storm, demonstrating his divinity.

Probably, Job's mention of "Rahab"[197] and the "fleeing ser-pent" are references to Satan. Such an interpretation would be consistent with a major theme of the book, because Satan was the instrument of Job's calamities (Chapters 1 and 2), and is a highly suspect candidate for the "Leviathan" mentioned by the Lord in Chapter 41. But whatever the case, Job understands that the Lord created the beast and maintains absolute control over his actions.

And, Job says, that's just for starters "[T]hese are but the out-skirts of his ways"; that is, these are merely the few things that we *do* see. Beyond that all we hear is a "small whisper," and when you get to "the thunder of his power, who can understand?" (26:14).

JOB REBOOTS

Sometimes, when you are utterly confused, when life makes no sense at all, when your brain is swimming with endless possi-bilities, you need to go back to the few things you do know. You need to isolate and reaffirm them, even though knowing them hasn't yet brought clarity. The computer needs a reboot; you need to restart the operating system.

No, Job is saying, I don't understand what God's purposes are. I can't explain what's happened to me, but I do know some of the facts and I am going to stick to them. Chapter 27 is Job's recita-tion of four relevant truths of which Job is absolutely convinced.

First, *God did this to me.* I know that God is the one who has brought on my trouble; he is the one who "has taken away my right," and "made my soul bitter" (27:2). And Job was right about this, though Satan was God's instrument (2:3).

---

197 Job had referred to Rahab previously: "God will not turn back his anger/ beneath him bowed the helpers of Rahab" (9:13), a likely reference to the devil's angels (Mt. 25:41). The beast is also paired with Babylon (Psa. 87:4), and men-tioned again in Psalm 89:10 ("You crushed Rahab like a carcass"; see Gen. 3:15: "he shall bruise your head"). Isaiah equated him with Egypt (Isa. 30:7), and also identified him as the object of the Lord's judgment ("Was it not [the LORD] who cut Rahab in pieces?") in Isaiah 51:9.

Second, *my trouble is not my fault.* I know that God has not done this because of some great sin that I've committed: "I hold fast my righteousness and will not let it go; my heart does not reproach me for any of my days" (27:6).[198]

Third, *God judges the wicked.* Even though it often appears that the wicked seem to get along well in life,[199] I wouldn't trade places with them. I know their final end. I know that God is just, and that ultimately, in his way and in his time, the wicked will be judged. This is "the heritage that oppressors receive from the Almighty" (27:13):

> He goes to bed rich, but will do so no more;
>> he opens his eyes, and his wealth is gone.
> Terrors overtake him like a flood;
>> in the night a whirlwind carries him off.
> The east wind lifts him up and he is gone;
>> it sweeps him out of his place.
> It hurls at him without pity;
>> he flees from its power in headlong flight.
>> (27:19-22)

Fourth—and here's Job's problem—*God is treating me just like the wicked.* What should and will happen to the wicked sounds eerily similar to what's happened to me. I went to bed rich one night, but when I opened my eyes, my wealth was all gone (1:13-19). Terrors overtake the wicked like a flood (27:20), and "the terrors of God are arrayed against me" too (6:4). And it's worse at night, when God scares me with dreams and terrifies me with visions (7:14). The great east wind sweeps the wicked out of his place (27:21), but it has wreaked even greater havoc with me; it bereaved me of all my children (1:18-19). God hurls calamity upon

---

198 Job is able to say this while recognizing his own sinful condition: "Why do you not pardon my transgression and take away my iniquity?" (7:21), and his consequent need of a Redeemer (19:25).

199 "The tents of robbers are at peace, and those who provoke God are secure" (12:6). See also 24:1-12.

the wicked *without pity* (27:22), and likewise with me: "[h]e slashes open my kidneys and *does not spare*" (16:13).

Of these four truths, Job is right, and he is certain. There is a great difference between being certain and being just stubborn. Job's friends are the stubborn ones, because they've adopted a position that is based on bare theory, contrary to fact, and have decided to adhere to that unfounded theory regardless. They've tried to wheedle a "fact" out of Job to fit their theory, but have failed because that supposed "fact," Job's particular sin, doesn't exist.

While Job is sure of these things, he is also at the end of his rope. He just can't figure God out. Why, he wonders, is God treating me like the wicked? What I need is wisdom, but—

WHERE IS WISDOM TO BE FOUND?

It isn't that Job doesn't believe there's an answer. Indeed, he is sure that there is, and that's why he now continues to search for it. But he also is beginning to recognize that it will take some brand of wisdom, well beyond his current capacity or intellect, to understand.

Chapter 28 is Job's description of, and cry for, God's precious wisdom. He knows, fundamentally, that that's where answers are to be found.

He first distinguishes it from man's wisdom, which, impressive as it may be, is really just knowledge. He illustrates this with a 'high-tech' expertise of his day: mining.

Mankind can do some amazing things. Iron, copper, gold and gems are dug from the earth. Men dig deep for them, and light up the depths of the earth in their quest:

> Man puts an end to darkness
> and searches out to the farthest limit
> the ore in gloom and deep darkness. (28:3)

What the miners are looking for, and what they find, are things of great value. But you have to dig deep, in dark, secret places—places "away from where anyone lives," and "forgotten by travelers" (28:4), places not apparent to those who only tread the surface of the earth, places not known to birds or beasts (28:7-8).

These men go to great lengths to get what they're looking for. They drill tunnels and snake down into the earth with their lamps, ladders, ropes, hammers and chisels, hanging in the air, swinging to and fro, illuminating the depths "as by fire" (28:5). They carve channels in the rock, and dam up subterranean streams to divert the flow of water (28:10-11). They "overturn mountains by the roots" (28:9). All of this just to extract earthly treasure, that which is deemed precious to mankind, treasures of gold, sapphires, silver, iron, copper, crystal, pearls, topaz and onyx.

Doubtless there was a day in Job's life when he'd been searching for those kinds of things too, but not now. On this day, he is seeking wisdom and understanding. If God is gracious, this day comes for all of us, and like Job, we'll find that it isn't to be found on the earth, in the deep, or in the sea (28:13-14). You can't buy it, not for any amount. "The price of wisdom is above pearls," Job says (28:18).

This kind of wisdom is unknown to natural man: "[i]t is hidden from the eyes of all living" (28:21). Abaddon[200] and Death say that "[o]nly a rumor of it has reached our ears" (28:22, NIV). Trying to find it here on earth can be like looking for someone you've lost touch with, like a long-lost cousin, or a neighbor. All you have to go on is rumor. You go up to a door, knock, and somebody answers. You say, "I'm looking for Wisdom. Does she live around here?" The person answering the door scratches his head, thinks for a bit, and says, "Now that kind of rings a bell. A

---

200   The "destroyer"; the "angel of the bottomless pit"; also called "Appolyon." See Rev. 9:11.

long time ago there was a rumor going around that Wisdom lived in the area, but I never met up with her, and I don't know if she's even around any more. Sorry."

WISDOM AND CREATION

But wisdom isn't a lost person to God. He understands the way to it, and he knows its place (28:23). Through King Solomon, he gives us some directions:

> I, wisdom, dwell with prudence,
>> and I find knowledge and discretion...
> When he established the heavens, I was there;
>> when he drew a circle on the face of the deep,
>> when he made firm the skies above,
>> when he established the fountains of the
> deep,
>> when he assigned to the sea its limit,
>> so that the waters might not transgress
>>> his command,
>> when he marked out the foundations
>>> of the earth,
>> then I was beside him, like a master workman,
>> and I was daily his delight,
>> rejoicing before him always,
>> rejoicing in his inhabited world
>> and delighting in the children of man.
>>> (Prov. 8:12; 27-31)

Who is this Wisdom, this "master workman," this one who the Apostle John calls the "beginning" of God's creation?[201] The Apostle Paul tells us:

> [B]ut we preach Christ crucified, a stumbling block to Jews and folly to Gentiles, but to those

---

201   Rev. 3:14. John also wrote: "All things were made through him, and without him was not any thing made that was made." (Jn. 1:3).

who are called, both Jews and Greeks, Christ the power of God and the *wisdom* of God. (1 Cor. 1:24)

Job didn't know about Jesus in specific. But he knew that what he needed was wisdom, and he has just laid out his quest for it in 28:1-22. Thus, whether he knew the particulars or not, he recognized his need for Jesus, just as when he expressed his need for a redeemer in 19:25.

As mentioned before, God alone knows the way to wisdom. In 28:23-28, by the unction of the Holy Spirit, Job begins to answer his own question, for the Holy Spirit, speaking through Job, reveals to us where wisdom is found—in creation, or more to the point, in the Creator:

> For [God] looks to the ends of the earth
>   and sees everything under the heavens.
> When he gave to the wind its weight
>   and apportioned the waters by measure,
>   when he made a decree for the rain
>   and a way for the lightning of the thunder,
>   then he saw it and declared it;
>   he established it, and searched it out.
> And he said to man,
> "Behold, the fear of the LORD, that is
>   wisdom, and to turn away from evil is
>   understanding." (28:24-28)

The Lord loves what he has made, values it highly, and speaks through it. Wind, lightning, thunder, oceans, lakes and rivers—these and all else in the created universe reveal his wisdom. And wisdom is shown in its highest degree in what the Lord said to man when he created him:[202] "the fear of the LORD, that is wis-

---

202 It's interesting that Job here indicates that the Lord made this statement to man at creation. Perhaps more conversation between God, Adam and Eve took place than is recorded in Genesis.

dom, and to turn away from evil is understanding." These were things for which the Lord had already commended Job,[203] so Job, whether he fully appreciated it or not, already possessed, at the least, the beginning of wisdom.[204] Being made righteous in Christ, every believer has that too, but like Job, we think we've lost it when we are beset by trouble.

Except for Job's final words in Chapters 29-31, the balance of the Book of Job is virtually all about creation. Elihu will speak, using most of his allotted time to talk about the awesome power of God displayed in the weather. Finally, the Lord himself will speak, and talk about nothing but his creation.[205]

Creation is of utmost importance in both the Old and New Testaments. Speaking of the wicked, the Apostle Peter wrote that they are "scoffers," mocking God as Creator, and "deliberately overlook this fact, that the heavens existed long ago, and the earth was formed out of water and through water by the word of God."[206] This they do, Peter says, because if they were to admit to the God of creation, they would also have to deal with that same God in judgment, the God who brought the Great Flood, and the God who has stored up creation for fire.[207]

I have previously argued that many of us, though we affirm creation, minimize its importance and significance. Yet it is exactly through creation that all men see God's "invisible attributes, namely, his eternal power and divine nature."[208] I've witnessed it in the courtroom.

---

203 See 1:1: "[Job] feared God and turned away from evil."
204 Psa. 112:1.
205 The first chapters of Genesis, of course, contain the creation story. However, there is no book in the Bible that contains as much material regarding the created order as the Book of Job.
206 2 Pet. 3:5.
207 2 Pet. 3:6-7.
208 Rom. 1:20.

I was once involved in a case in federal court where the plaintiff was a man who had undergone a surgical procedure to alleviate earaches in his right ear. The surgeon meant to remove debris, but dug a little too deep with his knife and severed the man's facial nerve. Serious permanent injury resulted. At trial, four different doctors specializing in ear surgery testified. In the process, the judge, lawyers, and members of the jury were treated to what amounted to a seminar about just how intricate and complex the human ear is. We got to hear about all the bones, tissues and nerves, every tiny part with a specific purpose, working together to gather little vibrations floating through the air, and then somehow assembling and translating them, sending them to the brain as information. There the information instantly produces smiles, frowns, words, or physical actions, and millions of other responses.

The doctors, who of course looked at patients' ears all day long, weren't at all matter-of-fact about the ear. They displayed enthusiasm and amazement themselves as they testified. When the case concluded, on the way out of the courtroom, one of the lawyers said, "I feel like I've been to a worship service!"

I think she had. She had just heard hours of sworn testimony about the Creator's "eternal power and divine nature." You could tell, too, from the testimony, that medical science had discovered only a little bit of what there was to know about the ear. So much remained a mystery. As Job said earlier, "these are but the outskirts of his ways" (26:14). Creation drives us to our knees, to worship and praise, because of God's infinite wisdom made manifest.

JOB THINKS GOD'S THOUGHTS

What Job has done in 23:23-28 is to give us a very short synopsis of what the Lord will later say to Job. Job was, as the early Christian astronomer Johann Kepler is believed to have said of his scientific discoveries, "just thinking God's thoughts after him." In these six verses he has set out a vision of the Lord's wisdom, authority and power as shown in the wind, oceans, rain, and lightning, representing all creation. Job's thoughts here were God's.

Job is on a mountaintop at the end of Chapter 28, when he concludes by saying "the fear of the LORD, that is wisdom" (28:28). In his mind and heart, he is looking up—not down, around, or at himself for an answer. We might wish for him that he could just stay there, basking in the wonders of the wisdom of God.

But he doesn't.

FOR REFLECTION

1.

When you haven't been able to figure things out and have become bewildered, have you found it helpful to "reboot" as Job did in Chapter 27? What kinds of basic facts or certainties did you consider? Did this help you?

2.

James 1:5 says: "If any of you lacks wisdom, let him ask God, who gives generously to all without reproach, and it will be given him." How does this relate to what Job says about wisdom, and man's quest for it, in Chapter 28? In particular, how does James 1:5 relate to Job 28:28?

3.

How does the created order come across to you as wisdom? Is God's wisdom as shown by creation something only believers can see, or can others see it too?

15.

JOB'S RETREAT

CHAPTERS 29-31

JOB was still in the flesh. He was still on an ash heap, still holding onto a piece of broken pottery, still using it to scrape his painful boils. He was discouraged, disillusioned, and disoriented. This was still his state, though he had just been to the top of the mountain at the end of Chapter 28. There he had grasped the true essence of wisdom: the fear of the Lord. He will remain anchored there, for sure. But in Chapters 29-31, we can detect some slack in the cable. Cognitively, he knows where wisdom is to be found, but you can't detect a present sense of consequent wellbeing. We know already that Job will persevere in the end, but for the moment, he takes a couple of steps backward.

These three chapters have more to do with how Job feels rather than what he knows; more to do with that which is seen than that which is unseen. Job should have kept his focus on that which can be seen only through the eyes of faith.[209] But when a person is discouraged like Job was, faith can weaken. We then try

---

209 "For this light momentary affliction is preparing for us an eternal weight of glory beyond all comparison, as we look not to the things that are seen but to the things that are unseen. For the things that are seen are transient, but the things that are unseen are eternal." (2 Cor. 4:17-18).

to sort things out based on our feelings and what we see immediately in front of us, setting aside for the moment what we know to be true. That, I believe, is what happened to our brother Job here. Sanderson describes a friend of his who had the same experience:

> A friend of mine lost her husband during the Normandy invasion of the Second World War. She told me that when the word first came, she rose to the occasion.[210] She was able to worship God. She was able to pray. She was able to thank God for the years that they had together. She felt buoyed up by the prayers and the comforts of other people. But then, as the days turned into weeks, and the weeks turned into months, the loneliness set in. That's when the real temptation came.[211]

The human body does this physically. A smashed finger instantly turns numb, with no feeling. If you haven't had a smashed finger before, you might think it's never going to hurt. But an hour later, when it turns painful and swells up to twice its normal size, you think it's the worst pain you've ever experienced. It's then that you realize how good the finger felt before, and how bad it hurts now. It takes time for reality to settle in.

Job didn't need to do much self-reflection to conclude that things weren't the way they used to be. He remembered good health, prosperity, family, and respect. He longed to go back.

JOB'S NOSTALGIA

Once when I went shopping at a department store, just as I crossed the threshold, something stopped me in my tracks. My

---

210 Job "rose to the occasion" immediately after the two catastrophes, when he asked his wife, rhetorically: "Shall we receive good from God, and shall we not receive evil?" (1:10). But now he himself wonders what the answer to that question should be.

211 5 JWS 75-120C-A.

sense of smell had put on the brakes, and I stepped back across the threshold. I had caught a scent from long ago. At first, I couldn't quite place it, and to this day have no idea why it came from the store's entrance. Then it came to me, suddenly transporting me into my grandparents' garage in the town of Holland, Iowa (then, Pop. 100), forty years earlier. It was unmistakable—the faint smell of oil, grass on the lawnmower, paint, a general sweet dankness—all mixed together, producing a kind of delightful mid-summer incense rising from a golden childhood long ago. I ached to go back.

We've all had such a moment. We call it nostalgia.

Chapter 29 of the Book of Job is a poetic record of Job's nostalgia. "Oh, that I were as in the months of old!" he begins (29:1). We can see him tilting his head back, closing his eyes, remembering. Those were great days, Job says, so much different from today. Those were

> the days when God watched over me,
>   when his lamp shone upon my head,
>   and by his light I walked through darkness,
> as I was in my prime,
>   when the friendship of God was upon my
>   tent,
>   when the Almighty was yet[212] with me.
>
>   (29:1-5)

In these five verses, Job is engaged in some heavy-duty nostalgia. Here he expresses a deep yearning for something wonderful he had experienced in the past, and it's not for something as fleeting as his grandparents' garage.[213] He is hungering for the presence

---

212   "Yet" implies that Job doesn't believe that the Almighty is now with him. In Job's pain and desolation, he has lost assurance of the presence of God in his life. So did Jesus, on the cross: "My God, my God, why have you forsaken me?" (Mt. 27:46).

213   Job's longing for the presence of God, which he had experienced in the past, is much like the elderly Jews' longing for Solomon's Temple, at the con-

of God, a presence he once felt. That is what he remembers, and that is what he misses. He believes the Lord has abandoned him. God's watchful eye, his lamp, light, and friendship—all of these Job casts in the past tense.

But why does Job now suppose that God is no longer with him? Does he not have confidence in God's promise that he will never leave, never forsake us?[214] Job does not leave us to wonder why he feels that God is gone. In 29:5-25, he recites in some detail what his life was like before (when God seemed present), and in Chapter 30:1-23 he describes what it's like now (when God seems absent). This is a dubious effort on Job's part, and is perhaps what King Solomon was talking about when he wrote: "Say not, 'Why were the former days better than these?' For it is not from wisdom that you ask this."[215]

Job's first and most poignant memory was "when my children were all around me" (29:5). The death of Job's ten children was, without doubt, Job's greatest loss. Parents who have lost children never fully get over it. A lawyer friend of mine, whose high school son had been killed in a car accident, told me years after the accident that "sometimes, at night, I still feel like I can almost reach out and touch him. I want to hug him. But I can't. My boy is gone." Those pangs of loss remain, but the pangs also prompt good memories. Job recalls when his children were "all around me," as the Psalmist has said, like olive plants around his table.[216]

With his head still tilted back, Job remembers other things that are now gone. Good things. Among them, he was *rich*: "my steps were washed with butter, and the rock poured out for me streams of oil." And he was *respected*: "when I prepared my seat

---

struction of the new, much smaller temple in Ezra's time: "But many of the priests and Levites and heads of fathers' houses, old men who had seen the first house, wept with a loud voice when they saw the foundation of this house being laid." (Ez. 3:12).

214   Heb. 13:5, citing Josh. 1:5.

215   Eccl. 7:10.

216   Psa. 128:3.

in the square, the young men saw me and withdrew, and the aged rose and stood; the princes refrained from talking and laid their hand on their mouth" (29:6-9). Job remembers with fondness the feelings he had then. Who wouldn't?

And, Job says, that was because I had earned their respect. They all knew that I was the one who "delivered the poor who cried for help." I was the one who helped the fatherless and the widow. I was eyes to the blind, feet to the lame, father to the needy. And I didn't always just wait for folks to bring their cases to me. If I saw oppression and injustice, I'd go after it. I was proactive. I even "searched out the cause of him whom I did not know" (29:12-16).

What great days those had been. So personally fulfilling! Such great ministry opportunities are available when everyone listens to you! People would wait to hear what his counsel might be, and when he spoke, they "opened their mouth as for the spring rain" (29:23). His smile gave them confidence. He was their chief; he "lived like a king among his troops" (29:25). When Job spoke, the world listened. That's a great memory.

We can assume that Job isn't bragging, nor exaggerating, but telling it like it really was. He was, indeed, a righteous man. The Lord has already said that "there is none like [Job] on the earth, a blameless and upright man, who fears God and turns away from evil"[217] (1:8). But clearly Job is savoring his late, great past, and it's not altogether healthy for him to do so. It's not doing him any good to rustle up what it felt like when he'd walk into the room and everyone would hush up and stand at attention.

But the real problem in this regard is that he clusters all of these past wonderful *things* in his life together with God's *presence* in his life, and their disappearance with God's supposed *absence* in his life.

---

217 Job's life had met the Apostle James' definition of "pure religion": "Religion that is pure and undefiled before God, the Father, is this: to visit orphans and widows in their affliction, and to keep oneself unstained from the world." (James 1:27).

Job believes that because these things are gone, God is gone. He is veering from what he had said earlier, when he asked his wife in the immediate wake of his catastrophes, "Shall we receive good from God, and shall we not receive evil?" (2:10). He meant that the Lord would remain present with them, whether the days were good or bad, just as in the wedding vow between husband and wife. But right now he is beleaguering himself with the suspicion that God might be absent in the "evil" part. Job really knows better, but is momentarily losing his footing.

DOWNHILL SLOPE INTERRUPTED

When Job had children, riches, and respect from everyone around, he believed this prominent and blessed state of affairs would continue for the rest of his earthly life. He had "arrived," and presumably, would stay there. He recalls saying to himself, "I will die in my nest," "my glory fresh with me, and my bow ever new in my hand" (29:18-20).

I had a Christian acquaintance, a chemistry professor at a large American university. He was well off, at the top of his profession, and an elder at his church. He and his wife had three children.

He reached retirement age during his youngest son's senior year in college. At semester break, just four months before graduation, the young man went out with friends to have some winter fun on snowmobiles. The fun turned tragic. My friend's son accidentally flipped his snowmobile upside-down, and he suffered a broken neck and fractured spinal column. He is now quadriplegic, requiring full-time care for the rest of his life. To make it worse, there was no medical insurance to cover the enormous costs of surgery, hospitalization and rehab, because the boy's birthday, celebrated just a month before the accident, had removed him from his parents' coverage and he had not yet obtained his own. The collection agencies pestered my friend with endless phone calls.

My friend later told me that prior to his son's accident, as he and his wife were making plans for retirement, he truly believed that the rest of their earthly existence would be lived on the "downhill slope." Of course, way back in their heads they had some concern that something might make life *up*hill. But they never dreamed that a catastrophe like this would intervene, so radically altering their lives. Like Job, my friend had hoped and believed that he would "die in his nest," but he found himself hurled down from it, ruthlessly, in a blink. His dreams had turned to nightmares, just as Job's had. Neither he nor Job could see much evidence of a loving God's presence in his life.

Who of us can blame Job for being disillusioned? No, but we can learn, and we squander the Lord's enormous investment in his servant Job if we do not take careful note. When we are disillusioned because we have misgivings regarding the presence of God in our life, we are in a precarious spot. This is so because if we are no longer looking up to the Lord, where our real help comes from,[218] we will still be looking, and it will be in all the wrong places.

Job had serious misgivings about the Lord's presence in his life. So he began to look down and around, rather than up. This would prove to be a bleak and fruitless enterprise.

THE SCUM OF THE SCUM OF THE EARTH

The first thing that Job looked at was what other people now thought of him.

This once great man Job, who had "lived like a king among his troops"(29:25), was great no more. He had been deposed. His fiefdom had evaporated. All respect went with it. It used to be that "[m]en listened to me and waited, and kept silence for my counsel" (29:21), but

> now they laugh at me,
> men who are younger than I,

---

218 Psa. 121:1: "I lift up my eyes to the hills. From where does my help come from? My help comes from the LORD, who made heaven and earth."

whose fathers I would have disdained
to set with the dogs of my flock. (30:1)

Job is here making reference not to the orphan, the widow, the underprivileged or the oppressed poor, but to the "rabble," the "riffraff," the "no-goods," those who had been "driven out from human company" (30:5) and "whipped out of the land" (30:8). These thugs lived like animals: "[a]mong the bushes they bray; under the nettles they huddle together" (30:7). They were that day's scum of the earth.

But now Job had become *their* scum. They would climb from their holes and slither out from under the rocks (30:6), taunting him with their mocking songs. Job had become a "byword" to them (30:9), probably something along the lines of a sing-song sneer at another who had suffered a tragedy: "Man, did you just get *Jobed* !"

In former days, this wouldn't have bothered him so much, because he could have just picked up the phone, made a quick call, and had the hoodlums locked up. But now he had no defenses, and they meant to take full advantage. Such was their nature, because they were hyenas—cowards until they saw that the way was clear. They sensed his vulnerability and smelled blood. They "cast off restraint," and it was "[a]s through a wide breach they [came]" (30:11, 14).

THE HEDGE WAS GONE

Who was responsible for opening the breach in the first place, to give them opportunity to so abuse Job? Who, now that the breach was opened, could defend him from these malevolent intruders, but refuses to do so? Job has no doubt:

> *God* has cast me into the mire,
>   and I have become like dust and ashes.
> I cry to you for help and you do not answer me;
> I stand, and you only look at me. (30:19-20)

If Satan was listening in on Job at this point, I'm sure he perked up, leaned forward in his seat, and scratched his claws together expectantly. Maybe this would be the moment he was waiting for. Satan had told the Lord at the outset that the reason Job feared God was that the he had "put a hedge around him and his house and all that he has, on every side" (1:10)—protecting him from just this kind of abuse. Satan had assured the Lord that when that hedge was removed, Job would collapse, and curse God to his face.

Well, the hedge was gone. Job doesn't see God's protection at all. Indeed, at this point he sees God only as his adversary: "You have turned cruel to me; with the might of your hand you persecute me" (30:21). It is as though the Lord has both quit Job's defense and joined up with the offense, eager to finish him off: "[f]or I know that you will bring me to death" (30:23).

It's interesting to compare the two different uses of the word "hedge." Sanderson notes that "in Chapter 1, Satan says to the Lord, 'You've hedged him in, with camels, and donkeys, and money, and a happy family. You've hedged him in; I can't get at him.' Job, having lost all that, now feels hedged in. He's hedged in because he's totally surrounded by ignorance, pain, exquisite suffering."[219]

Yet, Job did not curse God.

THE MISTAKE OF LOOKING AT OTHERS

Circumstances differ, but many of us have gone through something like Job went through here. Anyone who has been through a time of life where he has lost all control, and is at the mercy of those who vilify, scorn and berate him, knows something of what Job went through. Such a person knows the feeling of utter vulnerability. The magnitude of Job's suffering was immense, but the basic elements of his experience then and ours today are the same.

---

219   7 JWS 75-120D-A.

Someone once owed a friend of mine a large sum of money. He had signed a note, memorializing his indebtedness. When the date came for payment, my friend was dead broke, and was desperately in need of having the debt paid. He was so broke that he was three days away from having the electricity shut off at his home. The person who owed the money knew about my friend's circumstances, and took full advantage of him. For no reason other than to profit at my friend's expense, he essentially blackmailed him, and cut the amount he had agreed to pay by about twenty-five percent. He then required that my friend sign an "amendment" to the original note, reducing the amount owed to what he was willing to pay. My friend was in a fix, and had no choice but to accept, because he had to keep the electric company from doing the disconnect. Like Job, he was utterly vulnerable. It's an awful thing to be completely at someone else's mercy. It's humiliating and dehumanizing.

At such a time, it is not just possible, but typical, to lose perspective. The perspective we are tempted to lose is the Lord's, which is freely available and generously given.[220] If we succumb to that temptation, we "forfeit the mercy that could be [ours]" (Jon. 2:8, NET). But we are so beset by our miserable circumstances and the hardships imposed upon us by others that we don't remember to look up to heaven to ask for that mercy. Such a failure may be understandable, but it's terribly unwise. Unwise also for Job, but given his circumstances, not surprising.

VOLUNTARY SLAVERY

When we let others "get to us" by harking to what they say about us, or worrying about what they think of us, we give them far too much credit and simultaneously discredit the promises of God. What *he* says about us, what *he* thinks of us, is all that mat-

---

220 "If any of you lacks wisdom, let him ask God, who gives generously to all without reproach, and it will be given him." (James 1:5).

ters—and he thinks a great deal of us, measured by the infinite investment made by his Son on our behalf:

> You were bought with a price; do not become bondservants of men. (1 Cor. 7:23)

When we take to heart what others say when they abuse or demean us, we voluntarily sign up for slavery. It's slavery because we begin to think that they are in control of us, and particularly in control of our reputation. We are convinced that people will believe what they say.[221] We chafe at this, we get defensive, we spend lots of time and emotional energy striking back. But we have asked for it. We don't need to be in that position, and we absolutely don't need to stay there. We don't need to forfeit the mercy that could be ours.[222]

Furthermore, when we choose to stay there, for however long a time, we will discover that our discouragement, disillusionment and depression will spiral out of control. Our mental health will be affected. And we will hurt those around us. I know this to be so, because I've succumbed to this very temptation, and have hurt others as a result.

We must sympathize with Job here, because the abuse he describes was intolerable. We should always sympathize with those who are subjected to personal debasement. But (as my mother used to tell us) don't let what people say about you make you "moody." Maybe Job's mother had told him the same, and if so, Job might have forgotten what she said. I understand that Job 30 is in the Bible, but it seems to me that Job's ruminations about what the rabble had to say about him was an unnecessary waste of his time, did him no good, and served only to intensify his suffering. That was one thing he did not need.

---

221 Job worries about this, in the context of what others are saying about him: "my honor is pursued as by the wind." (30:15).
222 Jon. 2:8.

THE MISTAKE OF LOOKING AT YOURSELF

Let's look ahead to the end of the book, where the Lord's only mention of Job will be when he asks him some difficult questions, like "[w]here were you when I laid the foundation of the earth?" (38:4). God is not going to focus on Job; he's going to focus on God. Thus he will help Job focus on God. Knowing that now will help us to have a proper frame of reference for what Job says next in 30:16 through the end of Chapter 31, where Job rests his case.

In his *Institutes of the Christian Religion*, John Calvin begins by saying that "Our wisdom, in so far as it ought to be deemed true and solid wisdom, consists almost entirely of two parts: the knowledge of God and of ourselves."[223] Calvin proceeds to explain that the one cannot be had without the other. Thus, personal introspection is an essential part of the process of obtaining "true and solid" wisdom—but only when it is informed by the knowledge of God.

In 30:16-31, a span of just sixteen short verses, Job uses the words "I," "me" and "my" a total of thirty-three times. Maybe that's not surprising, because, after all, he's describing his own suffering. But maybe it's also an indicator of his deteriorating state, where he yields to a human propensity, the one that makes you want to just curl up in the fetal position, to despair, to think about nothing other than how bad off you are. And if you open your eyes when you're all curled up, the only one you can see is yourself. When we engage in that kind of introspection, it's at best damaging, and if unchecked, it's lethal, because we are intentionally disallowing ourselves to be informed by the knowledge of God. It is a choice; we do not have to stay curled up on the floor.

What can a person expect when he turns to look only at himself? Healing? Renewal? Joy? Life? Job didn't find any of that. He just got in deeper.

---

223 Calvin, John, *The Institutes of the Christian Religion*, translated by Henry Beveridge (Kindle Locations 657-658). OSNOVA. Kindle Edition.

IT'S NOT FAIR

What Job did see as he looked at himself was death, and he believed that he was staring it in the face: "[f]or I know that you will bring me to death" (30:23). He even describes for us what his pre-death appearance is like: "[m]y skin turns black and falls from me," displaying his skeleton, bones "that burn with heat" (30:30). He is in a "heap of ruins," he says.

Job argues that it's only natural for a person who's in a heap of ruins, who thinks he's going to die, to cry for help:

> Yet does not one in a heap of ruins stretch out his
> hand,
> And in his disaster cry for help? (30:24)

Job argues that in his case, such a cry for help is particularly understandable, even justified. I *deserve* help because I've got a good record. What you are doing to me, Lord, just isn't fair:

> Did not I weep for him whose day was hard?
> Was not my soul grieved for the needy?
> But when I hoped for good, evil came,
>   and when I waited for light, darkness came.
>   (30:25-26)

Job doesn't think he is getting a square deal. Surely he is telling the truth when he says that he wept "for him whose day was hard," and that his "soul grieved for the needy." But now that he is looking down and not up, his argument has degenerated into a "tit for tat" equation. Jesus did say: "Blessed are the merciful, for they shall receive mercy,"[224] but he did not say that the mercy they shall receive is provided to balance the books. In that case, it wouldn't be mercy.

It's hard to be sure exactly what Job is talking about when he says "I stand up in the assembly and cry for help" (30:28), partly because the picture given us in the Book of Job is that he is con-

---

224 Mt. 5:7.

signed to the ash heap, the town dump—and he's sitting there (2:8), not standing. Likely he's not speaking of "standing" or "assembly" literally, but of his pleadings before his three friends, who would then represent the "assembly of the righteous."[225] Whatever the case, by making reference to the assembly, Job means to say that he has now filed his petition with both God and man regarding his unfair treatment, and has gotten zero assistance from either.

He has exhausted all known remedies. He believes that God and man have rejected him, that they aren't even listening. His only brothers now are jackals, his only companions ostriches (30:29).

Where, then, can he go? Who can he approach for help?

JOB INVOKES HIS OWN RIGHTEOUSNESS

Chapter 31 is Job's mournful litany of his own righteousness. It doesn't smack of arrogance, and we must take it as truthful. It is an utterance of a sad man, a broken man, a man thrown from his nest,[226] a man who is gravely ill and believes he is about to die.

These are particular sins, he says, that he has successfully avoided:

> Lust, lasciviousness (vs. 1)
> Dishonesty, lying (vss. 5,33)
> Straying from God's law (vs. 7)
> Covetousness (vs. 7)
> Unfair dealings with others[227] (vs. 7)

---

225 Psa. 1:5.

226 29:18.

227 Perhaps this is the meaning of the term "if any spot has stuck to my hands." An ancient and universally accepted rule of law (the "clean hands" doctrine) is that a person seeking equitable relief in court must approach the court with "clean hands," that is, he must show that he has not dealt unfairly with the other party. David spoke of this principle when he said that the person who would "ascend the hill of the LORD" must have "clean hands." (Psa. 24:3-4).

Adultery, licentiousness (vs. 9)
Oppression of employees (vs. 13)
Refusing to help those in need (vss. 16-23)
Love of money (vss. 24-25)
Idolatry (vss. 26-28)
Gloating over the misfortunes of others (vs. 29)
Closing his door to immigrants, travelers[228]
(vs. 32)
Abuse of the environment[229] (vss. 38-40)

To all of these, Job pleads "not guilty." He makes it clear that if in fact he were guilty of these sins, his calamities would be appropriate and deserved. If, for example, he gazed at a young woman with lust in his heart, he could expect God's retribution. He asks, rhetorically:

What would be my portion from God above
and my heritage from the Almighty on high?
Is not calamity for the unrighteous,
and disaster for the workers of iniquity?
(31:2-3)

If I have committed adultery with my neighbor's wife, Job says, "then let my wife grind for another, and let others bow down on her" (31:10). If I have dealt unjustly with my servants, whom God made just as he made me, I could not plead innocent before the Lord (31:13-15). If I turned away the poor or the widow; if I

228 "When a stranger sojourns with you in your land, you shall not do him wrong. You shall treat the stranger who sojourns with you as the native among you, and you shall love him as yourself, for you were strangers in the land of Egypt: I am the LORD your God." (Lev. 19:3-4).
229 Job says "[i]f my land has cried out against me...let thorns grow instead of wheat." Mosaic law required that "in the seventh year there shall be a Sabbath of solemn rest for the land, a Sabbath to the LORD. You shall not sow your field or prune your vineyard. You shall not reap what grows of itself in your harvest, or gather the grapes of your undressed vine. It shall be a year of solemn rest for the land" (Lev. 25:4-5). The Israelites' failure to obey this law would later be a factor in God's judgment on Israel during the Babylonian captivity, as prophesied by Moses (Lev. 26:34-35). Cf. 2 Chron. 36:21.

refused to give a warm blanket to a needy person out there in the cold; if I "raised my hand" against the orphan because I thought I could get away with and profit by it—in any such case, I could expect "calamity from God, and I could not have faced his majesty" (31:16-23). He says the same for all sins mentioned.

FILTHY RAGS

Job's list of righteous deeds and avoidance of sin is impressive. Because he was a man of stellar character, and since he believed that he was about to die, surely he told the truth. But what did he hope to accomplish by compiling this list?

When our family returned from summer vacation one year, the front windshield of our station wagon was speckled with several dozen unfortunate butterflies, every one gone on to his or her reward. I picked up a rag from the garage to clean the glass. In the dimly lit garage, the rag looked clean. I dipped it into a bucket of sudsy water and started the cleaning project with a couple of large swipes of the rag over the driver's side.

I immediately realized that I needed better lighting in the garage. I had picked up a dirty rag. Instead of cleaning the windshield, I had just smeared dirty oil and grease all over it. At least I could see through the windshield before, but now I couldn't. I had to find a different, clean rag, and now, in addition, I needed some industrial strength detergent to remove the dirty grease. I had just made matters much worse by using a filthy rag.

Job's list, a tally of his righteousness, was like my rag: "*all* our righteous acts are like filthy rags."[230] Job's list didn't clean the windshield; it dirtied it. It just made matters worse. But it had looked clean in the dark.

This list of good deeds and virtues also sounds a little bitter, kind of like "what good did all this do?" After all, it wasn't easy to assemble this list. He had made it his life business. It took disci-

---

230   Isa. 64:6, NIV.

pline, self-control, and hard work. So it's not only a defense against the indictment his friends have levied against him; it is a negative commentary on God's justice. Sadly, Job has become cynical.

JOB'S RESUMÉ

Throughout the book, Job has put on an all-court press to gain access to the Lord. He wants a hearing. But when we begin to believe that our right to a hearing is based on how good we are, on how many of the Ten Commandments we have kept, we have assumed a burden that we cannot begin to bear, "[f]or by works of the law no human being will be justified in his sight."[231] Life becomes a nightmare when we begin to think that impressing the Lord with our good behavior will make the difference.

Chapter 31 is Job's resumé. He is pounding on heaven's door with his right fist while clutching his resumé in the left. He has an outstanding record. There's no doubt about that, because God certified it in Chapters 1 and 2. But neither his record nor ours can open heaven's doors; we are not able to tear the temple's curtain apart to enter the Holy of Holies. Access to the mercy seat in the Old Testament and the New is accomplished only "by the blood of Jesus, by the new and living way that he opened for us through the curtain, that is, through his flesh."[232]

There is no other way, and that's wonderful news because our burden is lifted. We who have repented and believe, whether our resumés are stellar, average, subpar, or just plain awful, are already "dressed in His righteousness alone, faultless to stand before the throne."[233] That's why Job expressed great confidence previously. But for the moment, his confidence has waned.

The Lord wants Job to leave his resumé in the drawer. He doesn't need it, and he's not even going to read it because he already knows it. He had already prepared a whole lot better one

---

231 Rom. 3:20.
232 Heb. 10:19-20.
233 "My Hope is Built on Nothing Less," Edward Mote, 1834.

on Job's behalf anyway, listing only one achievement: the work of Christ. And from eternity past, he had engraved Job's name at the top. Isn't it a wonderful relief, that at Heaven's gate, we will all have the same perfect resumé?

Job knew this well, not because he knew in specific about Jesus, but that his Redeemer stood in for him, representing him before God.[234] Perhaps one of the reasons Job prefaced that great confession of faith ("I know that my Redeemer lives") with the desire that his words be written down, inscribed in a book (19:23) was that he knew beforehand of his own human frailty, that he himself might weaken and lose perspective. In such a case (and Chapter 31 is such a case), he could repair to that truth, inscribed with an iron pen, and regain his perspective.

THE WORDS OF JOB ARE ENDED

It is kind of sad that Job finished all that he has to say by trying to prop himself up by his own righteousness. Chapter 31 is defensive and gloomy. Job doesn't exude any confidence in it at all, because good works don't produce confidence. As you read through these last forty verses, you can tell that Job was running out of steam. It's as though his life was ebbing away as he spoke, like the last movement of Tchaikovsky's *Pathétique*. Job had nothing more to say. Verse 40 reports, simply: "The words of Job are ended."

Job had come not only to the end of his words, but to the end of himself. It was the Lord, in his infinitely wise providence, because he cared so much for Job, who had brought him to that point.

---

234 19:25-27.

FOR REFLECTION

I.

When you've had trouble, have you sometimes looked back at your past, wondering why things seemed good then but bleak now? Did it help you to do this? What pitfalls might there be in looking back?

2.

Have you hoped that you might someday "arrive" as a believer, and that from then on life would be easier? Is there any basis in Scripture for this hope? Is it a proper hope?

3.

What dangers, particularly in times of trouble, might there be when you begin to compare what's happened to you with what's happened to others?

4.

Job 31 is a list of things that Job had done in his life that were right, that were obedient to God's commandments. In what ways was it helpful, or hurtful, for Job to recite these things?

16.

ELIHU

CHAPTERS 32-37

IF YOU flip to the chapters on Elihu in scholarly books on Job, you'll find that there are about as many opinions regarding him as there are scholars. Some think Elihu is bad, some good, somewhere in between, or no comment. Most are afraid to touch him, but not all. I read one who said he was a young, brash fool, and another who said he was God's chosen messenger. There certainly isn't any consensus on the man, except that he's hard to identify.

Elihu's parentage is given, unlike the more limited information given for Job and his three friends. He was the son of Barachel the Buzite, of the family of Ram (32:2). Barachel and Elihu are the only Buzites mentioned in the Bible. Possibly Elihu was related to Abraham, because Abraham had a nephew Buz, son of Abraham's brother Nahor.[235] We don't know.

Unlike Job's three friends, Scripture doesn't indicate what relationship Elihu had with Job. He isn't mentioned as a "friend"; he wasn't a participant in the appointment[236] arranged by Eliphaz, Zophar and Bildad to meet up with one another before they vis-

---

235   Gen. 22:20-21.
236   3:11.

ited Job when they first got news of his troubles. But Elihu was there to hear what Job, Eliphaz, Zophar and Bildad had to say,[237] and had kept his mouth shut, listening.

IS ELIHU SIGNIFICANT?

Some writers advise to largely discount Elihu, because he's not counted with Job's friends, and because he's not mentioned by the Lord at the conclusion of the Book,[238] that is to say, that the Lord ignored him. But the fact that the Lord didn't mention him is surely no evidence of his insignificance. He isn't presented as one of Job's friends in the first place, and he was younger than Job and the three,[239] making it less likely that he would have joined the group.

Moreover, the fact that the Lord didn't mention him at the conclusion of the book may be evidence that cuts the other way. The particular reason the three friends were mentioned by the Lord at the end is that the Lord was angry with them because they had "not spoken of me what is right, as my servant Job has" (42:7). Thus it's not unreasonable to conclude that the Lord was not angry with Elihu, because his counsel, in contrast to that offered by the three, might have had the Lord's approval.

More importantly, Elihu's words are contained in Holy Scripture, and for that reason alone what he had to say is worthy of our study, whether he was good or bad: "All Scripture is breathed out by God and profitable for teaching, for reproof, for correction, and for training in righteousness."[240]

ELIHU'S AGE

Elihu had silenced himself during the debate between Job and his friends. He did so because he was younger than they. In those

---

237   32:11-12.
238   The Lord mentions only Job, Eliphaz, Zophar and Bildad. (42:7-9).
239   32:6-7.
240   2 Tim. 3:16.

days, that was considered proper, out of respect for those with gray hair.[241] One bit his tongue in the presence of older folks. Such days are apparently over.

ELIHU A PROPHET

As Sanderson did for Job's friends and Mrs. Job, I'd like to "make out a case" for Elihu. I believe Elihu was a prophet.

Old Testament prophets did not derive their wisdom, nor their message, from being old, seasoned and experienced. Never in Scripture is it required that a prophet be old and seasoned. Indeed, it appears that the Lord often chose unlikely men to speak for him just to show that God's message is *God's* message, having nothing whatever to do with the life station of the messengers. God could use the old or the young. Theirs was not the "wisdom of this world, [which] is folly with God,"[242] but the wisdom that comes from the Holy Spirit.

Jeremiah, like Elihu, was reluctant to prophesy because of his youth. Although God had appointed Jeremiah a "prophet to the nations" before he was born,[243] when called on to prophesy, Jeremiah objected, because, he said, "I do not know how to speak, for I am only a youth." But the Lord answered him:

> Do not say, "I am only a youth";
> for to all to whom I send you, you shall go,
> And whatever I command you, you shall speak.
> Do not be afraid of them,
> for I am with you to deliver you,
> declares the LORD. (Jer. 1:7-8)

---

241 Lev. 19:32: "You shall stand up before the gray head and honor the face of an old man."

242 1 Cor. 3:19.

243 Jer. 1:5.

PROPHETS SPOKE BY THE HOLY SPIRIT

It was typical of prophets to claim to speak by unction of the Holy Spirit. That was not the only mark of a true prophet,[244] of course, because there were false prophets who made such claims. But Elihu does present himself as one speaking by the Holy Spirit:

> But it is the spirit in man, the breath of the
> Almighty, that makes him understand.
> It is not the old who are wise, nor the aged who
> understand what is right.
> Therefore I say, "Listen to me;
> let me also declare my opinion." (32:8-10)

Later, Elihu, referencing himself, will tell the four older men that:

> I will get my knowledge from afar
> and ascribe righteousness to my Maker.
> For truly my words are not false;
> *one who is* perfect *in knowledge is with you.*
> (36:3-4)

This is almost an Old Testament version of "Verily, verily, I say unto you." In substance, Elihu makes claim here to a true, God-directed message, which is, in essence, a claim to prophecy (though not necessarily a claim to the office). As such, he would have to be considered either a *true* prophet or a *false* prophet. I believe that the substance of Elihu's message as a whole, coupled with the Lord's failure to rebuke him at the end of the book, make the second alternative virtually impossible.

In making this claim to be speaking by the Holy Spirit, Elihu was like King David, the "sweet psalmist of Israel," who in his last words testified that "[t]he Spirit of the LORD speaks by me;

---

244 A prophet's message also had to be consistent with the Word of God, and if a prophet predicted a future event it had to happen. (Deut. 13:1-5; 18:22.) Thus Elihu's claim here, not predictive in nature, must be borne out by whether his message is consistent with the revealed Word of God.

his word is on my tongue."[245] Martin Luther marveled at David's seemingly boastful claim:

> What a glorious and arrogant arrogance it is for anyone to dare to boast that the Spirit of the Lord speaks through him and that his tongue is voicing the Word of the Holy Spirit! He must obviously be sure of his ground. David, the son of Jesse, born in sin, is not such a man, but it is he who has been called to be a prophet by the promise of God.[246]

Likewise, it is not Elihu, the son of Barachel the Buzite, born in sin, who could make such a statement on his own. It is only "he who has been called to be a prophet by the promise of God." True prophets in the Old Testament did not speak by their own power, or according to their own wisdom, but as the Holy Spirit gave them utterance.[247] It was only on that basis that Elihu could rightly claim that "one who is perfect in knowledge is with you." So, I think, Elihu was either a fraud or a prophet, and I don't think he was a fraud.

PROPHETS COMPELLED TO SPEAK

Old Testament prophets had to speak out, like it or not. Jonah, who prophesied to the City of Nineveh, abhorred the prospect, literally running away from it. The Lord had to compel him to prophesy, and Jonah fought it every step of the way. He surely regretted having to spend three days and nights in the belly of a whale, but he nonetheless was sorry he had prophesied after he

---

245 2 Sam. 23:2.

246 Martin Luther, "Treatise on the Last Words of David (2 Sam. 23:1-7)," trans. Martin Bertram, in *Luther's Works*, 55 vols., ed. J. Pelikan and H.C. Oswald (St. Louis: Concordia Publishing House, 1972), 15: p. 275.

247 "For no prophecy was ever produced by the will of man, but men spoke from God as they were carried along by the Holy Spirit." (2 Pet. 1:21).

had done so, and after the City of Nineveh had repented because of his preaching![248]

Jeremiah wasn't like Jonah, but he wasn't exactly thrilled at the prospect of prophesying either. Nobody seemed to listen, and Jeremiah knew he would be persecuted as a result of his obedience to God's command that he prophesy. But the Lord had kindled a fire in Jeremiah—not a comfortable, cozy fire that warmed the great prophet to the task—but one that fired up a pressure cooker inside him, so that no matter how hard he tried, he couldn't contain it. It just burst out, almost involuntarily:

> If I say, "I will not mention him,
>> or speak any more in his name,"
>> there is in my heart as it were a burning fire
>> shut up in my bones,
>> and I am weary with holding it in,
>> and I cannot. (Jer. 20:9)

Elihu was at first reluctant too; in fact, he was afraid to speak: "I was timid and afraid to declare my opinion to you" (32:6).[249] But he had to, because he felt the same Holy Spirit pressure building inside that Jeremiah experienced, and the geyser just couldn't be capped:

> Behold, my belly is like wine that has no vent;
>> like new wineskins ready to burst.
> I must speak, that I may find relief;
> I must open my lips and answer. (32:19-20)

---

248 After Nineveh repented as a result of Jonah's preaching, Jonah wanted to die: "But [Nineveh's repentance] displeased Jonah exceedingly, and he was angry. And he prayed to the LORD and said, 'O LORD, is not this what I said when I was yet in my country? That is why I made haste to flee to Tarshish; for I knew that you are a gracious God and merciful, slow to anger and abounding in steadfast love, and relenting from disaster. Therefore now, O LORD, please take my life from me, for it is better for me to die than to live.' " (Jon. 4:1-3).

249 Moses was afraid, too: "Oh, my LORD, I am not eloquent, either in the past or since you have spoken to your servant, but I am slow of speech and of tongue." (Ex. 4:10).

ELIHU THE FORERUNNER

John the Baptist was the forerunner of Christ. God proclaimed him in the Old Testament as "my messenger; he will prepare the way before me."[250] This prophecy of his identity was fulfilled in the New Testament, where he is introduced as the "voice of one crying in the wilderness: 'Prepare the way of the Lord' "[251] Elihu is similar to the prophet John the Baptist in three particular ways:

First—Elihu, like all the prophets, did not give a seminar on how to win friends. While remaining respectful, he spoke forth what he claimed he was charged to say, perhaps quite different from what the four older men were expecting to hear. John was like that too. He spoke the unadorned, harsh truth about sinners. He confronted the Pharisees and Sadducees directly, calling them "a brood of vipers."[252] Elihu says that he wasn't speaking to curry favor either. He says he speaks without "partiality to any man,"[253] and won't flatter because he's not expert in that area; he had failed to earn a degree in flattery! (32:21-22). He flunked that class.

In this manner both Elihu and John spoke as the greatest prophet Jesus did, because, like Jesus, they knew that all men are sinners. The sole manner in which we wretched sinners can be prepared for entry into the Kingdom of God is to recognize that we are, in fact, wretched sinners. This is so at the first, when we come to Jesus for salvation, and for the thousands of times later, when we are driven by our sin to him for forgiveness, wisdom, healing and help. And we will not recognize our plight until someone confronts us with that fact, as the prophet Nathan did with David.[254]

---

250 Mal. 3:1.

251 Mt. 3:3.

252 Mt. 3:7.

253 Elihu, speaking for the Lord, must be impartial, for "God shows no partiality." (Rom. 2:11).

254 2 Sam. 12:1-15.

True prophets, in contrast to false, always spoke the hard truth. Throughout Scripture, in both the Old Testament and the New,[255] false prophets typically told people what they wanted to hear. Jeremiah's Jerusalem was infected with false prophets who told the people that Jeremiah was wrong in predicting the Babylonian captivity. But they did so because it was what the people wanted to hear, not what they needed to hear.[256] Jeremiah, to his own hurt, said that these men refused to expose the iniquity of the Israelites, so that they might repent. This is a universal trait of the false prophet, but never of the true. Jeremiah, John and Elihu were of the second category.

Second—Both Elihu and John were echoes, not of past words, but prophetic echoes of words yet to come.[257] John spoke beforehand that "the kingdom of heaven is at hand,"[258] and Jesus said that "the kingdom of God has come upon you."[259] Elihu, from Chapter 35:24 through the end of his speech at 37:24, speaks with increasing specificity and intensity of God's creation, obviously overwhelmed by it. His testimony to God's awesome power displayed in creation merges directly into what follows, where the Lord speaks exclusively about the things that he has made. Sanderson[260] points out that Elihu criticizes Job for thinking he can figure everything out,

---

255   2 Tim. 4:3.

256   "Your prophets have seen for you false and deceptive visions; they have not exposed your iniquity to restore your fortunes, but have seen for you oracles that are false and misleading." (Lam. 2:14). This is illustrated when Ahab, Israel's king, wanted to go to war against Ramoth-Gilead. False prophets told him to proceed, that his mission would be successful: "Then the king of Israel gathered the prophets together, about four hundred men, and said to them, 'Shall I go to battle against Ramoth-Gilead, or shall I refrain?' And they said, 'Go up, for the LORD will give it into the hand of the king.'" (1 Ki. 22:6).

257   When Elihu addresses Job with the words "Answer me, if you can" (33:5), he "echoes" what the Lord later says to Job: "He who argues with God, let him answer it." (40:2).

258   Mt. 3:2.

259   Lk. 11:20.

260   Sanderson, in his lectures, treats Elihu favorably, but does not identify him

and God reiterates Elihu's charge, and the charge is just this: Job has tried to fill in the blanks. And when you try to fill in the blanks by yourself, you "darken counsel by words without knowledge."[261] This has resulted in error; this has resulted in confusion.[262]

Third—Both Elihu and John directly preceded the Lord. Elihu was still making what proved to be his final point at the end of Chapter 37, when the Lord unceremoniously interrupted all proceedings and spoke out of the whirlwind, not even allowing time to say: "the words of Elihu are ended." The Lord entered the picture right on Elihu's heels, almost as if what he had to say was a continuation of Elihu's speech. The human prophet, in both cases, found himself swallowed up by the majesty and power of the arrival of the Lord.

ELIHU REPROVES JOB

Elihu had listened patiently while Job and his friends had argued on and on, but he didn't like what he heard. A storm was building in his heart. He became angry at the whole lot—angry with Job "because he justified himself rather than God," and angry with the three "because they had found no answer, although they had declared Job to be in the wrong" (32:2-3). So, he cautions, "[b]eware lest you say, 'We have found wisdom.'" None of you, Elihu implies, has found true wisdom or provided an answer. And since you're just standing there, having given up because you have nothing more to say, I also will "declare my opinion" (32:13-17).

---

as a prophet.

261   The Lord will ask Job, "Who is this that darkens counsel by words without knowledge?" (38:2).

262   13 JWS 75-123A-A.

Elihu addresses Job first, beginning with a disclaimer. He tells Job that he need not be afraid of him[263] because he and Job are equals. God formed both from the dust: "I too was pinched off from a piece of clay" (33:6).[264] I'm just like you, Job. Job had earlier worried that he couldn't press his case with the Lord, because "he is not a man, as I am, that I might answer him, that we should come to trial together" (9:32). So at the outset, Elihu is attempting to calm Job's fears. Elihu will speak for the Lord, but like Job, he is just a man.[265]

GOD SPEAKS, ACTS, AND LOVES YOU

As we have seen, although Job maintained early on that the Lord would hear his cry, he had gradually wilted. God must not be answering his prayers, he worried, because nothing was changing,[266] and worse, God wasn't even talking. Though famous in Scripture for patience,[267] Job was like most of us in this regard. We worry and wither when God is silent, but the problem isn't with God; the problem is with our limited perception.[268] We may not

---

263   It is unlikely that Elihu would have said this unless Job had already displayed some fear of him, indicating Job's recognition that Elihu was speaking authoritatively for the Lord. There is no indication that Job had a similar disposition toward Eliphaz, Zophar or Bildad. Indeed, at times he responded with sarcasm to what they said, and even ridiculed them (12:2; 13:5). True prophets instilled fear in the hearer, but as to the false prophet, the Lord told the Israelites: "[y]ou need not be afraid of him." (Deut. 18:22). And when the greatest prophet, Jesus, came, his words were self-authenticating: "And they were astonished at his teaching, for he taught them as one who had authority, and not as the scribes." (Mk. 1:22).

264   "[T]hen the LORD God formed the man of dust from the ground..." (Gen. 2:7).

265   After the Israelites heard the voice of the Lord at Sinai, they petitioned Moses to speak to them, rather than hearing from the Lord himself. (Ex. 20:19).

266   Job had prayed, but as he did so, his suffering continued to increase. Moses complained of the same kind of thing: "[S]ince I came to Pharaoh to speak in your name, he has done evil to this people, and you have not delivered your people at all." (Ex. 5:23).

267   James 5:11.

268   "For God speaks in one way, and in two, though man does not perceive it."

see that the Lord is allowing the "withering" to cause us to ache increasingly for his presence and voice. He is using loneliness and isolation to stretch us. This kind of stretching feels unbearable if we depend on what we see through human eyes. But it feels solid, and strengthening (though it hurts), if we can see it through the eyes of faith, patiently waiting for the Lord to do his work. Godly patience is, in fact, faith.[269]

"Why," Elihu asks Job, do you contend against him, saying, " 'He will answer none of man's words'?" God does speak, "in one way, and in two"[270] (33:12-14). God sometimes speaks in dreams and visions, and it can be terrifying[271] (3:15-16). Perhaps Job had experienced such a vision, because he said that God did "scare" him with dreams, and terrify him with visions (7:14).

But the clear implication of what Elihu has to say here is that God is speaking to Job *principally* through his suffering. Without mentioning Job specifically, Elihu catalogues some of the particular physical issues that Job is dealing with. This itemization surely struck home with Job, because he had previously complained about all of them, and Elihu had been taking notes:

> Man is also rebuked with pain on his bed [30:17]
> > and with continual strife in his bones [7:4],
> > so that his life loathes bread,
> > and his appetite the choicest food [3:24].
> His flesh is so wasted away that
> > it cannot be seen [17:7],
> > and his bones that were not seen stick out
> > [19:20]
>
> > > (33:19-21)

(33:14).

269 Abraham, the man of faith, was stretched as well, waiting patiently, and thus he obtained the promise, God's answer to his prayers. (Heb. 6:15).

270 "Long ago, at many times and in many ways, God spoke to our fathers by the prophets[.]" (Heb. 1:1).

271 Abraham experienced such. See Gen. 15:12-21. Eliphaz testified to a terrifying vision as well, in 4:12-17.

But all of this, Elihu says, God does for man's good, to "keep back his soul from the pit"; to set man's feet in the right direction (33:17-18). In other words, God does these things because he loves his own.

GOD'S PROTECTIVE DISCIPLINE

In the early days of railroads, companies employed brakemen stationed atop the moving freight cars to apply the brakes when needed. The engineer would signal them with the whistle when the train had to slow or stop, and these brave men had to run from car to car while the train was moving to whirl down the brake wheels installed on the top of each car. This was dangerous business all the way around, but the greatest danger was that trains often passed through tunnels or under overpasses low enough so that the brakeman would be hit by the overhead structure if he didn't duck or lie down.

After too many injuries and deaths, laws were enacted requiring the railroad companies to erect "tell-tale"[272] devices a few hundred feet in front of each overpass. A tell-tale was a crossbar installed above the top of the train, with ropes or wires hanging down from it to within a few feet of the top of the passing cars. If a brakeman was still standing at the time the cars passed under the tell-tale, the dangling strands would strike him in the head and upper torso to warn him that the overpass was looming, and he'd better get down.

Now it's no fun to be going 60 miles per hour and get struck in the face by ropes and wires. But ropes and wires are flexible, won't kill you. It's a whole lot better than being struck in the head by solid concrete reinforced with steel I-beams. That will kill a man. The brakeman needs to be protected from the deadly overpass coming up. The protection is painful. When the tell-tale hits

---

272 One of the definitions of "tell-tale" is "discloser of secrets." In this case, the "secret" was the overpass.

him, he suffers. He probably will go home that night with welts on his face. But he's not going home in a coffin.

This is what Elihu was talking about. God was using suffering to protect Job from straying, from future sin. Elihu didn't tell Job what particular overpass Job was being protected from; he probably didn't know, and it didn't matter. That remained a mystery, known only to the Lord. But Elihu could testify with certainty that God sent suffering into Job's life in order to "keep back his soul from the pit."

If, as many believe, an issue addressed by the Book of Job is "Why do the righteous suffer?", Elihu may here be indicating an answer. It isn't the answer that the friends had proffered, that Job's suffering was due to unconfessed sin. Rather, Elihu is saying, God's purpose was to protect Job from some serious threat to his future wellbeing, from an overpass looming dead ahead. And in that way, Elihu is saying, God has already "given an account"[273] as to why he often sends trouble our way. Sanderson says:

> These are the kinds of things, you see, that show that God has given an account. God has appeared in history. And when God has appeared in history, he has very frequently done this to prevent sin. Notice, in verse 29, that "God does all these oftentimes with men." We don't have the details of the background here. But Elihu is able to appeal to the knowledge of Job, and to the knowledge of Job's friends, and they know that as a matter of fact God has intervened, and in various ways God has brought men back from sin; that is, he has kept them from sinning.[274]

We may not know precisely how suffering prevents future sin, but we know it is so because the Apostle Peter wrote that "who-

---

273   That is, given an explanation.
274   13 JWS 75-123A-A.

ever has suffered in the flesh has ceased from sin."[275] And I believe we can understand it to a point.

My parents grew up in the Roaring Twenties, when everything seemed to be on the uptick and people spent their money freely, many wildly. But by the time my parents got married in the late Thirties, the world was in the throes of the Great Depression. Everyone suffered terribly. There were no jobs. There were long soup lines because there was little to eat. Folks were scratching everywhere just to maintain a subsistence living.

By the time World War II had swallowed up the Depression, my parents' generation had learned some valuable lessons about spending money. These lessons were way, way deeper than head knowledge. These lessons registered in their guts. If you have been acquainted with folks from that generation, you know what they were, or are, like. They *felt* differently about wild spending. It wasn't merely that they had learned it was wrong—they didn't even need to know it; they were now allergic to it. They hated it. They had been immunized. They had been protected from profligacy, illustrating what it means to have your "*soul* kept back from the pit."

The Lord's purpose in allowing suffering in our lives is not to abandon us to twist in the wind. Right in the sanctifying troubles, God is teaching us. Though Job thought he couldn't hear God speaking, he actually was hearing him loud and clear, way down deep, because the Lord was speaking to his affections. This is what is meant to have the law written on our hearts.[276] None of us can truly or finally conquer sin and self apart from a change

---

275 1 Pet. 4:1. The Apostle Paul experienced this personally. Having been "caught up to the third heaven," he was vulnerable to pride, and testifies: "So to keep me from becoming conceited because of the surpassing greatness of the revelations, a thorn was given me in the flesh, a messenger of Satan to harass me, to keep me from becoming conceited." (2 Cor. 12:7).

276 Jeremiah said: "For this is the covenant that I will make with the house of Israel after those days, declares the LORD: I will put my law within them, and I will write it on their hearts." (Jer. 31:33).

in our affections, and the way God typically works this change is through suffering.

Job wasn't suffering because of his sin, but he would *feel* differently about things—particularly himself—in the future. He was being changed profoundly. He was being protected in his soul.

And in it all, Job was being preserved. He was being protected not only from potential future wanderings, but from present destruction. God's mercy was there in the whole matter.[277] The Lord had set limits: Satan couldn't touch his life (2:6). There was someone in heaven protecting Job, saving him from destruction. Job already knew this, so Elihu can remind him of his own words: God has provided a Mediator, a Redeemer.[278] This one remembers you, sees you, answers your prayers, accepts you, is merciful, renews your youthful vigor, and brings you joy (33:18-28). God loves you, Job.

ELIHU IS A BREATH OF FRESH AIR

Elihu is markedly different from Job's three friends. He puts his arm around Job. He assures Job right at the start: "I desire to justify you" (33:32). Elihu wants Job to know that he's really on his side, that he will work with him to locate an answer.

Surely Elihu, Eliphaz, Bildad and Zophar all wanted Job to recover. But the latter three never communicated that very well, and certainly didn't convey a desire to justify him. They just kept pounding away, employing the Eliphaz Formula, telling him that if he'd simply repent of his (mythical) sin and lies to cover it up,[279] God would accept, heal and restore him. Indeed, they said, nei-

---

277 "The steadfast love of the LORD never ceases; his mercies never come to an end; they are new every morning; great is your faithfulness." (Lam. 3:22-23).

278 Job, of course, had expressed personal confidence in just such a person. (19:25).

279 Recall what Zophar said of Job: "Though evil is sweet in his mouth, though he hides it under his tongue, though he is loath to let it go, and holds it in his mouth." (20:12-13).

ther God nor man could or should justify Job so long as he was hell-bent on keeping his precious sin and lies to himself.

It is earlier recorded that when Job's three friends came to see him, they saw him from a distance, and were unable to recognize him (2:12). They were Job's friends, but they never truly covered that distance separating them at the first; they never fully recognized him or what agony he was enduring; they never came alongside him. Their brittle theology wouldn't permit them to get close to him.

ELIHU ADDRESSES THE FOUR

Young Elihu, though he will speak bluntly and fearlessly with one arm around Job, now puts his free arm around the three friends—but only briefly. "Let *us* choose what is right," he says. "[L]et *us* know *among ourselves* what is good" (34:4).[280] But, Elihu implies, we won't get anywhere without the establishment, or the recognition, of some facts.

He rhetorically establishes the first fact in a way that makes him look like he doesn't have his arm around Job at all:

> What man is like Job,
>> who drinks up scoffing like water,
>> who travels in company with evildoers
>> and walks with wicked men?
> For he has said, "It profits a man nothing
>> that he should take delight in God.[281]" (34:7-9)

JOB, A SCOFFER?

Why would Elihu accuse Job of "scoffing"? Of course Job is a sinner, through and through. But in what sense could Job be called a "scoffer"?

---

280 Isaiah gives the same invitation in a different context, but with the same spirit: "Come now, let us reason together, says the LORD." (Isa. 1:18).

281 This is not an exact quote, but it is a fair summary of some of what Job has said. See 9:22-24, 9:30-31, 24:1.

Job had progressively faded during his debate with the three. More and more, he seemed to look at God cynically, as when he asked "Why are not times of judgment kept by the Almighty?" (24:1). A weakening Job thought that the wicked got away with their wickedness because God didn't bring their houses down on their children (although he had done so with Job).[282]

That kind of thinking is, by nature, "scoffing," because it scorns God's rules of justice: believing, if only "by the way," that it doesn't make any difference whether you keep the rules or not. And if you come to such a conclusion and begin to become settled on the matter,[283] the law of God will no longer be your "delight" as it was to David.[284] For the person who hunkers down and stays there, the law of God becomes a joke. It also gets personal, because you become the Lawgiver's mocker.

If you mock the Lawgiver it doesn't damage the Lawgiver at all, but it damages you. You will turn to "chaff" that the wind drives away. That's why Elihu used strong language, telling Job he was scoffing, "in company with evildoers." David, in Psalm 1, identifies this very item, because sinners, scoffers, the wicked— they're all in the same boat, because they trivialize God's law. It's a joke, they say, because obedience makes no difference.

Satan is the chief scoffer. He was scoffing when he predicted at the outset that Job would curse God to his face, after Job had found out that obedience to God, and delight in his precepts, was a joke. So we can see how close Job came to cursing God when he

---

282   Of the wicked, Job had said: "Their offspring are established in their presence, and their descendants before their eyes. Their houses are safe from fear, and no rod of God is upon them." (7:8-9).

283   Job was not there yet. He also said of the wicked, "They say to God, 'Depart from us! We do not desire the knowledge of your ways. What is the Almighty, that we should serve him? And what profit do we get if we pray to him?' Behold, is not their prosperity in their hand? The counsel of the wicked is far from me." (21:14-16).

284   David claims "delight" in the law of the Lord, setting himself apart from "scoffers." (Psa. 1:1-2).

said that "[i]t profits a man nothing that he should take delight in God" (34:9), and when he asked "What advantage have I? How am I better off than if I had sinned?" (35:3).

Elihu did not want Job to become chaff. Elihu's strong language should be read not as an indictment of Job but as a warning, much like the warning Job gave his wife when she advised him to "Curse God and die." Elihu is acting as a tell-tale device. You warn those you love. Elihu still had his arm around Job.

GOD IS JUST

People may scoff, Elihu says, but God's justice, his equity, is absolute, no matter how man evaluates it or what it looks like presently through human eyes.

I have a hard time watching documentaries of the Second World War, particularly the segments having to do with Nazi atrocities. Forcing defenseless Jews into cold boxcars in the dead of winter, separating children from parents, starving them in concentration camps, leading the women to believe they were headed for showers but murdering them by the millions in what proved to be gas chambers—there is no punishment known to man that could come close to achieving justice. It's tempting to question God's justice when viewing these horrors, because so far as we can see, they continued without his intervention. But, Elihu reminds us, God is just:

> For according to the work of a man he will repay
> him,
> and according to his ways he will make it
> befall him.[285] (34:11)

---

285 The Apostle Paul assures that there is no "slippage" in God's justice: "He will render to each one according to his works: to those who by patience in well-doing seek for glory and honor and immortality, he will give eternal life; but for those who are self-seeking and do not obey the truth, but obey unrighteousness, there will be wrath and fury. *There will be tribulation and distress for every human being who does evil*, the Jew first and also the Greek, but glory and

Elihu here speaks of the nature of God, and is telling the four that all the palaver he has heard from their mouths about whether or not the Lord is equitable can be put to rest immediately. God, by his very nature, is equitable. He is the sole source and definition of justice—indeed, to this all other definitions must yield. It's no problem for us to wonder about and feel tension regarding the unpunished crimes of the Nazis, but to conclude that God is not just because he didn't punish them is unbelief. We've substituted our standards of justice for his.

God's perfect justice is a given, not up for debate. So we start there, and we end there.

GOD HAS ALL THE FACTS

Not only is God's perfect justice a given, but in his court, the facts are a given as well.

I've tried hundreds of cases in the American court system and I can't recall a one in which some fact wasn't in dispute. But God's court isn't like ours. His court is fully informed of every tiny piece of evidence well before the trial begins. Nothing is in dispute; not a thing. He doesn't need a report from the FBI. He has already assembled all the facts:

> For his eyes are on the ways of a man,
>   and he sees all his steps.
> There is no gloom or deep darkness
>   where evildoers may hide themselves.
> For God has no need to consider a man further,
>   that he should go before God in judgment.
> He shatters the mighty without investigation
>   and sets others in their place. (34:21-24)

---

honor and peace for everyone who does good, the Jew first and also the Greek. For God shows no partiality." (Rom 2:6-11).

We cannot stand before or against the judgment of Jehovah God. Asaph wrote: "He calls to the heavens above, and to the earth, that he may judge his people."[286]

SONGS IN THE NIGHT

Elihu's main thrust here is to counter Job's expressed belief that God is silent. Elihu is saying that if Job will just listen, he'll hear him. He speaks in lots of different ways. Sometimes he's quiet; sometimes he's loud. Sometimes, Elihu tells Job, God gives us "songs in the night" (35:10). Sanderson remembers when the Lord spoke personally to him in this way:

> Have you ever had a song in the night? Have you ever had one?
>
> I have discovered that the older I get, the harder it is for me to sleep. About a year ago, I woke up at around three o'clock in the morning, and I couldn't get back to sleep again. And the Old Boy came around, and he started reminding me of when I was a kid, and I was a pretty nasty kid. I began thinking about that, and I really got down in the dumps. And then he reminded me of the nasty kid that I was in high school. And then he reminded me of college. Then things really got bad. At three o'clock in the morning everything's bad enough anyhow. It was really depressing.
>
> So this went on for more than fifteen minutes, and I was literally crying. And then all of a sudden the verse came into my mind, that all of these sins God has forgiven. All of them. And that for Christ's sake he has declared me righteous in his sight. Then, all of a sudden, everything changed.

---

286 Psa. 50:4.

Then I did something. I'm not sure it was theologically correct, but I deliberately said to the devil, "Tell me some more things that I can remember, that I have been forgiven for." I mean, I just had a celebration. Well, that's a song in the night. May God give us all songs in the night. Because of course God is far off. He is exalted, he's transcendent, and all the theological and philosophical jargon that you want to use. But he's also the God who is here. And he does give us songs in the night.[287]

Sanderson's song in the night sounds like God was speaking kind of quietly. But Elihu sees something coming up on the horizon where it looks like the Lord's voice will be pretty loud. It's beginning to sound that way, too.

ELIHU THE METEOROLOGIST

Elihu is looking at Job with one eye when he rebukes him, but his other eye is trained on the sky. It looks like a low pressure front is moving in across the desert. It's getting darker, and it's begun to sprinkle. He sees lightning, and hears claps of thunder:

> For he draws up the drops of water;
>   they distill his mist in rain,
>   which the skies pour down
>   and drop on mankind abundantly.
> Can anyone understand the spreading of the
>   clouds, the thunderings of his pavilion?
> Behold, he scatters his lightning about him
>   and covers the roots of the sea. (36:27-30)

Job has suffered from the sultry heat out there on the pile of ashes ("you whose garments are hot when the earth is still because of the south wind" [37:17]), and maybe cooling showers would

---

287   14 JWS 75-123A-B.

bring some relief. But then he also had to worry about the lightning, which God commands to "strike the mark" (35:32). That's the way it is with storms. God's judgment and mercy come at the same time.[288]

Just watch and listen. This is an unusual storm, because you can hear the thunder, the roar of God's voice. It's going to be a big one. You can see the animals running for cover[289]; they somehow always know when a storm is coming. And now I see funnel clouds! (37:9)—this storm is really kicking up its heels, and coming fast. Just a few minutes ago the sky was like bronze, just like it will be after the storm has cleared (37:18), but now black clouds, lightning, thunder and maybe even a tornado. (37:1-20). This is serious for all five of us, and not just because of lightning and thunder. It's serious because God is in this storm. Though he's invisible and we can't find him, he's about to speak: to show us his nature, his power, his justice, his abundant righteousness, and why men fear him:

> The Almighty—we cannot find him;
>> he is great in power; justice and abundant
>> righteousness he will not violate.
> Therefore men fear him;
>> he does not regard any who are wise in their
>>> own conceit. (37:23-24)

Maybe Elihu has more to say, but if so, he doesn't get the chance. The thunder sounds like someone clearing his throat, like a father at the dining room table with his children, who've been arguing. When Dad clears his throat, it's a signal to the children to stop arguing, be quiet, and listen up to what he's about to say.

---

288 "Whether for correction or for his land or for love, he causes it to happen." (37:13).

289 "[T]he beasts go into their lairs, and remain in their dens." (37:8).

FOR REFLECTION

1.

In view of what Elihu said in Job 32-37, do you think he was a "young, brash fool," a prophet of God, or somewhere in between? How is what he said relevant to Job's situation, if at all?

2.

As you look back on your life, can you see times when the Lord exercised "protective discipline," that is, when he did something in your life that you can see protected you from future sin? Or can you see that he was protecting you from future sin in other ways, apart from discipline?

3.

Was Elihu right in calling Job a "scoffer"? Did this help Job? In what ways might it be said that Job had "scoffed"?

4.

As Sanderson asks, have you ever had a "song in the night"? What were the circumstances, and what effect did it have on you in the future?

17.

THE LORD ANSWERS JOB

CHAPTERS 38-41

THE BOOK OF JOB begins with a storm and ends with a storm. Both storms were terrifying. The Lord sent both of them,[290] and he meant to speak to Job in each. But they were very different. The first was an evil storm; the second was a *perfect* storm, in all senses of the word.

In Chapter 1, though the Lord sent it, the storm was Satan's evil deed. Being evil, it was meant to kill and destroy, and it succeeded. It killed Job's children, those he loved most, those he had persistently prayed for. It destroyed everything Job had. It was savage and murderous, straight from hell. It was the kind of storm Satan invents and delights in.

But the storm that Elihu described in Chapters 35-37 is from heaven. Elihu testifies that God is speaking to Job through lightning, thunder, rain and whirlwinds, in an awesome display of the power of the Almighty:

> Keep listening to the thunder of his voice
>   and the rumbling that comes from his mouth.

---

290 After the first storm, the Lord took responsibility for it, in saying to Satan: "[Job] still holds fast his integrity, although you incited me against him to destroy him without reason." (2:3).

Under the whole heaven he lets it go,
  and his lightning to the corners of the earth.
After it his voice roars;
  he thunders with his majestic voice,
  and he does not restrain the lightnings when
    his voice is heard.
God thunders wondrously with his voice. (37:2-5)

All through the book, Job had beseeched the Lord to speak to him, that God would appear so that Job could have a hearing before him. Typical of this was his request in 13:3: "But I would speak to the Almighty, and I desire to argue my case with God." Now, suddenly, the Lord grants his wish in an awesome display of power and glory. Job got what he wanted, but maybe didn't want what he got:

> Then the LORD answered Job out of the whirl-wind and said: "Who is this that darkens counsel by words without knowledge? Dress for action like a man; I will question you, and you make it known to me." (38:1-3)

GOD THROWS DOWN THE GAUNTLET

Do you really want to argue your case before me, Job? Then get ready: put on your fighting clothes. I've got some questions for you, and I want to hear your answers, if you have any. I'll begin way back at the beginning. I'm going to ask you some questions about creation.

GOD SAW THAT IT WAS GOOD

Once before, long ago, the Lord commented on his creation. Several times in Genesis 1 he stepped back to look at what he had just made, and evaluated it. In each case he called it "good." Then on the sixth day, after he had created man, he stepped way back, and "saw everything that he had made, and behold, it was *very* good."[291] In Genesis, God gives us an astonishing insight into what he himself thinks of the things he has made, and he thinks very highly of them.

But nowhere in Scripture are we given anything close to the degree of insight as to what God thinks of his creation like that revealed in Job 38-41. Here he will tell us what he thinks about the foundation of the earth, stars, seas, clouds, mornings, mountains, topology, birth, death, light, rain, snow, hail, rivers, erosion, constellations, lightning, lions, ravens, mountain goats, wild donkeys, wild oxen, ostriches, horses, hawks, the proud, Behemoth, Leviathan, and more. What a panorama!

I'm no carpenter, but I once made a dish cupboard. There was a crudely shaped recess in our dining room wall beckoning for a built-in cupboard. All I had was a saber saw, yardstick, hammer and nails. But I did it! Nice, swinging glass doors on top, bright brass hinges, wooden doors on the bottom. No particle board, either. Beautiful, I must admit. It still looks great, thirty years later. This was a project unlike any others I ever attempted, because it turned out well. I have no idea how that happened, but I'm happy with it. So is my wife (it was her idea in the first place), and that's the acid test.

It's natural, even good, for us to do a job well enough to be happy with it. We are made in the image of God, and he delights in everything he's made. As you read Chapters 38-41, you get the sense that the Lord is excited and joyful in "showing Job around." It's as if the Lord is bragging on his work and wants Job to join in.

GOD IS GOD AND MAN IS MAN

Before God shows Job the beauty and majesty of his creation, he reminds Job of something that he actually knew well, but had forgotten.

---

291   Gen. 1:31.

Once, when Job was pretty much out of control, he said: "Here is my signature! Let the Almighty answer me!" (31:35). It is as though Job were in court, knew he was losing, angrily scribbled out his demands, signed the paper and thrust it at the judge. I've seen lawyers do this kind of thing, to their later regret. Job demands, "Let the Almighty answer *me!*"[292] but the Lord here bangs his gavel and says, "No, you answer *me!*"

> Where were you when I laid the foundation of
>   the earth?
> Tell me, if you have understanding.
> Who determined its measurements—surely you
>   know!
> Or who stretched the line upon it?
> On what were its bases sunk,
>   or who laid its cornerstone,
>   when the morning stars sang together
>   and all the sons of God shouted for joy?
>   (38:4-7)

THE PRIMACY OF CREATION

As mentioned before, the secular world refuse to admit to creation, because they don't want to deal with the Creator. The Apostle Peter says that "they *deliberately* overlook this fact, that the heavens existed long ago, and the earth was formed out of water and through water by the word of God."[293] It's not just an innocent error on their part; it's intentional. And it is to their own hurt.[294]

---

292 Regarding Job's outburst in 31:35, Sanderson comments: "And now, Job, I think you've gone too far. Because when you talk to *El Shaddai* like that, you've forgotten that he is *El Shaddai*. God is not your equal, and you can't call God to account any more than the clay can say to the potter, 'Why have you made me thus?' " (13 JWS 75-123A-A).

293 2 Pet. 3:5.

294 The Apostle Paul, speaking of the unbelieving world, says: "For [God's] invisible attributes, namely, his eternal power and divine nature, have been clearly perceived, ever since the creation of the world, in the things that have been made. So they are without excuse." (Rom. 1:20).

Today's Christians are not exempt. We don't deny creation, and we believe in the Creator. But we often minimize it, and it's to our hurt too. We treat it as a footnote to the Gospel, when the Holy Spirit has placed it in the main text. The Apostle's Creed, which is the history of redemption in creedal form, puts creation front and center, beginning with the words "I believe in God the Father Almighty, maker of heaven and earth." It's central to redemption, because we will bow before the Lord, as Creator:

> For the LORD is a great God,
>   and a great King above all gods.
> In his hand are the depths of the earth;
>   the heights of the mountains are his also.
> The sea is his, for he made it,
>   and his hands formed the dry land.
> Oh come, let us worship and bow down;
>   *let us kneel before the LORD, our Maker!*
>   (Psa. 95:3-6)

In his miracles, Jesus demonstrated that he was Creator God. It was no problem for him to calm the sea,[295] because he made the sea. He could cure a woman of her twelve-year-long "issue of blood,"[296] because he created her. Demons knew that they had to yield to his authority,[297] because he even created demons.[298]

JOB MUST BOW DOWN

"Job," the Lord is saying, "before you can begin to understand your plight, you must bow before your Creator." Job had lost perspective. He needed a different pair of glasses. Job had had a proper set when he said "the fear of the LORD, that is wisdom" (28:28), but he had misplaced those glasses by the end of

---

295 Mt. 8:23-27. This was the same Person who, at creation, commanded the waves to halt. (38:11).

296 Mk. 5:21-43.

297 Lk. 8:26-39.

298 The Lord will talk about this comforting fact in Ch. 41, when he describes Leviathan.

his speeches, when he mumbled through all his righteous deeds (Chapter 31). The Lord now gives Job a prescription for a new pair, and during the Lord's speech, he fills the prescription.

God is not trying to make Job feel like dirt. Though we were made from dirt, we aren't dirt. God made us in his image, and it is because of that that we joyfully bow in his presence. But we weren't around when things started up.

"Where were you when I laid the foundation of the earth?" he asks Job. "Tell me, if you have understanding" (38:4). God, it appears, also created sarcasm.

The Lord won't make dirt out of Job, but he's going to lay him low. He hits Job with a volley of unanswerable questions, that is, unanswerable if your response were to be anything other than "*You* did!" Who laid the earth's cornerstone? Who measured it? Who anchored it so as to make it stable in orbit? Who established limits for the oceans? Who commanded the "proud waves" to stop in their tracks, not to come one inch closer? (38:5-11).

These questions, while meant to humble us, are also designed to make us think about God's massive undertaking in the creation of the universe. He did not do it magically, but with real, hard, diligent work. This work took place in real space and time. There were real challenges in the project, requiring practical, workable solutions. These questions are designed to make us think about that.

For example, if you're operating in open space, where do you put the cornerstone? Cornerstones have to be anchored to something, but there's nothing to anchor it to (the best we can do is to come up with the fanciful "sky-hook"). And all of a sudden, units of and instruments for measurement become essential—we can't go forward with much of anything until we have that, because we will need to know how much, how long, how short, how big, how heavy, just so that everything will be coordinated. What we know as scientific principles and law had to be defined and employed.

You could take any of man's inventions to illustrate. One such invention is the gyroscope.

If we were constructing the universe, we'd have to figure out a way to keep what we had made "up there," so it didn't just aimlessly wander off. We'd have to come up with something like a "device consisting of a wheel or disk mounted so that it can spin rapidly about an axis that is itself free to alter in direction."[299] This constantly-spinning device would promote stability, which is what we're after. Then we've got to model all the billions and billions of stars, constellations, galaxies and planets on that principle, because they're going to have to spin freely, yet stay where they belong.

Probably, of course, the stars and galaxies came first, and the gyroscope was modeled after them. But maybe not. It's very possible that God designed little models first, and went from there.

The point is that God wants Job to look at creation from a practical standpoint, because it is only then that we'll see God's true glory in it. It's exciting to study the details of creation. God is glorified when we see that creation took hard work; that it wasn't an "abracadabra" or "poof" event. It was an awesome project, took time, and had sequence.[300] Every detail had to be worked out before the finished product could be unveiled, but when that great day came,

> the morning stars sang together
> and all the sons of God shouted for joy! (38:7)

GOD IS JUDGING THE WICKED

God made the universe, and he can shake it.

When we get up early enough to see the sun rise, it is beautiful, but it is also a marker for judgment. What's going to happen that day, and every day, is that the sun will "take hold of the skirts

---

299 "Gyroscope." Merriam-Webster.com, 2016.
300 See Gen. 1. Creation progressed through a period of seven days.

of the earth, [that the wicked will] be shaken out of it" (38:13). Every day. We don't see it, nor did Job see it when he asked, "Why are not times of judgment kept by the Almighty, and why do those who know him never see his days?" (24:1). The Lord here answers Job's question. Job, don't worry about it: it's happening!

The sun was shaking the wicked out of the earth in Judge Deborah's day, when she led Israel's troops against the Canaanite king Sisera, soundly defeating him and his armies who possessed chariots of iron. After the victory, she sang a song of praise to the Lord:

> So may all your enemies perish, O LORD!
> But your friends be like the sun as he rises in his
>   might! (Judges 5:31)

It used to be that when we arose at sunrise, we'd collect the morning paper from the front yard and read the headlines. Now we head for virtual newspapers, our computers. The technology has changed, but the headlines remain the same. Every morning we are confronted with a smorgasbord of mass bombings, beheadings, rapes, wars, new slaveries, oppressions of every imaginable kind. We are tempted to ask with Job, "Why are not times of judgment kept by the Almighty?"

But when the sun comes up, we should open our Bibles before we open our laptops. God's headline reads:

"THE WICKED ARE BEING SHAKEN OUT OF THE EARTH TODAY!"

There will be a final judgment, but the Lord has already begun the process. He's judging on a daily basis.

CLIMATE CHANGE

I don't have a position on climate change, just a strong hunch: the experts don't know. It might be happening, it might not. But reading 38:16-30, I doubt that anyone can know for sure, because it looks like a secret that the Lord means to keep to himself. The

Lord sets out a list of queries in these verses, all bearing on climate. Even today, with all our sophisticated apparati, we don't have answers to his questions. Although we now know some amazing facts about the "springs of the sea"[301] (38:16), as evidenced by a 2015 study of "seafloor hydrothermal circulation,"[302] and though some brave souls have descended to the deepest parts of the ocean floor,[303] we have never been to the "storehouses of the snow" or hail (38:22), mainly because we don't even know where they are; they're not on our maps.

But we do know the Lord brings about climate change, and for his own purposes.[304] He is able to cause the globe to warm for 100 years, and cool it off for the next 200. He can change the weather whenever he wants, and some of the rain, snow and hail he has "reserved for the time of trouble, for the day of battle and war" (38:23). He has used some of those reserves for such purposes in recent history.

As is known to anyone who lived through or has studied the Second World War, weather played an enormous role. Dense fog provided cover on D-Day, rain and mud swamped tanks in western Europe just after D-Day, snow and sub-zero weather abruptly halted the Nazi advance on Moscow in the winter of 1941-42. Man lived or died at the hands of the weather, but no-one had control

---

301　These "springs" are probably the same as those described in the history of the Noahic Flood, when "all the fountains of the great deep burst forth." (Gen. 7:11).

302　"Sustainability and dynamics of outcrop-to-outcrop hydrothermal circulation," by Dustin M. Winslow and Andrew T. Fisher, *Nature Communications* 6, Article 7567 (June, 2015).

303　Ker Than, "James Cameron Completes Record-Breaking Mariana Trench Dive," *National Geographic* (March, 2012).

304　The Lord has graciously restrained himself, however, as to an important aspect of atmospheric change: the continuation of the four seasons. After the Great Flood had devastated the earth, he promised Noah that "[w]hile the earth remains, seedtime and harvest, cold and heat, summer and winter, day and night, shall not cease." (Gen. 8:22). Global warming, if it is happening, will not end the seasons, as some fear.

over it, or even claimed to, because no-one but God can direct where the wind is to be "scattered upon the earth" (38:24).

The Lord seemingly mocks Job in 38:21, where he reminds him that he wasn't around when any of this was in the planning or building stages: "*You* know, for you were born then, and the number of your years is great!" Job must have needed this kind of needling sarcasm because the Lord gave it to him. But surely, by this time, he already had his face on the ground.

JOB'S FIELD TRIP

Next is what Sanderson calls "Job's Field Trip."

As mentioned before, many think that the primary subject addressed in the Book of Job is the question "Why do the righteous suffer?" And without doubt, the question is raised throughout the book. But that's just a *question*. If the Lord meant for that to be our primary concern, you'd think he would have answered that question, straight out. But you can read what God says in Chapters 38-41 time and again, backwards and forwards, and you're not going to find a definitive answer to it. That isn't to say that there isn't an answer; God just doesn't divulge it.

Sanderson says:

> I suppose that traditionally, it has been argued and urged that the book of Job deals with the problem, "Why do the righteous suffer?" And if you have someone who is very sick, well, you give them the book of Job. And as they read the book of Job, they will find a complete and full explanation of suffering as it goes on in this world, and then they'll feel better.
>
> Well, I'm not exactly sure that that traditional interpretation is at all a very good one. Let's try it out on you for a moment. Let's suppose you were Job; you've lost all your wealth, and your family, and

now you are a very sick man or woman, sick with a terrible disease, expecting to die. And also, let's suppose in good pastoral fashion, I should drive up to your house, with an ambulance, and I would put you into the ambulance, and you would expect me to be taking you to one of these hospitals around here for special treatment.

But we drive past all the hospitals, and you see us going down Route 40 and we get off at Forest Park, and you say "wait, where are you taking me?" and then "oh yes, that's right, Barnes Hospital *is* right near Forest Park."[305]

But we don't go to Barnes Hospital, we go to the zoo!

And then we take you out of the ambulance, and put you on a stretcher, and we just wheel you around and show you the giraffes, hippopotami, and all kinds of animals, ostriches, and things like that. And then we say to you, "Well, now that you've gotten that lesson, let's go over to the planetarium and let's look at Orion, and Pleiades, and Arcturus, and then when we're done looking at that, we'll just take you back to the house."

You will say "Okay, fine, I've enjoyed the sightseeing trip but when am I going to get well? How does any of this relate to my problem?"[306]

But it was the Lord who was wheeling Job around the zoo, and he wasn't going to let Job presume the issue.

---

305 Sanderson's 1975 lecture series, from which this is excerpted, was delivered at Covenant Theological Seminary in St. Louis, Missouri. Forest Park and Barnes Hospital are adjacent, located just north of U.S. Highway 40. Forest Park featured both a zoo and a planetarium.

306 I JWS 75-120A-A.

THE PLANETARIUM

The Lord tells Job to look up, *way* up, into the sky on a starry night. He did the same with Abraham, when "he brought him outside and said, 'Look toward heaven, and number the stars, if you are able to number them!' "[307,308] The specific purpose there was to reveal to Abraham the vast number of his covenant offspring yet to come. Yet in both of Abraham's and Job's cases, God's purpose was to give his servants a different perspective. Both of them were in a spot where they needed new perspective.

There comes a time for all of us when we must look up—away from the ash heap, from the boils and scabs, from the pus-smeared shards of broken pottery, from the "body which was as good as dead,"[309] from the unmitigated wretchedness of our lives, and from our abject inability to do anything about it, to gain a fresh perspective that God alone can give.

It's a perspective that you really can't obtain unless you're first brought down flat on your face as Job was here. He had been reduced to nothing. The Lord appointed Satan to begin the process in Chapters 1 and 2, then Job's friends took over, then Elihu, who told Job that he "drinks up scoffing like water" (34:7), and now the Lord himself, who riddles Job with sarcasm: "You know, for you were born then, and the number of your days is great!" (38:21).

Though the Lord continues, and will continue to the end, to impress upon Job his low estate, he is at the same time lifting Job up to the heavens. It is essential that every one of us understand that "God is in heaven and you are on earth,"[310] but that's not all

---

307 Though a bit gentler, this is the same kind of "divine sarcasm" that God employed with Job in 38:4.
308 Gen. 15:5.
309 "[Abraham] did not weaken in faith when he considered his own body, which was as good as dead (since he was about a hundred years old)." (Rom. 4:19).
310 Eccl. 5:2.

we need to understand. God also wills for us to obtain *his* perspective on things. For the rest of what the Lord says to Job, it's as though he has swooped his child up on his shoulders so that he can get a better view. My father used to do that with all eight of us Belz kids (though not all at once), and it was a grand feeling. It's as though God is holding Job firmly on his shoulders with one hand and points at the stars with the other so he can see them like he does, so he can see everything from a different point of view:

> Can you bind the chains of the Pleiades
>   or loose the cords of Orion?
> Can you lead forth the Mazzaroth in their season,
>   or can you guide the Bear with its children?[311]
> Do you know the ordinances of the heavens?
> Can you establish their rule on the earth?
>
> (38:31-33)

Job, when he heard these questions, must have been laughing and crying at the same time. I'm not in charge of anything anymore! I'm no longer in charge of any cattle, servants, or donkeys. I sure can't control my wife. I'm not even in charge of myself. No, I'm going to have to leave the chains of Pleiades and the cords of Orion to someone else. The Lord then asks him:

> Can you lift up your voice to the clouds,
>   that a flood of waters may cover you? (38:34)

Can you do a rain dance?—I mean, one that works? When it's really needed, when it hasn't rained for months, and it's hellishly hot and dry? But you don't need to, because I make it rain! I see when the "dust runs into a mass and the clods stick fast together[.]" That's when I "tilt the waterskins of the heavens" (38:37-

---

311   Throughout this divine commentary on creation in Chapters 38-41, the Lord uses the names mankind has ascribed to both the animate and inanimate, even names arising out of ancient pagan mythology, as in the constellations mentioned here. It seems to be a pattern, instituted at Creation, where the Lord brought the beasts and birds to Adam, "to see what he would call them. And whatever the man called every living creature, that was its name." (Gen. 2:19).

38), so that the thirsty land will have something to drink, grass will turn green, the grain will grow, and you'll have something to eat.

This has been a quick but stunning trip for Job to the planetarium, looking up at the sun, stars, constellations, and contemplating the snow, ice, rain and hail. But that lesson is over, and Job is wheeled out of the planetarium. Though the Lord has smacked him down pretty soundly, Job had lived through it. That in itself was a special mercy of the Lord, because God had told Moses that "you cannot see my face, for man shall not see me and live."[312]

GOD'S SPECIAL RULES OF EVIDENCE

Job had expected a very different kind of hearing before the Lord. He had thought that if and when God broke through the awful, suffocating silence that persisted all the way from the beginning of Chapter 3 through the end of Chapter 37, he would grant Job a formal kind of trial, a more typical kind, the kind Job used to preside over when he judged others' disputes at the gates of the city.[313] Job knew firsthand what trials were like, and how to conduct them. Both sides were permitted to present evidence, make opening and closing statements and the like. It wouldn't be a proceeding where Pleiades and Orion would be allowed into evidence, because quite obviously, they're not relevant.

And at the end of the hearing, Job had believed that God would vindicate him outright in front of his three friends:

> Oh, that I knew where I might find him,
>   that I might come even to his seat!
> I would lay my case before him
>   and fill my mouth with arguments.

---

312   Ex. 33:20. Similarly, Gideon, like many others, feared death after he had seen the angel of the LORD, but experienced the same mercy: " 'Alas, O LORD God! For now I have seen the angel of the LORD face to face.' But the LORD said to him, 'Peace be to you. Do not fear; you shall not die.' " (Judges 6:22).

313   29:7-17.

> I would know what he would answer me
>> and understand what he would say to me.
> Would he contend with me in the greatness of his
>> power?
> No; he would pay attention to me.
> There an upright man could argue with him,
>> and I would be acquitted forever by my judge.
>> (23:3-7)

Only two of these expectations had been fulfilled thus far: Job had "found" God (actually God found Job), and the Lord was *really* paying attention to him.

But the rest of it looked like it was going down the tubes. Job wasn't able to lay his case before the Lord, nor fill his mouth with arguments, because he didn't have any. Clearly Job hadn't known what the Lord would answer him. Would he "contend with me in the greatness of his power?"—well, apparently so. And Job had been expecting full acquittal, complete vindication, not a discourse on the heavenly bodies, constellations and weather patterns.

THE ZOO

But the proceeding is now being conducted on the Lord's shoulders now, and that's far better than sitting in a stuffy courtroom anyway. The two leave the planetarium and head for the zoo. They'll spend the rest of their time together there.

Our zoos are cramped, and not really all that good for the wild animals and birds they house. My family has visited the St. Louis Zoo many times (it's free), and it's always seemed to me that the tigers, monkeys, polar bears and the like all have a kind of sad expression on their faces, like "I really don't like this place very much." Well, they weren't designed to like it, all caged up. They were designed to enjoy the wild, the free range, so that's the kind of zoo the Lord takes Job to. It's the "genuine article" zoo, way out there in the jungles, marshes and prairies.

First stops are the lion's lair and bird sanctuary:

> Can you hunt the prey for the lion,
>> or satisfy the appetite of the young lions,
>> when they crouch in their dens
>> or lie in wait in their thicket?
> Who provides for the raven its prey,
>> when its young ones cry to God for help,
>> and wander about for lack of food? (38:39-41)

The lion and raven aren't very much alike, except that both have eyes and claws. But, for example, ravens don't have teeth and lions don't have beaks (that's so we can tell them apart). But they are alike in other ways, one of which is that they both need food. They need to eat to survive. Every living thing, plant or animal, needs food. Otherwise, they die.

We'll pause a bit here and focus on the raven.

THE WORKS OF CREATION AND PROVIDENCE

When the Westminster divines wrote the catechism in 1647, they asked the question "How does God execute his decrees?"[314] The answer they gave for us to memorize was that "God executes his decrees in the works of *creation* and *providence*."[315] And here the Lord is giving Job and all of us a tiny but awesome glimpse into what that means.

First, God created everything. He's been showing Job this because he wants Job to understand clearly that he's the designer, architect and manufacturer of all things, that neither Job nor anybody else had a thing to do with it, and that we know very little about it. This humbles us, and brings us to our knees in worship.

---

314 The decrees of God are defined as "his eternal purpose, according to the counsel of his will, whereby, for his own glory, he has foreordained whatsoever comes to pass." *Westminster Shorter Catechism*, Q. 7.
315 Ibid, Q. 8.

But second, the Lord is talking to Job about his providence, or ongoing provision, for everything he has made. That's where the raven comes in.

THE LOCKHEED MARTIN F-35 LIGHTNING II

God made the raven, and endowed man with the ability to copy it and make the airplane. The raven is more advanced than the airplane though, because it produces little ravens, and the little ravens are at no cost. Man has not yet built an aircraft that reproduces, which is unfortunate, because the Lockheed Martin F-35 costs more than $100 million per unit. The Pentagon plans to buy 2,457 of them and have the entire fleet deployed by 2040. It's a very ambitious project, financially and technologically.

However, at this writing, Lockheed has run into numerous problems, not having to do with the aircraft itself, but the complex software designed to make a pilot almost unnecessary. Most of this software is earth-bound, not in the aircraft itself. This software is basically a world-wide infrastructure, provided to take care of every F-35 launched into the skies. It will keep the aircraft alive and flying. It is every bit as important as the birds it supports.

GOD'S GREAT INFRASTRUCTURE

When the Lord tells Job about the raven he created, he's telling him about something else he made: an infrastructure specifically designed to keep the raven alive and flying. Like the massive computer base designed for the F-35, this infrastructure is essential for the raven's survival; the difference is that it has never had glitches. The Lord did this for all his millions of different kinds of creatures, including people.[316] His computer banks are specifically designed to take care of ravens when "its young ones cry to God for help, and wander about for lack of food" (38:41). The Lord created so great an infrastructure that it can answer a bird's cry

---

316 "And out of the ground the Lord God made to spring up every tree that is pleasant to the sight and good for food." (Gen. 2:9).

and provide food for a baby raven, just so the tiny creature can live and grow up to fly.

Whether he had time presently to think about it or not, this fact should have been a great encouragement to Job. He wasn't crying out for food, like the baby raven was, because he had lost his appetite (3:24; 33:20). But he was crying out for just about everything else that a person needs to survive. And he, like every one of us, was much more important to his Heavenly Father than birds.[317]

WE'RE NOT REALLY NEEDED

Important as Job was to the Lord, Job is also being told that he's not really needed in running the universe. None of us are. God takes care of what he's made, and he does it without assistance from anyone. This is humbling to someone who thinks, as natural man does, that he's the center of the universe. But it's also freeing, because we are being assured that we do not have to bear such an impossible burden.

Man has a little bit to do with the environment, and God requires us to be good stewards of what we have been given to control. But that part is tiny compared to the entire project. Modern man tends to believe that we can, or should, make all the difference, because the secular mind does not and cannot accept the One who sovereignly created and now sovereignly provides.[318] People could be freed from this burdensome misconception by simply bowing the knee before the One who created and sustains the universe,[319] but natural man refuses to do so. Men and women have exchanged the real freedom that could be theirs for a self-imposed slavery to the upkeep of the universe.[320]

317 Jesus told his disciples: "Fear not, therefore; you are of more value than many sparrows." (Mt. 10:31).
318 "For the mind that is set on the flesh is hostile to God, for it does not submit to God's law; indeed, it cannot." (Rom. 8:7).
319 "And he is before all things, and in him all things hold together." (Col. 1:17).
320 This is consonant with the "great exchange" the Apostle Paul talks about

WILD KINGDOM

It's not just the F-35 that is unable to give birth. Nothing that man makes is able to perform that miracle, and surely never will. Male and female computers? Little computers toddling about? Childhood and adolescence? Computers suffering through puberty? Every one of them a little different from the other, so we can recognize them as individuals? We know very little about God's birth and growth processes:

> Do you know when the mountain goats give
> birth?
> Do you observe the calving of the does?
> Can you number the months that they fulfill,
>   and do you know the time when they give
>   birth?
>   when they crouch, bring forth their offspring,
>   and are delivered of their young?
> Their young ones become strong;
>   they grow up in the open;
>   they go out and do not return to them. (39:1-4)

And consider the wild donkeys. God has made the wild donkey independent, frisky and free, providing the "arid plain" and "salt land" for his habitat. He likes it, too, and "scorns the tumult of the city." He doesn't like to live where we live![321] The wild ox lives in the wild too, not in man's domain. He can't be domesticated. Imagine giving him instructions in the morning, like harvesting the wheat: "Do you have faith in him that he will return your grain, and gather it to your threshing floor?" (39:5-12).

---

in his letter to the Romans: "[they] exchanged the glory of the immortal God for images resembling mortal man and birds and animals and creeping things." (Rom. 1:23).

321   15 JWS 75-123B-A.

WHY DID YOU MAKE THAT?

The Lord has created all kinds of animals with brains and habits peculiar to each. For some of them, their usefulness to us is obvious: cattle for milk and meat, hens for eggs, horses for riding, dogs for petting and loving. But a whole slew of them are hard to figure out, and the principal reason is that we can't see how they are of any use to *us*. Take the hippopotamus, for example. Sanderson said:

> One of the great reasons for visiting the zoo is to be confronted with a lot of animals that you don't understand. I mean, what's the good of a hippopotamus? Stupid looking, awkward, ugly—just a great big mound of blubber. I'll be honest with you, I haven't the ghost of an idea. And that tells me something. Because if I can't figure out a hippopotamus, that tells me that there is a lot that I don't know. And that's why you and I ought to take some time to go down to the zoo for a half hour, and just look for the whole time at a hippopotamus. Because God does know, and God had a reason, and God doesn't make any mistakes. And it may not be necessary for you to know what a hippopotamus is all about. Just so God does. And God says, "I do." And the glory of God comes across as *wisdom*.[322]

Our chief end is not to figure out all God's creatures in terms of their usefulness to us, or to figure them out at all. Man's chief end is to "glorify God, and enjoy him forever."[323] We do that *particularly* when we don't understand something he's made, because it's then that we are aware of his greatness, of his "beyond-ness," of his unfathomable wisdom, of his glory. Creation is chock full

---

322   2 JWS 75-120A-B.
323   *Westminster Shorter Catechism*, Q. 1.

of secrets like this, things that we don't understand at all, and it is thus that "*the whole earth is full of his glory.*"[324]

MOTHER OSTRICH

Take the ostrich, for example:

> The wings of the ostrich wave proudly,
>> but are they the pinions and plumage of love?
> For she leaves her eggs to the earth
>> and lets them be warmed on the ground,
>> forgetting that a foot may crush them
>> and that the wild beast may trample them.
> She deals cruelly with her young,
>> as if they were not hers;
>> though her labor be in vain,
>> yet she has no fear, because God has made her
>>> forget wisdom
>> and given her no share in understanding.
> When she rouses herself to flee,
>> she laughs at the horse and his rider. (39:13-18)

She puts on a big show, flapping her wings proudly, but she's really stupid. Her flapping wings are impressive, but they aren't "the pinions and plumage of love" at all, because she has no concern for the baby ostriches that she hatches. She just lays her eggs and takes off for a night on the town; she even forgets where she lays them. Why? Because "God has made her forget wisdom, and given her no share in understanding." He did it intentionally! God can make his birds and animals stupid if he wants to; he can do anything he wants. She's stupid, but *boy is she fast*! When she races horses, she wins every time, and "laughs at the horse and his rider."

---

324   Isa. 6:3.

HORSES

Speaking of which, the Lord says, the horse laughs too, not at ostriches, but at men, at men trained for battle. The horse laughs at fear, unafraid of man's weapons. And though ostriches win races against the horse, the horse is really fast too: he gallops forward, he "swallows the ground" (39:24). We see this every May when we watch the Kentucky Derby: the cameras can barely keep up. And when the horse hears the trumpet for battle, he can't stand still. This is what he's been waiting for, the "thunder of the captains, and the shouting" (39:25).

GOOD EYESIGHT

The eye is an amazing organ. Mammals have two of them; some insects and fish have dozens. It's so complex that many evolutionists can't see how the eye came to be pursuant to their theory, because it had to "come to be" all at once. The theory of evolution says that body organs developed over millions of years, during which time little, incremental advantages to beasts increased their overall advantage, and gradually improved their chances of survival. This weeded out the poor creatures not so well endowed—those with something less than 20-20 vision, for example.

But, for evolutionists, the problem with the eye is that it would be of no advantage at all until it could actually *see*, and a little bud on a monkey's forehead couldn't do that. So the eye, in order to be of any advantage to the monkey, had to have been fully developed, all at once. That doesn't fit the millions of years theory. (An easier solution might be that someone designed and made the eye all at once).

Hawks (39:26-30) have eyes, and their eyes are a great advantage to them. Their survival depends on how far they can see, and they can see their prey from a very long way off—experts say from as much as a mile. I don't know how these hawk experts came to that conclusion. Perhaps they put the big bird in a chair and placed an eyesight chart in front of him, a mile away, clinically arranged with pictures of chipmunks and mice. Then they would have to ask the hawk if he could identify them. I'm just guessing. But I do know that God created the hawk, that he gave him everything he needs to live on, that his eyes worked fine the first day out without any trial runs, that man can't do it, and that on the fifth day of creation, "[God] saw that it was good."[325]

INTERMISSION

"So," the Lord says to Job, "do you believe you should argue with the Creator?"

> Shall a faultfinder contend with the Almighty?
> He who argues with God, let him answer it. (39:2)

The author doesn't tell us what Job's physical posture was when the Lord asked this question. But we are told that Job was through arguing, and that from now on he would be still[326] and know that God is God. He cupped his hand over his mouth. He was pretty much speechless, managing only a timid response:

> Behold, I am of small account;
>   what shall I answer you?
> I lay my hand on my mouth.
> I have spoken once, and I will not answer;
>   twice, but I will proceed no further. (39:4-5)

Job had been brought very low. He had come a great distance since he boldly asserted: "But I would speak to *El Shaddai*, and I desire to argue my case with God" (13:3), and "I will argue my ways to his face" (13:15). Now, feeling very small and insignificant, he doesn't even want to talk, not to utter a single syllable.

I've felt that way when I've been in court. I once represented a woman who, at the beginning, had a passably good case (so

---

325 Gen. 1:20-23.
326 "Be still, and know that I am God. I will be exalted among the nations, I will be exalted in the earth!" (Psa. 46:10).

I thought). The other lawyer didn't think our case was all that good, so it went to jury trial. By the time all the evidence was in, I didn't think our case was even *passably* good any more! But I had a responsibility to my client, and I was required to argue her case to the jury. I did so as best I could, but I really wanted to cover my mouth just as Job did. When you don't have anything to say, it's hard to say it.

Job had spent months trying to justify himself. He remembers that he had even *confronted* the Lord, that he had gone so far as to question God's justice, as when he asked: "Why are not times of judgment kept by the Almighty?" (24:1). But now he presses his hand against his mouth because he's utterly embarrassed about what he had said. He's thinking, How could I ever have thrust a paper at the Judge, and said such things—like "Here is my signature! Let *El Shaddai* answer me!" (31:35). How could I be so cocky and brainless? Job wishes he could take it all back, but he can't, because it's in the transcript.

When you are arguing with someone, it's devastating when they start quoting you, when you both remember what you said. "Will you even put me in the wrong? Will you condemn me that you may be in the right?" the Lord asks Job (40:8). Job knew that he had done so, time and again, as he mounted a defense against the accusations of his three friends.

The Lord towers over Job, who is sick, filthy, weak and almost dead. "Adorn yourself with majesty and dignity," the Lord thunders down; "clothe yourself with glory and splendor." Again, divine sarcasm. If you can do that, and "[l]ook on everyone who is proud and bring him low," then I'll yield, I'll cry "uncle!", and "acknowledge to you that your own right hand can save you." (40:10-14).

BEHEMOTH

In the previous chapter of this book we talked about the fact that commentators on the Book of Job don't know exactly who

Elihu is. Behemoth, described by the Lord in 40:15-24, is the same. Not so much in physical appearance, because Behemoth had a tail and Elihu probably didn't. Their similarity lies in the fact that both are hard to identify.

Some scholars believe that both Behemoth and Leviathan[327] were mythical beasts. But these two beasts aren't denominated as mythical, and further, all of the other things and creatures that the Lord has described up to this point were real. Stars, ravens, ostriches and horses are real, physical things or beings. God is describing his *creation*, which consists of real things.

That's the whole point: he is telling Job that I *really* made these things. God is displaying his glory when he describes Behemoth and Leviathan, and it wouldn't be any glory at all if he were describing fanciful beings. Children can do that, and may impress us with their imagination when they draw pictures of dragons that don't really exist. But God's glory is revealed through what really does exist, what he has actually made. God is not drawing a picture of something that he *might* have made, like a unicorn, because we can all do that.

Many have thought that Behemoth is a hippopotamus and Leviathan a crocodile.[328] Some of what the Lord tells us about them would fit those hypotheses. Behemoth is a herbivore because he "eats grass like an ox"; in this respect, he is like the hippopotamus. He has powerful abdominal muscles, and his bones and limbs are like "tubes of bronze" and "bars of iron." He lies under the lotus tree for shade; he likes the marshy area; he lies in the river and "is confident though Jordan rushes against his mouth." (40:15-23). Perhaps all of these attributes fit the hippopotamus.

But there are other things the Lord tells Job about Behemoth that don't fit the hippo so well. Behemoth is "the first of the

---

327 The Lord describes Leviathan in Chapter 41.
328 Samuel Rolles Driver and George Buchanan Gray, *A Critical and Exegetical Commentary on The Book of Job* (T. & T. Clark, Edinburgh, 1921), p. 352.

works of God" (40:19). Amazing as a hippopotamus may be—weighing in at up to 10,000 pounds, for example—it's hard for me to believe that the Lord would put him at the top of his list. And then there's the tail, which the Lord says the behemoth can make "stiff like a cedar." The hippopotamus' tail doesn't do that; it just basically dangles.

I think in this case a better candidate is a dinosaur. It would have to be one of the plant-eating variety, it would have to be big with strong bones, and it would have to have a tail that could be made "stiff like cedar." Several species would probably fit these criteria, and (it seems to me) one of them would be *Triceratops*. These rhinoceros-like beasts were herbivores, eating massive amounts of grass and other greenery every day. They are estimated to have weighed up to 26,000 pounds, and were up to 30 feet long and 10 feet tall. They were quadrupeds, with exceptionally strong bones and a powerful muscular build. Their tails were relatively short and stiff.

Whether these characteristics would qualify *Triceratops* over the hippo as a candidate for "the first of the works of God" billing is hard to say. But personally, I would defer to a charging 13-ton *Triceratops* even more readily than I would to a hippopotamus weighing 8 tons less!

Whatever, or whoever, Behemoth was, it's clear that the Lord is now shifting his emphasis. In his previous descriptions of animals and birds, he did not stress power, but with Behemoth and Leviathan, it's all about size and power.

NO CONTROL

When the Lord talked to Job about the ostrich, he was telling Job that there is a whole lot out about creation that people just don't know and don't understand. In this, God was implying that they don't have to understand, because, as Sanderson says, God knows and that's all that really matters.

But God is saying something additional when he describes Behemoth and Leviathan. Not only don't you understand these beasts, Job, or why I made them to be like they are, but you can't control them. Regarding Behemoth, he asks Job,

> Can one take him by his eyes,
>   or pierce his nose with a snare? (40:24)

and regarding Leviathan,

> Can you draw out Leviathan with a fishhook
>   or press down his tongue with a cord?
> Can you put a rope in his nose
>   or pierce his jaw with a hook?
> Will he make many pleas to you?
> Will he speak to you soft words?
> Will he make a covenant with you
>   to take him for your servant forever?
> Will you play with him as with a bird,
>   or will you put him on a leash for your girls?
>   (41:1-5)

Job had to check the "no" box for every one of these questions. These creatures are overwhelming, and the Lord uses them to show Job that life on earth is a series of Behemoths and Leviathans, that is, a series of things and events that people can't control.

And it is exactly because they are overwhelming that God is describing them to Job. He wants Job to feel so overwhelmed that he will be forced to look for answers and protection from a source other than himself.

In reminding Job of the vastness and the intricacy of his creation, the Lord is both humbling and freeing him. Humbling him, because Job is learning that he has a very limited understanding of creation, and virtually nothing to do with running it. Freeing him, because he doesn't have to run it. God sovereignly controls and provides for everything and everybody he created, including Job. It also includes Satan.

LEVIATHAN

God created Leviathan. He is mentioned elsewhere in Scripture, and he lives in the sea but apparently also on land.[329] He differs from all the other animals and birds described here in Job because he is characterized as evil: "You crushed the heads of Leviathan,"[330] and "In that day the LORD with his hard and great and strong sword will punish Leviathan."[331] He has multiple heads.[332]

He has become famous in literature and art, including that geared to children. The Lord describes him like this:

> His sneezings flash forth light,
> and his eyes are like the eyelids of the dawn.
> Out of his mouth go flaming torches;
> sparks of fire leap forth.
> Out of his nostrils comes forth smoke,
> as from a boiling pot and burning rushes.
> His breath kindles coals,
> and a flame comes forth from his mouth.
> (41:18-21)

Reading this description will doubtless rustle up story-book pictures in the reader's mind, pictures of enormous, vicious, fire-breathing mythical beasts. Unfortunately, however, Leviathan is not mythical, but an actual created monster. At the same time, it's "fortunate" that this beast is an actual *created* monster, because that means the Creator has control over him.

---

329 The Psalmist says: "You crushed the heads of Leviathan; you gave him as food for the creatures of the wilderness" (Psa. 74:14), indicating that the monster lived in the wilderness with other land creatures. He is also described as a sea monster here in Chapter 41, as well as in Psa. 104:26.

330 Psa. 74:14.

331 Isa. 27:1.

332 Psa. 74:14.

Leviathan isn't named *per se* in Revelation, but the beast or dragon described there sounds very much like him: "And I saw a beast rising out of the sea, with ten horns and seven heads, with ten diadems on its horns and blasphemous names on its heads."[333] The dragon of the Apocalypse is identified as Satan himself.[334]

The Lord ends his description of Leviathan with this summary:

> On earth there is not his like,
>> a creature without fear.
> He sees everything that is high;
>> he is king over all the sons of pride. (41:33-34)

I believe there is little doubt but that Leviathan is Satan. Who other than Satan can rightly be called the "king over all the sons of pride?"[335] This is the Evil One who "takes his seat in the temple of God, proclaiming himself to be God."[336] And no one on earth can come close to matching his power. Luther wrote:

> For still our ancient foe
>> doth seek to work us woe;
> His craft and power are great,
>> and armed with cruel hate,
>> on earth is not his equal.[337]

People today too often treat Satan as a joke, a little imp whispering suggestions of harmless practical jokes into our ears. All in fun. But Satan is no joke. Have you ever had a battle with Satan, and tried to handle it on your own? If you have, you'd have the same advice for Job that the Lord gives him: "remember the battle—you will not do it again!" (41:8).

On Halloween night, 1975, I suffered a total mental collapse, a psychotic episode, secondary to what the doctors later diagnosed as bi-polar disorder. I had not known that I suffered from bipolar

---

333   Rev. 13:1.
334   Rev. 20:2.
335   See Eze. 28:1-19.
336   2 Thess. 2:4.
337   "A Mighty Fortress Is Our God," Martin Luther (1483-1546), stanza 1b.

disease, but learned through that experience that it is indeed very serious, life-long, and treatable.

In that "episode" I learned something else: the terrifying reality of Satan. He sees openings and exploits them. Just like a lion going after his prey, he'll go after the zebra who runs with a limp. I was the one running with a limp, and from the night of the psychosis on, through the following six months of intensive treatment, Satan invaded my brain and whole being. I was afraid to go to bed at night because that was when he'd attack—every night. I seriously believed that I was going to die, and I think I would have if the Lord hadn't intervened.

On a day in early May, 1976, when I was alone in the car, I literally screamed out to the Lord for help. I told him that I was dying; that (though my doctor was doing his best) it was obvious to me by this time that no one could help me but God alone. I shouted back to him, in desperation, his promise in Psalm 91, which I had been required to memorize as a child:

> You will not fear the terror of the night,
> > nor the arrow that flies by day,
> > nor the pestilence that stalks in darkness,
> > nor the destruction that wastes at noonday.
> > > (Psa. 91:5-6)

That night, when I lay down on the bed, I was just trying to doze off when I had the sense that something above me was shattering like glass, then falling softly all over the bed, like tiny crystals of ice. The terror evaporated. Quiet peace came at once, and it came to stay. I have had no attacks like that since. I still find myself thanking God when I remember it because it was altogether his work. I no longer fear "the terror of the night." But I will remember the battle. I never want to lay my hands on Satan again.

A COMFORT TO JOB

Do you think Job gained any comfort from the Lord's fearsome description of Leviathan? On the surface, it seems as though it might have had the reverse effect, and would have kept Job from being able to sleep at night, just like me.

Satan had attacked Job twice in the first two chapters of the book. Satan had nearly devoured him, and would have finished him off had the Lord allowed him to. Because, for a time, God had removed the "hedge" around Job he was vulnerable to Satan's attacks and utterly helpless. The Lord had told Satan that Job "is in your hand" (2:6). But Satan is in someone's hand too.

In Chapter 41, the Lord is describing for Job the one who had attacked him—the one who had taken all he had, killed his children, and ruined his health. We said previously that Job's possessions, mentioned in Job Chapters 1 and 42, provide bookends. But Satan amounts to a second set of bookends—terrifying and evil ones. The description the Lord gives is all about the fact that man has no control over, or defense against, this mighty dragon. "Terror dances before him" (41:22), "the mighty are afraid" (41:25), and man "is laid low even at the sight of him" (41:9). That's why Luther wrote that "on earth is not his equal."

The Lord's underlying assurance to Job is this: *I created Satan.* I control him. He's mine, for "[w]hatever is under the whole heaven is mine" (41:11). I made Pleiades, the wild donkey, ravens, and Satan. I made everything and everybody. And I made you right along with them![338] You can't do any of that, nor can you provide or care for them, but I can and I do. No creature of mine can do anything apart from my permission and control. You need not be terrified of the devil; you need to fear me.

What an awesome God, and what a comfort to Job! It turns out that the Book of Job isn't first and foremost all about Job—it's all about God and his glory. Sanderson says that the Book of Job is *"a revelation of the glory of God, and of the implications which that revelation has for our faith in binding us back to God."*[339]

---

338 "Behold, Behemoth, which I made as I made you." (40:15).

339 I JWS 75-120A-A.

That's exactly where Job finds himself, still prostrate on a heap of ashes, but *bound back to God*.

In Chapter 1 he's described as a man of prayer, a man of faith, a man who trusted God enough to accept evil as well as good from his hand. Job had been severely challenged in his faith, now and again had taken some detours, and had wobbled, but here he is— battle-scarred but intact. The Holy Spirit had preserved him, and he discovers that though all the fury of hell had been unleashed against him, it had accomplished nothing other than to drive him back, to bind him back, into the loving hand of the God who made him. Luther, who encountered Satan head-on more than once, wrote these wonderfully comforting words:

> And though this world, with devils filled,
> Should threaten to undo us,
> We will not fear, for God hath willed
> His truth to triumph through us:
> The Prince of Darkness grim,
> We tremble not for him;
> His rage we can endure,
> For lo! his doom is sure,
> One little word shall fell him.
>
> That word above all earthly powers,
> No thanks to them, abideth;
> The Spirit and the gifts are ours
> Through Him who with us sideth:
> Let goods and kindred go,
> This mortal life also;
> The body they may kill:
> God's truth abideth still,
> His Kingdom is forever. [340]

---

340 "A Mighty Fortress Is Our God," Martin Luther (1483-1546), stanzas 3 and 4.

FOR REFLECTION

1.

Why do you think the Lord spoke only of his creation in his theophany? How did this help Job, if at all? Was what he said at all relevant to Job's problems? How did the two relate, if at all?

2.

Did God answer any of Job's questions in what he said about creation, either directly or indirectly? If so, which ones?

3.

Can you think of some reasons that the Lord might have had for not telling Job (or us) why he had been put through this trial? That is, give possible reasons why God did not specifically answer the question "Why do the righteous suffer?" Did what God said to Job in the theophany in any way give Job some answers to this question?

4.

Sanderson says that it's helpful for us to look at the hippopotamus, because the beast seems inexplicable. How does seeing something in creation that you can't explain help you in dealing with life's problems? How would this have helped Job?

5.

Have you ever had what you believed to be a direct confrontation with Satan? How did you deal with it? Is there anything that the Lord said in his description of Leviathan that reminds you of that experience?

MARK BELZ

18.

JUDGMENT DAY

CHAPTER 42:1-9

IN THE YEAR that King Uzziah died, Isaiah the prophet "saw the LORD sitting upon a throne, high and lifted up, and the train of his robe filled the temple." Isaiah heard the seraphim cry out: "Holy, holy, holy is the LORD of hosts; the whole earth is full of his glory!" The foundation of the temple shook, and it was filled with smoke.[341]

Isaiah's immediate response was: "Woe is me! For I am lost; for I am a man of unclean lips, and I dwell in the midst of a people of unclean lips; for my eyes have seen the King, the LORD of hosts!"[342]

It's an awesome event when the Lord comes to visit. His presence alone brings an overwhelming sense of lostness, insufficiency, uncleanness and shame.

JOB REPENTS

Like Isaiah, Job had seen the King, the Lord of hosts, had witnessed firsthand that "the whole earth is full of his glory," and had Isaiah's same reaction. After the Lord had finished, Job answered

---

341 Isa. 6:1-4.
342 Isa. 6:5.

him with a confession that has become a confession of believers to this day who know what it means to "repent in dust and ashes":

> I know that you can do all things,
>> and that no purpose of yours can be thwarted.
> "Who is this that hides counsel without
>> knowledge?"
> Therefore I have uttered what I did not
>> understand,
>> things too wonderful for me,
>> which I did not know.
> "Hear, and I will speak;
> I will question you, and you make it known to
>> me."
> I had heard of you by the hearing of the ear,
>> but now my eye sees you;
>> therefore I despise myself,
>> and repent in dust and ashes. (42:2-6)

These five verses are wonderfully composed. We should memorize them and make them our own. The first sentence is an acknowledgement of God as God Almighty, *El Shaddai*: "I know that you can do all things" (you can do anything you want), and "no purpose of yours can be thwarted" (no-one can stop you). "Lord," Job is saying, "you are who you say you are. I believe you. I unreservedly acknowledge your infinite, sovereign, wise power. I own that as the pinion of my faith."

We will never get the rest of our faith straight until we come to this understanding. We may have to go through the trials of Job to get there, but whatever it takes, it's worth it. And where God needs to "get" us is deep in our hearts, so we feel it, and don't have to recite it to remember. Everything in our lives flows from the sovereignty of God, and a deep joy results when we fully own that great truth.

Job is there now, and based on that humble and happy acknowledgement, he takes care to respond to two things that the

Lord had said when he first spoke to him out of the storm. Job recites the Lord's words, almost like a child repeating a catechism question, because he believes he is responsible to respond specifically to the Lord's specific question. After all, *El Shaddai* told me to respond, so I'd better respond!

The first was the rhetorical question the Lord had asked Job in 38:2, the first words out of the Lord's mouth: "Who is this that darkens counsel without knowledge?" Because it was rhetorical, Job really didn't need to respond. The answer, of course, was obvious. But he painfully and dutifully recites the question, and his response is unreserved penitence: "I uttered what I did not understand, things too wonderful for me, which I did not know." It's as though Job is pointing at himself, and saying, "Over here, Lord! I'm the one you're looking for! I'm the one who said those things! And I didn't know what I was talking about."

Job's second response is to the Lord's challenge in 38:3 and repeated in 40:7, where he had said to Job: "I will question you, and you make it known to me." Job recites that as well, but doesn't endeavor a response, except to say that before God appeared to him in the storm, he had only heard about him. Now, however, he says that "my eye sees you; therefore I despise myself, and repent in dust and ashes." There is an enormous difference between hearing *about* God, and hearing *from* God.[343]

What was the object of Job's repentance? What had he done to make him despise himself in the presence of the Lord? In general, as mentioned, any mortal will immediately react with Isaiah's "Woe is me!" because man is instinctively aware of his sinful state

---

343 Abraham felt the same as Job, when he pled directly with the Lord for his nephew Lot: "Behold, I have undertaken to speak to the LORD, I who am but dust and ashes" (Gen. 18:27). Simon Peter had the same reaction when Jesus miraculously filled the disciples' nets with fish: "[W]hen Simon Peter saw it, he fell down at Jesus' knees, saying, "Depart from me, for I am a sinful man, O Lord." (Lk. 5:8).

when he is brought into the presence of Holy God. Job felt this, of course, just as Isaiah did.

But with Job there's something more. Job had questioned the wisdom of God. True enough, at the start, his response to the first catastrophe was unquestioning faith in God's wisdom: "The LORD gave, and the LORD has taken away; blessed be the name of the LORD" (1:21). But after his health was ruined, and the grinding pain worsened, he began to see that God wasn't intervening, and gave ground. He began to question God's justice, both in the way God treated the wicked and the way God treated him. In Chapter 31, he polished off his speeches with a filthy rag, a litany of his own good deeds, the implication being that the Lord had *failed*— failed to give adequate consideration to Job's righteousness.

Job repents now because the theophany has brought him up short. Maybe it was his trip to the zoo, when the Lord showed him the hippopotamus, which Sanderson described as "stupid looking, awkward, ugly—just a great big mound of blubber." Job couldn't make sense of the fact that God had created such a seemingly ridiculous beast, nor could Job understand why God had brought calamity on him. Both were ugly; both were inexplicable. But as Sanderson said, there are all kinds of things God has made and done that we can't understand, and that's okay, because "God does understand, and God doesn't make any mistakes." When we entrust the hippopotamus and everything else to him, we find, as Job did, that "the glory of God comes across as *wisdom*."[344] Job now rests in that wisdom, and repents for having risen up to question it.

No answer is given in the Book of Job as to why Job was made to suffer so. Was it deserved? No. Was it needed? In God's economy, apparently yes. Do we know why it was needed? No, and it's not our responsibility and certainly not our right to know why. Like Job, we must confess that these things are "too wonderful"

---

344 2 JWS 75-120A-B.

for us, and we simply leave the matter there, in God's sovereign, protective and loving hand.

THREE FRIENDS IN THE DOCK

The Lord had pretty soundly rebuked his servant Job, but he's done with that now, and Job has repented. And though the Lord's words from 38:1-41:34 had been addressed to Job, the three friends were paying close attention.

What was going through their minds as they heard the Lord speak? They had been permitted to tag along with the Lord and Job to the zoo and planetarium, and like Job, they probably wondered what all this had to do with their debate. But they could also see that the Lord was rebuking Job, and he wasn't even mentioning them. That was a good sign. It sounded a whole lot like they were going to be vindicated, that the verdict would be in their favor.

If that's what they thought, they were mistaken, because the Lord next turned to Eliphaz, committee chairman, and said: "My anger burns against you and against your two friends, for you have not spoken of me what is right, as my servant Job has" (42:7). This had to be shocking to Eliphaz, Zophar and Bildad. This seemed a divine non-sequitur.

First, in what way had they not spoken of God what was right? That was a head-scratcher, because they had argued, all the way through, that God was transcendent, perfect, omniscient, gracious, and just. Is there any way in which they had transgressed the Westminster Divines, who wrote that "God is a spirit, infinite, eternal and unchangeable, in his being, wisdom, power, holiness, justice, goodness and truth"[345]? In this regard (and what other 'regard' could there possibly be?) their theology seemed air-tight. Maybe they had missed something, but still, they were fiercely and doggedly orthodox. Just examine the transcript.

---

345 *Westminster Shorter Catechism,* Q. 4.

But even more shocking to Eliphaz and the other two was the second half of the Lord's verdict: Job has spoken of me what is *right*. How is that possible? Didn't the Lord, just moments before, thoroughly castigate Job? We were listening when God asked Job "Who is this that darkens counsel by words without knowledge?" (38:2), and when he riddled Job with sarcasm. How could someone who darkens counsel by words without knowledge be *right*? It sounded to us like the Lord was scolding Job because he hadn't said anything right about him at all!

WHERE DID THE FRIENDS GO WRONG?

We know, from the Lord's verdict, that the three friends had gotten off track—so far off track, in fact, that they had incurred God's wrath. But we must be humble in judging them, because if they erred in their judgment, we can do so just as easily. Besides, it is not ours to judge. The Lord has judged them here, and has revealed his judgment to us. We can't judge, but in light of God's judgment, we must examine what they said so that we can avoid similar error.

Surely a fundamental error in their thinking, and their subsequent approach to Job, was the Eliphaz Formula: during this life, sin always produces trouble, and trouble is always proof positive of sin. That was their foundational theology, and it was false. They had refused to give it up in spite of Job's repeated and truthful protestations that he had no hidden sins to confess. Thus their theology became accusatory and mean-spirited. In doggedly pursuing Job's guilt when he wasn't guilty, they had hurt their friend terribly.

And while injuring their friend, they also said something wrong about God. They had put God in a box: God *must* punish sinners with a troubled life, and God *must* reward righteousness with a trouble-free life. Always. Never mind the evidence that many unrepentant sinners don't have much trouble. Never mind the evidence that obedient children of God often have terrible trouble. They couldn't allow themselves to consider the possibility that God may be doing with Job what he did with the Apostle Paul, when he told Ananias: "I will show him how much he must suffer for my name."[346] They also couldn't allow for the possibility that someday a perfect man would atone for their sin, suffering death on a cross. To them, any cross would have to have been deserved, and would constitute proof of sin committed by the person hanging there. No, they had said of God what was wrong.

THEY DID NOT PRAY FOR JOB

There was a second error in the friends' theology. It wasn't that the words or phrases they used to describe God were wrong, but it was an error evidenced by their grammar. Perhaps you noticed, as they waxed eloquent in lecturing Job on the nature of God: not once did they speak in the second person. *Not once.* They always spoke of God in the third person. They spoke much *about* God, but never *to* God.

Really, this is remarkable. They were obviously godly men. They were Job's good friends. They were concerned about him so much that when they heard of his colossal losses, bereavement of ten children, and life-threatening illness they met together to arrange a time to visit him. When they arrived for the visit they suffered with him, sitting in a semicircle around him for a week, not uttering a word. They loved Job dearly, they really did. But from the time Eliphaz opened his mouth in 4:1 all the way through Bildad's abrupt, final statement in 25:6 where he essentially called Job a maggot, these men uttered not a syllable of prayer for their dying friend. As mentioned previously, Sanderson says, with regard to the friends, that they teach us in the negative: "You might read their speeches, and learn how *not* to do hospital counseling—and how not to do a few other things too."[347]

---

346   Acts 9:15-16.

347   I JWS 75-120A-A.

Of the four, Job is the only one on record who prayed. His responses to his friends' arguments become shorter and quieter, and his cries to the Lord grew longer and louder. It's as though the three are standing in his hospital room on one side of the bed, preaching away at him, reading him sections of the Confession of Faith and Catechism, while Job turns his face to the opposite wall to cry out to God for help, as a sick and dying King Hezekiah did centuries later.[348]

Whenever I see a new doctor for some new ailment, I'm required to sit in the waiting room with a clipboard and list all the hospitalizations I've had during my life. I realize, of course, that this is basically a subtle way of administering a memory test; I don't think they are really interested in why I've been in the hospital through the years. I start with the tonsillectomy I had at age 3, and try to remember all the other times I've been so incarcerated up through, right now, age 73. For whatever reasons, I have been hospitalized way more than the average person.

At such times, Christian friends have always come to visit. I cannot remember one time when such a friend visited that he or she didn't pray for me. And I can also testify that in every case, God graciously chose to answer their prayer by healing me. My friends believed that God was a God of mercy, the Great Physician, the God who was right there in the hospital room with us, the God who hears and answers prayer. When they prayed, they were speaking *to* God, and in doing so, they were making a profound statement *about* God. They were "speaking of God what is right," because they treated God as a person, not as a thing, a concept, or a systematic theology. And for those reasons, when

---

348 When Judah's King Hezekiah was sick and about to die, he beseeched the Lord for healing: "Then Hezekiah turned his face to the wall and prayed to the Lord, and said, 'Please, O Lord, remember how I have walked before you in faithfulness and with a whole heart, and have done what is good in your sight.' And Hezekiah wept bitterly" (Isa. 38:2-3). The Lord answered his prayer and granted him an additional 15 years of life.

Eliphaz, Zophar and Bildad failed to pray for their friend, they were "speaking of God what is wrong."

THEY BLAMED JOB

The third, and I think most significant, error that the friends committed is related to the first, the Eliphaz Formula. That theology falsely held that trouble is always a result of sin. So in telling Job that his trouble was a result of his unconfessed, hidden sin, they placed the entire burden for his suffering on his shoulders. Thus they savaged the sovereignty of God. "Job," they had said, "you brought this on yourself because of your sin. You are choosing to keep it *on* yourself because you insist on keeping it *to* yourself. As long as you persist in hiding your sin, there's nothing that we can do, and what's more, there's nothing God can do either. The whole thing is up to you. Your life is in your hands."

But Job's life wasn't in Job's hands. It was in God's hands. Job couldn't do anything about it at all; he had no control whatever over his plight. The friends could not see that the whole matter was a subject of God's sovereign purposes, because that would admit to mystery, and too many theologians can't bear mystery; they have to figure everything out and get it nailed down. But you can't nail down *El Shaddai* because, as Sanderson taught, he would then no longer be *El Shaddai*.[349] That was the friends' chief error.

POETIC JUSTICE

So the guilty verdict has been handed down against Job's three friends. What to do? If God were now to adopt their theology, the Eliphaz Formula, things looked really bleak, for that theology holds, in part, that sin always means trouble. What's more, serious sin means serious trouble. That's what Eliphaz had tried to impress upon Job in Chapter 22. And now God has told Eliphaz that their sin was so serious that "[m]y anger burns against you."

---

349   13 JWS 75-123A-A.

Unfortunately for the three, the principle of poetic justice is in Scripture. It's in the Sermon on the Mount, where Jesus said "Judge not, that ye be not judged."[350] And it's exemplified in many other ways in the Bible. The Israelites had been delivered from the plagues of Egypt, but if they turned from God to serve other gods, Moses warned them, "God will bring upon you again all the diseases of Egypt, of which you were afraid, and they shall cling to you."[351] Wicked Haman experienced fatal poetic justice when he was hanged on the very scaffold he had built to hang righteous Mordecai.[352] Even a Canaanite king, Adoni-bezek, recognized the principle after he had humiliated seventy other kings, and Joshua then humiliated him by chopping off his thumbs and big toes. Adoni-bezek reflected on what had just happened to him: "Seventy kings with their thumbs and their big toes cut off used to pick up scraps under my table. As I have done, so God has repaid me."[353] Eye for an eye, tooth for a tooth.[354]

So God knows how to exercise poetic justice, and the three friends had no good reason to expect that he wouldn't employ it here. If there ever were a perfect case for it, this would seem to be it.

REBUKED BY GRACE

But we must remember that *El Shaddai* refuses to be nailed down. He's unpredictable. You just can't figure him out. He does a surprising, amazing and wonderful thing for Job's friends. He will humble them, he will rebuke them, and he will prove to them that they were second-rate theologians. But he is not going to hang them on the scaffold they had built for Job.

---

350 Mt. 7:1, KJV.
351 Deut. 28:60.
352 Esth. 7:10.
353 Josh. 1:7.
354 Lev. 24:20.

What the Lord will do is teach them in the most powerful and loving way that their theology is wrong. He is going to show them this by sparing them from suffering for their sin. *He is going to show them that their theology is false by forgiving them.*

They may have thought that their flocks and herds would be destroyed, that their children would be killed by a tornado, that their bodies would be covered with boils. Poetic justice would have been served in that way, but it's not going to happen. Why? Because sin doesn't always bring suffering. God's abundant grace often alters that outcome. The Eliphaz Formula was wrong. They hadn't factored grace into the equation when they met together on their way to see Job. They hadn't factored in the power of the cross.

REPENTANCE AND FORGIVENESS

For these men, the cross was still two thousand years in the future. They didn't know about Jesus. But in the Old Testament, God taught his people much about the cross, about substitutionary atonement through blood sacrifice and repentance. God now not only makes this available for Eliphaz, Bildad and Zophar, but he *commands* them[355] to avail themselves of it:

> "Now therefore take seven bulls and seven rams and go to my servant Job and offer up a burnt offering for yourselves. And my servant Job shall pray for you, for I will accept his prayer not to deal with you according to your folly. For you have not spoken of me what is right, as my servant Job has." So Eliphaz the Temanite and Bildad the Shuhite and Zophar the Naamathite went and did what the LORD had told them, and the LORD accepted Job's prayer. (42:8-9)

---

355   When the Apostle Paul addressed the Areopagus in Athens, he told those gathered there that "[God] *commands* all people everywhere to repent" (Acts 17:30). Refusal to accept the free offer of the gospel is the ultimate disobedience.

The Lord is doing many things here, both to discipline and to bless. He is God, and directs the whole transaction.

REBUKED BY INTERCESSION

He first tells Eliphaz that he's appointed Job as the mediator. The one whom Eliphaz had accused of withholding bread from the hungry,[356] whom Zophar had called "stupid,"[357] and whom Bildad had called a "maggot,"[358] God now appoints as their intercessor. And he tells them to "go to my servant Job," indicating that they were to approach their friend and ask him for help, to ask him to act as their representative before *El Shaddai*.

Obviously, this was humbling for Eliphaz, Bildad and Zophar. In their persistent, blind criticism of Job, it had never occurred to them that Job would later be appointed as their mediator. They had not thought that they would ever need one anyway, but in case they did need one—*Job*? He's the maggot!

But the Lord's lesson for the three is meant not only to humble, but to teach. They had expounded truths about God to Job for days on end but had failed to pray for him. God is going to teach them to pray for others by having Job pray for them. God is showing them that he's a personal God, not a systematic theology. He's right there in the hospital room, right there on the ash heap. He hears and answers prayer. Prayer changes things, and when Job prays for Eliphaz, Bildad and Zophar, it's going to change things radically for them, and all for their good: they will be forgiven for their foolishness, "for I will accept his prayer not to deal with you according to your folly" (42:8).

HUMBLING FOR JOB, TOO

When the Lord commissioned Job to pray for his friends, it was humbling for Job too. He maybe wasn't all that excited about

---

356   22:7.
357   11:12.
358   25:6.

praying for the three so soon after they had insulted, abused, and wrongfully accused him. It might take some time for his feathers to be smoothed. But the Lord doesn't ask Job if he's up to it, or willing. He simply states, as a matter of fact, what's going to happen: "Job shall pray for you." God is sovereign, and he always makes a particular point of his sovereignty in the business of salvation, because salvation belongs to God alone.[359]

The friends obeyed. Job obeyed. God accepted Job's prayer.

And as mentioned, God was doing more than one thing here, all clustered around a simple intercessory prayer. He was actually performing a miracle.

RECONCILIATION ACCOMPLISHED

The miracle was that these four men became reconciled—reconciled to one another, and reconciled to God.

Reconciliation isn't just getting along. That's done every day without miracles. Biblical reconciliation, the kind that really matters and lasts forever, is love, a fruit of the Holy Spirit, accomplished in us by him alone. It's divine, supernatural love. Reading the last two-thirds of the friends' speeches yields no evidence of love from these men, but the opposite. Job's speeches don't evidence love either. From a worldly point of view, their relationships seemed irreparable. But when God enters the picture, and works in us, things are no longer from "a worldly point of view." Paul says: "from now on we regard no one from a worldly point of view."[360]

This could happen only because the men were first reconciled to God. The men were brought near to God when Job prayed for them and God answered his prayer. When we come near to God, of necessity we come near to one another, like it or not! And when we come into the presence of God, pride evaporates in the

359 Psa. 3:8, 62:1; Rev. 7:10.
360 2 Cor. 5:16, NIV.

blinding light of his glory. Pride is what had blocked us from loving and praying for people who have called us "maggots."

So the relationships were wonderfully healed. It's possible that Job had been physically healed by this time as well; we aren't told. Because of what follows in 42:10-17, it's obvious that he was healed at some point, because he lived another 140 years!—but the poor man is still poverty-stricken and bereaved of his children. The Lord has a pretty remarkable surprise for Job along those lines too.

FOR REFLECTION

I.

After the Lord spoke, Job said "I repent in dust and ashes." What was he repenting of? Was he admitting that the three friends were correct in their claim that he had hidden, unconfessed sin? If not, then why was he repenting, and was repentance merited?

2.

In what ways do you think the three friends "spoke of God what was wrong"? In what ways did Job "speak of God what was right"?

3.

Was God really equitable in delivering the three from punishment, when they had sinned, while making Job suffer so much, when he had not sinned? What truths can be learned from this apparent disparity?

19.

JOB'S SECOND LIFE

CHAPTER 42:10-17

AND THE LORD RESTORED the fortunes of Job, when he had prayed for his friends." Note that in dismantling the Eliphaz Formula, the Lord did not say that obedience always results in suffering. Praise God for that! Here, Job obeyed God's command, prayed for his friends, and God blessed him greatly. If he had been called the "greatest man in all the east" in Chapter 1, he ought now to be called the "greatest *greatest* man in all the east" because his portfolio, and his family, double: "And the LORD gave Job twice as much as he had before" (42:10).

JOB'S SHOWERS

Just about everything in the Book of Job happened *to* Job. These things were like showers—some wonderful and welcome showers; some not so wonderful and most unwelcome. They were different kinds of showers, three of them literal, and the rest figurative.

The first was a shower of blessings, when God blessed Job with great possessions, a great family, great friends, great wisdom, and a great reputation. *Everything* was great. The second was a shower of destruction, Satan's work, taking all his possessions and killing his children (the storm that took Job's children was literal). The third was another storm from Satan, this one destroying his health and very nearly taking his life. The fourth was a long, long shower—not a shower of blessings or compliments, but a shower raining down criticism, accusation, and vitriol, as Eliphaz, Zophar and Bildad went at him tooth and tong.

The fifth was another literal shower, the rainstorm and twisters that Elihu predicted and then described. It may have been a bit unwelcome when it started, because it was scary, but welcome because it brought relief from the hot weather, and more significantly, ushered in the Lord himself.

The sixth was a divine shower of stars, ostriches, horses, hippos and dinosaurs. It was raining cats and dogs! This shower made Job feel very, very small.

THE SEVENTH SHOWER

The seventh shower was one of the welcome variety. And it was literal. But in this case the word "shower" had a different meaning. It was a housewarming, like a bridal shower. It was tender and loving. Typically, men don't get showers like this, but Job did, because his friends and family knew he needed help:

> Then came to him all his brothers and sisters and all who had known him before, and ate bread with him in his house. And they showed him sympathy and comforted him for all the evil that the LORD had brought upon him. And each of them gave him a piece of money and a ring of gold. (42:11)

As a lawyer, in my earlier days, and having been told by a senior partner that it was important to appear prosperous, because people think prosperity is a sign of success,[361] I would fight people for the check at restaurants. A couple of times it became physical, as in arm-wrestling. In the physical ones I lost out. But in the others I usually won, and as a consequence, my credit card was perpetually maxed out. In my case, it was vanity, not generosity.

In 2003, I had a serious financial collapse, altogether due to my mismanagement. During this time, I took our three grandchildren to a hamburger joint—nothing fancy. We ordered and ate, and the waiter handed me the check. As I remember, it was about $18, but I looked in my wallet and I had only a ten-dollar bill, and two credit cards that I knew had "declined" written all over them (I hate seeing that word pop up at checkout). I was embarrassed, of course, and feared I'd have to wash dishes, or possibly be jailed and executed.

It was opportune, though, that I had brought our grandchildren. They were of course the cutest, smartest and sweetest kids in the world, and an older couple seated two tables away could see that that was true. The lady came to our table and said what a wonderful family we had, and that she had some extra coupons for free hamburgers and others for half-off shakes. That's just what we had ordered and already eaten! I thanked her profusely and yanked those precious coupons from her hand. I wound up paying only about $5 for the whole thing. I was very, very grateful for someone else "picking up the check," and for the fact that I still had money in my wallet.

It's almost impossible to accept financial help when you have just enough room on the card and want to appear prosperous. But it's easy as pie when the card is maxed out.

I'm thankful my wallet wasn't sufficient to buoy my vanity that evening at Steak 'n Shake because that experience worked a profound change in my life. It really did, and the change has been

---

361   Not every lawyer believes this silliness. Another older partner told me never to fake anything; that dishonesty shows.

(I hope) permanent. I no longer feel it mandatory that I pick up checks at restaurants or anywhere else. It was humbling and freeing.

The picture we get of Job is that he was not a vain man, but I'd venture a guess that he had been accustomed to picking up the check too. People expected him to, because of his wealth. But now, like me, he just wasn't able to pay the bill, and like me, being forced to recognize that inability brought *freedom*. Humility, even when forced on you, always brings freedom.[362]

This seventh shower also blessed Job with a depth of intimacy he likely had not had a chance to experience in his first life (Chapter 1). Look who turned up at the party: all his brothers and sisters and all who had known him before. A Jimmy Stewart moment! Sometimes it turns out to be a great thing to fall $8,000 short at the Savings and Loan, or to lose all your camels, because all your brothers and sisters and all who knew you before come over to visit. And they help you out. Here they gave Job what they could: each a piece of money and a ring of gold (they were well organized), just what he needed to start up housekeeping again.

Job was becoming a different man. He was being sanctified, though not because he had sinned as Eliphaz had claimed. Sanctification includes much more than dealing with past sin. It's broader, deeper, and more profound. It is "the work of God's free grace, whereby we are *renewed in the whole man* after the image of God, and are enabled more and more to die unto sin, and live unto righteousness"[363] (emphasis added). Jesus himself, amazingly, participated in sanctification by being *perfected*: like Job, in his life on earth he was being made "perfect through suffering."[364]

This little shower proved to be a big shower, showing Job that he didn't have to bear everyone else's burden like he thought he

---

362 "The ransom of a man's life is his wealth, but a poor man hears no threat." (Prov. 13:8).

363 *Westminster Shorter Catechism,* Q. 35.

364 Heb. 2:10.

did in his first life. He could relax, and let others help. The Lord, through Pleiades and everything else in the created order, had taught him that he wasn't responsible for the maintenance of the universe by showing him that he couldn't maintain it and that it would function just fine without his help. Now God is using his friends and family to teach him that he's not ultimately responsible for his personal finances either—certainly not now that he's broke (they're taking care of him)—and not in the future either, because he now knows he'll be able to give them a jingle if he ever again gets "down on his luck." Pleiades, an empty wallet, family and friends were sanctifying Job.

Job's experience with his family and friends here, and the new intimacy he discovered, was a much greater blessing than the material blessings that follow. I love it that 42:11 is placed right here in the text, as one of the last things mentioned about Job. Isn't it true that in your own life, mended, renewed, intimate relationships with friends and family mean everything? No, you might say, certainly not *everything* because my relationship to Jesus is at the top of the list. True, and that's the point: he's your friend,[365] and he's your sibling.[366]

Christ was present at the shower mentioned in 42:11 because whenever and wherever his family meets, he attends.[367] This is part of Christ's divine humiliation. He endured death on the cross to make us family, and looks forward with as much anticipation as we do to the family banquet in heaven, so much so that he's not

---

365 "No longer do I call you servants, for the servant does not know what his master is doing; but I have called you *friends*, for all that I have heard from my Father I have made known to you." (Jn. 15:15).

366 "For it was fitting that he, for whom and by whom all things exist, in bringing many sons to glory, should make the founder of their salvation perfect through suffering. For he who sanctifies and those who are sanctified all have one source. That is why he is not ashamed to call them *brothers*, saying, 'I will tell of your name to my brothers; in the midst of the congregation I will sing your praise.' " (Heb. 2:10-12).

367 "For where two or three are gathered in my name, there am I among them." (Mt. 18:20).

even going to sample the food and drink until the whole family arrives.[368]

Jesus, what a friend for sinners.[369]

THE EIGHTH SHOWER

The story could have ended with friends and family coming over. But the Lord had one more shower in store for his servant:

> And the LORD blessed the latter days of Job more than his beginning. And he had 14,000 sheep, 6,000 camels, 1,000 yoke of oxen, and 1,000 female donkeys. He had also seven sons and three daughters. (42:12-13)

Double everything! Wow. We often think that God places no value on material things, but obviously he does. When he spoke out of the whirlwind all he talked about was material things. The created order is material, and in Genesis 1, God called it "good." We get into trouble when we fall in love with material things, but God meant for us to possess them. And God considered Job highly qualified to possess them, because he doubled everything. You can go back to Chapter 1 and compare: everything is *exactly* doubled.

Except for the children. Job only got ten of them, and though three of them were girls of extraordinary beauty, named Jemimah ("little dove"), Keziah ("*cassia*, sweet-smelling spice") and Keren-happuch ("horn of make-up"), there were still only ten.

Ten children is plenty for any couple, and possibly the Lord meant to spare Mrs. Job from having to endure twenty more pregnancies. But the numbers here are interesting, because they are exact. Exact in the doubling of livestock, exact in the number of children—ten at the beginning, and ten at the end. It seems al-

---

368 "I tell you I will not drink again of this fruit of the vine until that day when I drink it new with you in my Father's kingdom." (Mt. 26:29).
369 "Jesus, What a Friend for Sinners," J. Wilbur Chapman, 1910.

most like a puzzle, begging to be solved. And I think that's exactly what it is, and we're meant to do our best to solve it.

TWENTY CHILDREN TOO

Surely the answer is to be found in the resurrection. Children are not "beasts that perish."[370] They are eternal.[371] Job and his wife had had ten children at the beginning, and those children were alive even now, though their bodies were resting in the grave until the resurrection.[372] Job would join them in the grave, although it would be another 140 years!—but that's hardly a blip, considering eternity. And then the entire family would be raised together: "For the trumpet will sound, and the dead will be raised imperishable, and we shall be changed!"[373] How many, in Job's case? Twenty-two, counting Job and his wife. Job had twenty children, not just ten.

This had to be solid comfort to Job. He had prayed for his children, specifically for their relationship to the Lord, and thus their eternal welfare. This he did "continually" (1:5). He later expressed his confidence in the resurrection in the famous passage in Chapter 19, where he testified that "after my skin has been thus destroyed, yet in my flesh I shall see God" (19:26).

By giving him only ten children in Chapter 42, the Lord was assuring Job that his prayers for his first set of children had been answered. If the Lord had given him twenty children at the end, it would raise the question as to whether the first ten children were "like the beasts that perish." But they were children, not beasts.

---

370 Psa. 49:20.

371 For an insightful study of the eternality of man, see R. Laird Harris, *Man—God's Eternal Creation: Old Testament Teaching on Man and his Culture.* (Moody Press, 1971).

372 "The souls of believers are at their death made perfect in holiness, and do immediately pass into glory; and their bodies, being still united to Christ, do rest in their graves until the resurrection." *Westminster Shorter Catechism,* Q. 37.

373 1 Cor. 15:52.

The Lord was assuring Job that his covenant children were in heaven.

AS IT IS, YOUR CHILDREN ARE HOLY

But Job's foundational confidence regarding his children was not based on his ability to solve a puzzle. It was based on the covenant.

The covenant was real to Job. We saw how real it was for him in Chapter 1, where he prayed for his children continually. His was a covenant family, and he treated them as holy or "set apart" for the Lord. He asked God to protect them, and believed that he would. They were special to him, and he knew that they were special to the Lord. He believed that through the covenant his children would be forgiven even if one of them cursed God in his heart. He believed that God had made them righteous and that he would keep them righteous.

My father died in 1978. Just days before he died he sent all eight of his children a handwritten letter, and I think every one of us has kept it. He was frail and his handwriting shaky. But his message wasn't shaky. He said that only recently he had come to understand what the Apostle Paul meant in 1 Cor. 7:14, when he addressed believing parents regarding their kids: "*as it is, they are holy.*" He said that gave him peace and joy.

When I received the letter, it gave me pause. How could Dad know that? He had seen his children's sin and shortcomings. He had even discussed some of mine with me. There was no way that he could know by observation of us alone that "as it is, they are holy." It seemed to me that Paul would have been better advised to say "as it is, they're *not* holy, but let's hope against hope that someday they will be." But that's not what the Apostle said.

Dad told us in the letter how he knew, and why he had confidence regarding his children. It was just because of what Paul said: you can know it because I have bound your children to me.

And because Scripture says it, it becomes an article of faith. "Faith is the substance of things hoped for, the evidence of things *not seen*."[374] Dad's hope was founded not on what he saw in his children but on the promises of God. Christian parents, take heart!

MORE BOOKENDS

I said previously that first Job's possessions, and then Satan, provided two very different sets of bookends for the Book of Job, because each is mentioned in the first chapter and in the last. Maybe that should be revised. Perhaps the real bookends are God's covenant promises. The covenant is where we begin at birth, and where we end when we pass into eternity.

Job's new covenant family was to be enormous. I wonder how many there were? There must have been some awfully big crowds when the family met for Thanksgiving and Christmas, for "after this Job lived 140 years, and saw his sons, and his sons' sons, four generations" (42:16). And the first batch, the first of those four generations, was ten! So there might have been hundreds—all covenant children, "[f]or the promise is for you and for your children and for all who are far off, everyone whom the Lord our God calls to himself."[375]

What a great, covenant-keeping God.

And Job died, an old man, and full of days. (42:17).

---

374   Heb. 11:1, KJV.
375   Acts 2:39.

FOR REFLECTION

1.

Why do you think God blessed Job again with material things and a family, all double, after Job's suffering? Does this seem to undermine the truths set out in Job 1 and 2, that Job's love for the Lord was not based on what blessings the Lord had given him?

2.

Have you ever been so financially embarrased that you needed others to help you out? If so, as you look back on the experience, was this good for you, or bad? What did you learn from it? Did it help or hurt your relationships with others? How?

3.

How was Job different, or how had he been changed, from the beginning of Job 1 to the end of Job 42? Is it possible to see, in retrospect, that some things needed to be changed? What?

POSTSCRIPT
FORT BENNING, 1968

HEBREWS 12:1

A BOUT ONE HUNDRED would-be law students, already admitted to the Iowa School of Law prior to fall semester, 1967, really wanted to follow through with their plans, and get their licenses to practice law. But the War in Viet Nam meant that many of them would have to become draft-dodgers in order to do so. I was one of those students, but didn't get to be a draft-dodger, because the United States Army drafted me first.

There was a temporary way out, though, and I took it. The Reserve Officer Training Corps (ROTC) was the escape route, so I signed up for it. It's true that I had to agree to serve two years active duty after graduating law school, but I actually looked forward to the prospect. I wanted to be in the infantry, and wanted to "GO AIRBORNE!"

All of us law students who were in ROTC had to go to military training classes that year, and in the summer of 1968, we were slated to attend basic training. Being in Army ROTC, that meant Fort Benning, Georgia.

Anyone who's been to Fort Benning in the summer can tell you how hot it is, and anyone who's been through basic training in any branch of the armed services can tell you how grueling it is. Trust me: no matter what they tell you, it's an understatement. We all thought we were in good physical shape before we went. We had no idea. Pushups all the time, running while holding a rifle over your head, the horizontal ladder, ten-mile forced marches. It ran from 5 in the morning until 10 at night. It was all hard, and most of us believed after the first couple of days that there was no way we were going to make it.

I have two memories of basic training that are particularly poignant. The first was entirely pleasant. The cadets had a day off about the third week in, and the army financed a trip to Fulton County Stadium in Atlanta so we could see the Braves play. It was on Sunday afternoon, July 14, 1968. The Braves were playing the San Francisco Giants. We didn't know what we were going to witness that day, but it turned out to be the day Atlanta's Hank Aaron hit his 500th home run. A great memory, and I've found that it impresses even my grandchildren, so I tell it often.

The other memory didn't start out so great, but ended wonderfully. About a week before basic training was to end, we were put to a test that our drill sergeant Willie told us was the toughest physical test in basic training's book. We were going to have to run around a quarter-mile track eight times (two miles, total). Didn't sound bad at all, considering we had already been on a ten-mile forced march. But he continued: this will be with your fully-loaded back packs or duffels, the M-14 rifle, bayonet, two cases of ammo, enough rations for a week, grenades, two canteens filled with water, a pup tent, and on and on. I mean, I didn't think I could even stand up straight with all that materiel loading me down, and when the day came, I did buckle a few times.

The day was hot, over one hundred degrees. The Georgia sun was unrelenting as we began our run. I'm not exaggerating when I tell you that after the first lap—only an eighth of the required distance—I had had it. I wanted to be anywhere on earth other than Fort Benning. But though by now I had slowed to little more than a walk, I somehow kept going and finished a mile. Still, that was just half way.

As I began the fifth lap, something happened that I've never forgotten. By this time my head was bowed, and I was looking only at the sweat raining down on my heavy, hot, dusty boots. But suddenly I saw something right beside my boots that I wasn't expecting. It was another set of black boots, shiny ones, moving stride for stride with mine. I looked up and saw who was running in those boots, and recognized him. It was Company D's first officer, the lieutenant that cadets were not even supposed to talk to.

He was smiling at me, and shouted: "You're doing great, Mark! You're going to make it just fine!"

I couldn't believe what I was seeing and hearing. He had called me by my first name! I hadn't heard my first name in six weeks. That alone came as a shock. But it did sound friendly, and encouraging. I can't remember that officer's name, but I do remember that he ran that last mile right beside me, all the way. And then he pounded me on the back at the finish line, just as though I had hit a home run, like Hank Aaron. He made me feel like a hero! That last mile was the easiest, most energizing mile I've ever run, fully loaded or not.

The officer who ran beside me had endured basic training too. It had been rough for him, just like it was for me, just like it is for everybody. But that's the very reason he *could* encourage me, and why he *wanted* to encourage me. He could sympathize with me, because he had been through it. He could encourage me, because he had been through it. He was a living witness to me that a man, fully loaded, can make it around the track all eight times. And I could feel it in every stride.

Job is that officer to me, but not to me alone. He's that to every believer, and has been for 4,000 years. It's in the Bible:

> Therefore, since we are surrounded by so great
> a cloud of witnesses, let us also lay aside every

weight, and sin which clings so closely, and let us run with endurance the race that is set before us, looking to Jesus, the founder and perfecter of our faith, who for the joy that was set before him endured the cross, despising the shame, and is seated at the right hand of the throne of God. (Heb. 12:1-2)

Job isn't specifically mentioned in Hebrews 11, the text immediately preceding that quoted here, but he's clearly included in the "great cloud of witnesses." The author of Hebrews felt that there were just too many of them to mention: "time would fail me," the author writes.[376]

God put Job through the traces for *us*. God put the Book of Job in the canon of Scripture for *us*. And when we look over and see Job, we see someone else running beside both of us. We see Jesus, "the founder and perfector of our faith." He is the one who is the believer's ultimate officer, the one who runs beside and encourages us. And he has appointed many others to do the same, because he knows that you and I need encouragement. We need it because "Even youths shall faint and be weary, and young men shall fall exhausted."[377] But

> they who wait for the LORD shall renew their
> strength;
> they shall mount up with wings like eagles;
> they shall run and not be weary;
> they shall walk and not faint. (Isa. 40:31)

Are you weary? So was Job. Are you faint? So was Job. Are you sick, maybe expecting to die? So was Job. Have you had suicidal ideations, as the psychiatrist calls them? Job wished he had never been born, and cursed the day of his birth. Have you gone bankrupt? Job lost everything, and didn't have a nickel. Have you

---

376 Heb. 11:32.
377 Isa. 40:30.

lost your reputation and respect? Job's friends spit him in the face. Are you convinced that God isn't there for you? Job looked east and west, backward and forward, and couldn't find him. Is God not answering your prayers? For thirty-seven chapters, Job pled with the Lord for an answer to his prayers, and God was silent.

But Job *made it*, and it was altogether in God's providence that he made it. God helped Job get past the finish line not only for Job, but for us. Perhaps that's why God allowed Job to suffer so awfully, because there's not one thing that we could possibly suffer that's beyond, or outside, the scope of his suffering. Everything is included. You'll make it too.

So perhaps God does answer the question after all, "Why do the righteous suffer?" Perhaps the answer is given in Hebrews 12:1: so that we will be able to "run with patience the race that is set before us."

MY FATHER,
GOD'S SERVANT

By Rob Sanderson

1916

AD 1916 WAS A HORRIBLE YEAR to be alive for plants, animals and mankind the world over. Unremitting agents of destruction were refashioning our landscape; tremendous advances had been made in the ways and means of snuffing out life: mustard gas, depth charges, "New! Improved!" land mines, Big Bertha. (Back then it wasn't a golf club.) Trench warfare was quickly becoming obsolescent in the face of new artillery, a face unseen even with binoculars, hurling explosives more powerful than ever before willy-nilly into every trench and hiding place. We'd even devised things to navigate the heavens, new machines to drop lethal parcels into the trenches and homes that the artillery couldn't reach. War was becoming scientific. In the hideous carnage more than sixteen million people met their Maker, almost half of them non-combatants, which of course means mostly women, children, and old men. We were carrying on and perfecting the Oldest Profession handed down to us by Cain, author of fratricide some six millennia before, when there were fewer than sixteen persons, never mind sixteen million, on the planet. It was a deadly year in the middle of one of the deadliest conflagrations in history, the one we came to call The Great War. Millions of survivors were asking themselves, "Who are we, to be doing this to ourselves?" The United States had yet to enter the fray, so in this little part of the globe few of the millions of tears shed during 1916 were for lost sons, brothers, husbands, or fathers. In fact, 1916 was an auspicious twelve-month: many tears were shed for joy over new babies who first saw the light of day in that very same year. To select just a few from the Who's Who, consider

> Gleason Archer, Francis Crick, Walter Cronkite, Olivia de Havilland, Kirk Douglas, Shelby Foote, Glenn Ford, Jackie Gleason, Betty Grable, Donald Guthrie, James Herriot, C. Everett Koop, John D. MacDonald, Robert McNamara, Gregory Peck, Bernard Ramm, Enos Slaughter.

Doyens all: 1916 infants who would become masters in their chosen professions, many of them now household names. It was in Weston Favell, Northamptonshire that the sun first shone upon Francis Harry Compton Crick, and the sun must have been especially bright that day because he turned out to be brilliant. Some like to call him Sir Francis though he refused the proffered knighthood; some even call him Lord Crick though his veins didn't course with the blood of nobility. His august suffixes include OM and FRS, and did he ever deserve them. Cambridge initially rejected him, perhaps because he hadn't mastered Latin, but on second thought granted him a PhD after an interruption we call WWII. Amazingly his doctorate was in Physics, not Molecular Biology. But forty years after his birth he revolutionized the way we look at ourselves and life itself in much the same way that Dr. Einstein had brought us new eyes with which to view the cosmos: energy, matter, light. Dr. Crick looked inward.

At about the same tender age that our Lord found his way to the temple to teach the teachers (and brought gray hair to his parents, strolling off like that!), young Francis had already decided he'd had quite enough of religion and announced to his parents that he'd accompany them to church no longer. This twelve-year-old decision would be brought to fruition in later years, after he had grown in knowledge by longer leaps and further bounds than most of us can imagine. He would go on to co-found the mighty triumvirate of Crick, Watkins & Wilkins, honored with the Nobel Prize for discovering the molecular structure of DNA and, so they thought, the secret of life. For an outsider like me his work is easy neither to read nor to understand. Codons, helical diffraction, complementary replication, ribonuclease, icosahedral symmetry, directed panspermia, crystallographic calculations: to me this stuff is bafflegab. But to him and his colleagues it assuredly wasn't, and their Nobel Prize was no mistake. Dr. Crick was a 1916 gift to mankind and his insight was nonpareil.

But did he see through a glass, darkly? He, too, asked the question, "Who are we?" and where did we come from. Had he stuck it out a bit longer in Sunday School, had he benefited from an evangelical pastor (John Stott comes to mind) and a couple of parents who took him to church and had Bible study at home regardless of his pubescent preferences, he might have encountered and come to believe Paul's words in Colossians 1, "by him all things were created: things in heaven and on earth, visible and invisible... all things were created by him and for him... in him all things hold together." His answer to the question is noteworthy for it illustrates the gaping chasm between knowledge and wisdom, noesis and understanding. He swapped his Bible for Darwin – even advocating the establishment of Darwin Day as a national holiday—and passionately embraced humanism in disdain of all religious "fables." One religion he held in particular derision. "Christianity may be okay between consenting adults in private but should not be taught to young children," he opined. "Who you are is nothing but a pack of neurons." Christian apologists would have used *reductio ad absurdum* on that one, but no doubt he'd have simply thought they were the dolts: science, not faith, provides the answers.

ON THE OTHER SIDE OF THE POND in that very same year, in a place called Baltimore—the cognoscente, namely the gentleman himself, informs us that it's properly pronounced Bawldmr with a nearly inaudible D and in two syllables, not three—another baby was born. Like Francis Crick, John Wilmer Sanderson, Jr. had been saddled with four names, to one of which he wasn't particularly partial, which may explain why there was never a John Wilmer Sanderson, III. Of Clan MacDonald, his name, I'm told, has nothing to do with "son of a sander," the craftsman, but is Scottish for "son of Alexander." Johnny was reared a Lutheran, probably due to his mother's influence, and perhaps it's that background which came to the fore later in life when at services' end he always alternated a Benediction with a Doxology. (My own brief Lutheran experience led me to prefer the symmetry of that liturgy's nomenclature, "Benediction / Benedicamus": He blesses us / we bless Him.) There are hundreds of both in Scripture, but he seemed always to incline as to the former to the Aaronic version in the sixth chapter of Numbers, and as to the latter to the Judean variety in 24-25, a sentence he might well have loved to parse and preach twenty-four or twenty-five hundred times.

I can hear him quipping that he and Crick "went to different schools together." John Sanderson, who had mastered Latin, might have been accepted at Cambridge, but he applied to Wheaton as had his older sister Grace Sanderson MacRae. It was there, probably in the mess hall, that he met a young lady named Pearl Hetrick, who he learned had been born on the very same day as he, just one year later; upon her graduation in 1939 they were married. Somewhere along the line, I don't know by whom, he got Presbyterianized. And like Crick he too looked inward, but found very different stuff, through a very different microscope. "The fear of the LORD—that is wisdom..."

I FIRST MET HIM IN AUGUST OF 1950, and I cannot recall being overly impressed. I had my mind on other things at the time, namely my mother's milk and warmth—it's cold out here, even in a Delaware August, compared to nine months in paradise; that probably explains it. Over the years I came to appreciate him very much indeed. It wasn't always easy. Fast forward from 1916 about four-and-a-half decades. "Who are you to tell anybody anything?" Dad asked me. I had been on the planet for nine or ten years, and thought pretty highly of myself; after all, I was John Sanderson's son, that's who I was. Obviously that argument was not about to work with Dad. I'd been having an altercation with a little 7-year-old compatriot—just a kid, much my junior—about his keeping our day's catch out of the water slung over the bow of the boat, to die in the air on our way back home to port. I was clearly the environmentalist here and he was unspeakably cruel, so I let him have it. It didn't matter that the heads of the fish were to be soon chopped off and find their way into the garbage bin, and most of the rest of them into various human stomachs; never mind that I was something like the fifteenth guest thrice removed and the person I teed off on was royalty—a blood-relative of the owner of the boat we were in, of the pier at which we docked, of the estate in which we were vacationing. Dad forcibly brought me back to reality: just who did I think I was?

It wasn't the first time or the last I had to confront the perennial existential question. I once stepped up behind John Murray, a colleague of Dad's at Westminster Seminary, to ask him quietly if he knew where a special ping-pong friend of mine was at the moment. (I spent hours in Westminster's "ping-pong room" every day after school, many treasured moments spent with the likes of Susumu Uda, George Marsden, Edmund Clowney.) Dr. Murray, quite startled, turned and said "Ach Roby, ya came oop on me blind side!" (It's impossible to put his beautiful brogue into written English; the R was very long and very rolled, the o long and very pure; Ian Maclaren, one of Dad's treasured authors, comes far closer than I in transcribing Scottish.) Someone had told me that a Luftstreitkräfte gunner had taken out one of his eyes in The

Great War while serving in the Royal Highlanders' Black Watch, to be replaced by glass, and I should have been more careful. "O my goodness," I blurted, "I'm so sorry!" "Boot laddie," replied the theologian a bit sternly but with a smile, "ya have na gudeness in ya!" Who did I think I was?

An exquisite memory is the day Clowney came down—a rare occasion!—to find Uda, Marsden and unfortunately for them, me, a 12-year-old kid: an unusual foursome to say the least. Uda was I think the best ping-pong player I've ever encountered. In classic Japanese style, he held his paddle "all wrong," and crouched about ten feet or as much as the little room allowed back of the table; he taught me very quickly that what we call ping-pong 'English' is rightly named 'Japanese.' A whole lot of his shots I returned either directly into the net, or way off the end of the table, depending on the spin he put on it. He once told me, "I meet you in the robby, Lobby" but I didn't laugh: he spoke English a whole lot better than I spoke Japanese. It was he whom I'd been seeking when I scared Dr. Murray in the lobby. Marsden was the fiercest competitor one could imagine, and he put a blunter, more American slant on things: he answered every slam in kind, and much harder on the U-turn. Clowney was certainly no slouch either, and that day he very graciously condescended to accept me as his partner against Uda and Marsden. At one point in the match Marsden slammed and I barely got my paddle up to meet it: Irresistible Force merely reciprocating on the Movable Object with no help from me. The paddle's tip sent the ball arcing in the other direction, nearly colliding with the fluorescent light above, descending to nestle right on the very top of the net. Which way would it go? In what seemed a few seconds later but was no doubt only a fraction of one, it dropped quietly on their side and there was absolutely no way to return it. With his inimitable wit Dr. Clowney exclaimed, "Great shot, Robby! Perfect it!" After the four of us stopped laughing I came to realize, there was the nagging metaphysical question once again: was I just a beneficiary of luck on which I somehow had to learn to improve?

DAD LOVED WORDS—HE WAS AN AVID CRUCIVERBALIST and he always did them in pen—but 'luck' was not one of them; the sovereignty of God was one of his constant themes. He wasn't in Gleason Archer's league: Dr. Archer reportedly committed at some point to learning a new language every year, and by the time of his death had become fairly comfortable in twenty-seven! But like Archer, Sanderson was a linguaphile. "There is no accounting for taste," he'd often say in Latin. "*Sine qua non*" ("something absolutely necessary") and "*par excellence*" were a preferred phrases in class, the latter sadly but justifiably never spoken in my direction. (To me he liked to say, though with a twinkle in his eye, "Your best is none too good.") The word "amoral" intrigued him: a pure Latinism with an alpha privative attached—he attributed this observation to J. Gresham Machen. Still ringing in my mind is "subjunctive, contrary to fact." Self-deprecatingly, he liked the aphorism that "Those who can, do; those who can't, teach"; he always added that "those who can't teach, teach education." He called my bride-to-be "totally unreconstructed," for the precise meaning of which I've searched in vain. (Upon her introduction to the Sanderson household, the very first thing she did was swap the heads of the condiment shakers behind all of our backs, so that both Dad & Mom got a tasty surprise when they were expecting "S" and got "P"; that behavior gives me a hint. He was, after all, Dean of the Faculty of the college we both attended! That didn't faze her a bit.) He had an incisive mind; I think he would have liked the late Antonin Scalia a lot. He used Dr. Quine's text on mathematical logic to educate us in the 'fell sweep' and the 'full swoop' to test an argument. He loved the books in which these words and ideas were found. Most of all he loved the Word, the inspiration and inerrancy of which he passionately advocated.

(Whenever he wanted a bit of errancy, he joyfully turned to P. G. Wodehouse whose characters, especially Wooster, may have given Mom some gray hair; she would have liked to engage in a pinch of bowdlerizing. He loved Psmith [the "P," Psmith loved to remind us, is silent] and Mr. Mulliner, and even Claude Pott, a corpulent P.I. someone compared to a leopard. In just four words, Wodehouse corrected that discrepancy: "Leopards pad; Pott waddled." Dad laughed out loud every time he read that sentence.)

Despite living in St. Louis for only four years, the Cardinals were his lifelong team, and Stan his man. Born in Wilmington, I became a Phillies fan, but during one game he took me to, he and Bob Gibson had me almost persuaded.

DAD LIKED TO HANG HIS STATEMENTS and his questions at home, forcing his family members to fill in the ending for him. I got in trouble a couple of years ago and was rebuked when I forgot where I was and audibly finished one of my pastor's sentences for him during a sermon. Oops, my bad; a Presbyterian worship service is not a Presbyterian home! Dad never played games in the pulpit, but he did put a wrinkle on the hanging technique and the very same pastor who recently rebuked me lovingly wrote me: "your father was indeed one of my favorites. One of his distinctions: the 'Sandersonian pause.' Your father could say more in a pause than many can in 10 minutes."

A journey with him on a Sunday morning required a roadmap, the Bible, because he might start in John, jump to 2 Timothy, go back to Deuteronomy, catch a lesson from Nahum, mention something from 1 Kings, visit Lamentations and end up in Hebrews. Wherever he led, he helped us discover the Lord Jesus, and forced upon every one of us the eternal question, who are we? His answer was never "a pack of neurons." And because he loved Wisdom, one of his favorite books was the Book of Job. It isn't all that common to find our Creator sarcastic, but try re-reading Job 38-40, where He practically dripped with it: who are you? where were you when I...? do you...? can you...? How about that behemoth, that leviathan? Just who do you think you are?

In preaching the Gospel, Dad was never convoluted or complicated; never inchoate; never smart-alecky, though he certainly had it in him. One time in Greek Philosophy class he spent a while writing five questions on the blackboard—we used them back then!—and announced to the class that these five would appear nowhere on the final exam. Sap that I was, I actually believed him and I was the only guy in the room to have lived with him for twenty years! I studiously avoided those questions. Of course they were the exam. Apparently he could be Jesuitical when he wanted.

He'd been invited to lecture to a bunch of theological students and was scheduled to continue doing so the following day. The Accuser or one of his deputies was roaming Earth that night, invaded his bedroom about 3 am, woke him up, and for twenty-five minutes or so presented him with a catalog of his sins. If you've ever experienced this, you know it's excruciating; Satan is a meticulous bookkeeper. The very question Dad had asked me came back to haunt him: "Who are you, Sanderson, you cluster of evil, to teach anybody anything?" He took it as long as he could and then said "Enough!" The words of Job may have reverberated in his mind: "I know that my Redeemer lives!" "My hope is built on nothing less, than Jesus' blood and righteousness!" That was all it took for the Adversary to depart. Dad rolled over and slept well, protected by his Savior, and went on the next evening to teach the gospel once again.

Our family was certainly initiated into initials: KJV, ASV, RSV, NASB, NEB, NIV—Dad didn't live long enough (here!) to do the ESV or the GNT. We enjoyed J. B. Phillips (who had been nudged to get started by C. S. Lewis) and Ken Taylor's paraphrase, which seriously lengthened our devotions by insisting on "pause, and calmly think of that!" every time he hit a "selah" in the Psalms. Many of them Dad found too new, too revised, too paraphrastic, some even too standard. But they were all the Word of God even if imperfectly translated, and we read it daily.

CIRCA 1916 B.C.

BACK TO THE YEAR 1916, this time about four millennia before Crick and Sanderson were born. (I might be a couple of hundred years off either way, but I love the symmetry and, as Dad would frequently say, "Never ruin a good story with a few facts." In this case, we have few facts to work with.)

Some consider Job a great-grandson of Noah, others the grandson of Esau and the king of Esau's land, Edom. Whoever he was, he was a fabulously wealthy plutocrat, but look! A merito-crat as well: 'blameless and upright'. The Lord Himself actually said "there is no one on earth like him"! How's that for an en-dorsement? So He offered him to Satan and said take your best shot. The Adversary was quite certain that, robbed of all his re-sources, he would curse God just as his wife advised him to do, and join his forces; so he dispatched some friends to "comfort" him. Of course they all did nothing of the sort, instead charging him with sin. (Had they never read the one about the Tower of Siloam?) Then God had a little family intervention, an interrup-tion, and all of them including Job were silenced. It's interesting that the Lord spoke to him out of a whirlwind. Not many of us have experienced a whirlwind, but here on the east coast, just an hour's ride north of 'Bawldmr', I've been in some hurricanes, and they're no fun. (Mom was literally displaced quite a few feet by Hurricane Hazel in the early fifties.) I'm told that ancient Hebrew made do with a single word for the entities we enjoy describing in three: Breath; Wind; Spirit. Here, the Spirit spoke from the Wind and Job was resuscitated with the Breath of life.

If Dr. Crick ever read Job, especially the first and last chapters, he would have concluded that Job lived in the land of Oz, not Uz, and the book about him was either an Aesop Fable, a Grimm Fairy Tale, or an episode of Star Wars: white-clad troops reporting to the commander-in-chief, Darth Vader marching into CCU (Command & Control, Universe) just after "roaming the earth" in his starship, the Commander inviting him to try his best against the most upright man to be found. One could hardly make this stuff up. The paragraphs detailing his monumental losses on the same day, each one reported to him by a servant who "alone escaped to tell you" cause even the believing reader to question Job's hiring abilities: where did he find these wimps, and why did he ever employ them? Had they never passed through Parris Island, where even in boot camp the Marine learns never to leave a brother behind? And at the end, twice what he lost was restored? How do you restore a son or daughter whom you've buried, even if the new daughters are the most stunningly beautiful women in all the land?

Of course there is always a grain of truth in the Adversary's temptations, else he'd never gain any traction. Later he'd dare attempt to make his own Creator question who He was, offering Him ten thousand angels, food to a man who hadn't eaten for forty days, the splendors of the world, of which Jesus knew nothing as a craftsman from Nazareth. Satan is the inventor and the master of the Imposter Syndrome. Christ Jesus replied with citations from His own writings: Man can't live by bread alone but by the Word; don't try testing your God; worship the Lord your God. As he had done with Job, so from the Lord his God he departed, temporarily to roam somewhere else in the solar system in the time he had left before his annihilation.

Circa 1492 b.c., and a.d. 33

THE VERY SAME QUESTION, TWICE AGAIN: Who are you? But look! Now the challenged one isn't just somebody or other, it's the Creator of the universe! Moses had every right to ask; he was an AWOL prince of Egypt and a criminal who couldn't speak either Egyptian or Hebrew very well anymore after forty years, and here he was being ordered to return to his home base, slip by the MPs, and announce the end of chains to the people of Israel and the end of slave-mastering to his father, Pharaoh of the mighty empire. Moses knew who he was alright: just an old Midianite shepherd. The pressing issue, as he realized he wasn't being invited to a mere causerie or tailgate party, was who are you? "Sir, if they just happen to ask who sent me, What's your name?" As a result of that quite pertinent question we are the beneficiaries of the holiest Tetragrammaton, YHWH, or JHVH, a name so sacred that the translators of the Septuagint didn't even attempt to bring it into Greek. An extremely enigmatic answer that the marvelous scholars of the 'Authorized Version' did their best with: I AM THAT I AM. Bring it forward about four centuries and today's scholars render it I AM WHO I AM, which is interesting since the KJV wordsmiths were without question in possession of the word 'who'. Graciously and epexegetically, the Lord had already declared with a bit of context that He was "the God of Abraham, the God of Isaac, and the God of Jacob" a total of four times in that one conversation. But He said, "Tell them I AM has sent you." Just as you and I are given our names by our fathers, so the Lord Jesus was given His "Name above every name" by His Father. He's the only one who can say "I am," period.

A millennium and a half later, the high priest of Israel, who should have been flat on his face, stood before the High Priest of the Universe and had the gall—likely mixed with vinegar, so acidic was his tongue—to ask, "Just who are you? Are you really the son of the Blessed One?" Once again, according to Mark, He answered with exquisite double entendre, I AM. But this time He wasn't the Sender, He was the Sent. This time He wasn't the prosecutor, He was the prosecuted. After creating the lamb, He now was the Lamb.

A.D. 1998

MY FATHER WAS INVITED TO JOIN six other outstanding preachers to speak to his co-residents at the Quarryville Presbyterian Retirement Community on Good Friday, 1998 about the seven sayings of Christ on the cross. (One of them was his nephew John MacRae who presented an excellent sermonette on "Mother, here's your son; John, here's your mother"; I found that particularly apropos). The median age of the audience was probably around 75, the overwhelming faith Christian, the status devout. None of that impeded him from preaching the Gospel, and taking his six or seven allotted minutes to speak as directly as he could, as individually as he could, of the Good News. He was assigned the final saying: "Father, into your hands I commit my spirit." Three weeks later he committed his own and met his Lord face to face. I'm certain "face to face" is not the correct representation: the Lord Jesus greeted him in His resurrected body; Dad was welcomed for the moment only in spirit, and I know his spirit was either genuflecting or utterly prostrate in worship and thanksgiving, if spirits can do that. He also met Mr. Job. They had a lot to talk about, and it was a long and precious conversation. Horatius Bonar, one of Dad's favorite lyricists, probably joined them, and they sang one of his hymns together. Maybe Herr Luther strolled over and they sang Mit unser Macht ist nichts getan, wir sind gar bald verloren! "Did we in our own strength confide, our striving would be losing." Dad loved every word of Dr. Luther's hymn and every note of his composition. And the Right Man was indeed by their side, the Man of God's own choosing: the only reason they were all there.

I'VE OFTEN WONDERED WHAT WORD might be next to John W. Sanderson's name in the Lamb's Book of Life, if the Lord writes epitaphs for a man. I don't think it would be 'Professor', 'Pastor' or 'Preacher'; I think he'd had enough of "split P's" in his life— PCUSA, OP, BP, EP, RP, PCUS, PCA—and had done all he could to unsplit the P's. The *mot juste* might well be 'Evangelist'. Dad always carefully considered his audience, but he knew that whether it were academicians, MDiv's in training, college students, the General Assembly of the PCA, or just a bunch of regular folks like me, the crowd was comprised of sinners saved by grace just like him, or sinners still asking who they are and yet to be saved by grace. No matter the audience, even if he was "preaching to the choir," he always pressed it home: Who are you, and will you, with Job, Mark Belz, and me, repent and bow before our Creator, our Lord, our Savior?

Dad will never have OM or FRS after his name, never have encyclopedia articles written about him; but I think the honor to which he most passionately aspired might be simply, profoundly, the appellation the Lord gave Job: "My Servant." Selah.

INDEX OF SCRIPTURE

66001877R00202

Made in the USA
Lexington, KY
03 August 2017